THE REINTERPRETATION OF EARLY AMERICAN HISTORY

JOHN EDWIN POMFRET

From a sketch by Sam Patrick, prepared for the Los Angeles HERALD-EXAMINER.

THE
REINTERPRETATION OF
EARLY AMERICAN HISTORY

Essays in honor of

JOHN EDWIN POMFRET

Edited by

RAY ALLEN BILLINGTON

THE HUNTINGTON LIBRARY · SAN MARINO, CALIFORNIA

1966

Contents

Section III

Approaches to Early American History

Foreword

To LIST JOHN EDWIN POMFRET'S CONTRIBUTIONS to the rejuvenation of early American history studies that has occurred since World War II is to underline the debt owed him by every scholar immersed in that discipline and every American concerned with the nation's formative era. He, more than any other individual, deserves the title of founder of the Institute of Early American History and Culture. He was primarily responsible for converting the *William and Mary Quarterly* from a provincial state journal into a quarterly publication of national scope and unexcelled excellence in colonial history. He has, during the past fifteen years, helped make the Henry E. Huntington Library and Art Gallery a principal depository for the records of early America. And, by no means least, his own extensive writings, particularly those on early New Jersey, have shed light on hitherto unexplored aspects of the nation's history. These are major accomplishments, worthy of the applause of all concerned with the national heritage.

John Pomfret's retirement from active administration (but not from scholarship) on October 1, 1966, offers a few of those who have benefited from his dedicated labors an opportunity to express their thanks through this volume of essays.

Clearly no ordinary tribute would properly honor Jack Pomfret, for he has been no ordinary scholar-executive. Hence this *festschrift* departs from the pattern set by most of its kind in two ways. First, those invited to contribute were only men who have known him well, either as co-workers at the Institute of Early American History and Culture, or as fellows and readers at the Huntington Library. Second, it emphasizes a theme intimately connected with the man it honors: its purpose is to survey and appraise the writing of colonial history since 1943 when he helped establish the Institute of Early American History and Culture. Each author was invited to summarize and criticize the literature in his own field of special competence; some to evaluate scholarly publication concerning a region or era of colonial America, others to appraise approaches to the subject that have gained prominence in recent years. The resulting volume, it is hoped, will stimulate the study of early American history, just as Jack Pomfret stimulated that study as student and administrator.

Foreword

The idea of this tribute originated in the permanent research staff at the Huntington Library, and all have contributed to its pages. Allan Nevins has drawn on his long friendship with Jack Pomfret to prepare a biographical sketch that reveals the warmth as well as the talents of the man it describes. A. L. Rowse has contributed a moving reminiscence of the Huntington Library during the fifteen years of Jack Pomfret's directorship. John M. Steadman has been attracted from his Miltonian studies to compile a bibliography of Pomfret's published works. I have been pressed into service as editor, despite the obvious fact that any knowledge I possess is not in the field of early American history. The trustees of the Library—John O'Melveny, Jonathan B. Lovelace, Lee A. DuBridge, Jesse W. Tapp, and Homer D. Crotty, chairman—have generously appropriated funds necessary to make this book possible.

Because of the time pressure inevitable in the preparation of such a volume, the exacting editorial supervision that makes Huntington Library publications models of their kind has not been possible. While an attempt has been made to achieve uniformity in style and footnoting, this remains a goal rather than an achievement. Neither quotations nor footnotes have been checked against original sources. Such editorial respectability as does exist is due in part to Professor H. Trevor Colbourn of Indiana University, who was a reader at the Huntington Library during the volume's preparation, and who read and criticized all essays.

Those who have contributed—either as authors or in a more humble capacity—have done so with only one purpose in mind: to honor a good friend on his retirement from active administration. Their hope is that the volume he has inspired will stimulate the quest for truth in a field in which he has played a major role for a generation. Jack Pomfret would want no higher tribute.

May, 1966   RAY ALLEN BILLINGTON

Section I

JOHN EDWIN POMFRET AND EARLY AMERICAN HISTORY

John E. Pomfret: Scholar-Executive

BY ALLAN NEVINS

Since his retirement in 1958 from a professorship at Columbia University, Allan Nevins has served as Senior Research Associate at the Huntington Library. There his daily associations with John E. Pomfret have engendered a warm affection that finds eloquent expression in the biographical sketch that follows. In its preparation he talked or corresponded with dozens of Pomfret's friends—those who knew him in his graduate-school days at the University of Pennsylvania, during his early teaching career at Princeton University, as a dean at Vanderbilt University, as president of the College of William and Mary, and in his multitudinous other capacities, as well as during the period since 1951 that he has presided over the Henry E. Huntington Library and Art Gallery. The result is a wealth of anecdotal detail that will make Jack Pomfret come alive to his many friends and will make all others wish that they had been a part of that wide circle. Allan Nevins tells the story with a gusto and spirit that helps explain why he is among the most respected of all American historians.

A REPRESENTATIVE ACADEMIC LEADER? Far from it. He has been too much a scholar to be a typical college president, and too much an administrator to be a typical scholar. And then he has qualities of moderation and poise all his own. In a well-known essay called "Aequanimitas" Sir William Osler used the word to denote the virtue that he deemed most needed by a strong humanistic leader. Probably few people who have served with John Pomfret have been able to do full justice to his personality. But they would agree that equanimity or evenness of mind and temper has stamped all his thought and acts, and that his balanced serenity has never failed even under severe trials.

These trials he has had in plentiful array. He began his career as a scholar apparently bound for a safe haven as an expert in British or British-American (that is, colonial) history; he ended it in the relative calm of a great library. But in between he changed his course several times, took on greater and greater burdens, and had to breast heavy storms. In doing this he never abated his natural geniality, moderation, and calmness. He united a strong but undemonstrative interest in intellectual pursuits with an even stronger delight in sociability and the practical demands of academic policies and government. He was always at the same time a good citizen. His liberalism of outlook in political, intellectual, and social affairs was repeatedly tested, and as a highly pragmatic liberalism was found effective. His feeling for the scholarly life, its dignity and nobility, has seldom burst to the surface in an ebullition of literary enthusiasm, but has often been expressed in a phrase of Johnsonian scorn for the superficial, inaccurate, and pretentious. Just so, his regard for decency and elevation in politics and society is stated in a sharp repudiation of falsities. Like Bacon, he has "no moderation for the vulgar." Yet he is the kindliest citizen of both the everyday world and the learned world, urbanely tolerant of all honest people however blundering.

A career fuller of quiet activity in the intellectual and social betterment of various communities it would be hard to find. He has labored well in New Jersey, Pennsylvania, Tennessee, Virginia, and California. Yet few indeed are the administrators with so deep a dislike of the glare of publicity. He never aspired to the spotlight; he would have said modestly that brilliant display was beyond him. But he brought into very different circles a sanity and wholesomeness that permanently enlarged their outlook. A shrewdly perceptive realism entered into this sanity. The genial calmness of his conversation is often broken by a bit of perceptive bluntness that both proves his realism and deepens the impression of his sincerity. His bluntness, however, is never contentious. "He never quarrelled with anybody," testified a Princeton colleague. "It was impossible for any of us to quarrel with him," remarked a Williamsburg associate. A simple man, his moral philosophy has excluded the aggressive; rather, he has spread an equable sunshine about him. Yes, aequanimitas is the best word for his nature.

John Pomfret has illustrated and assisted one of the most striking recent changes in American life, the progressive decentralization of scholarship, art, and thought. When he began his career, Boston, New York, and Philadelphia were our recognized centers of authorship and publishing. The belt from Cambridge to Baltimore held the greatest universities, laboratories, and public libraries; this belt governed American culture. As he worked at Princeton, Vanderbilt, and William and Mary, however, the scene changed. Before he left Williamsburg several southern universities—Virginia, North Carolina, Duke—possessed some departments as distinguished as any in the land, while four or five large Mid-western seats had even greater strength. When he removed to the Huntington Library other shifts were plain.

The Pacific slope, with increasing vigor, was claiming parity in various fields with the East. Stanford and Berkeley sheltered communities of scholars and scientists as able as almost any in the country, and the Statewide University of California was soon to assert, with reason, that it was the greatest of American universities. The California Institute of Technology achieved more Nobel laureates than its Massachusetts sister. Important art galleries adorned San Francisco and Los Angeles, nourishing schools of painters and sculptors. Among libraries of source materials for the study of British and American letters, economic development, and politics, the Huntington, crammed with manuscripts and rare books, held one of the proudest stations in the world. The national balance was changing. The first California President strode upon the stage, followed by the first Texas President, and California took primacy in population. The arrival of such men as Max Farrand and John Pomfret in the West to take charge of the Huntington Library and Art Gallery was an event of wide cultural significance.

Any record of Pomfret's work, however condensed, must take account of his mellow traits of character and mind, and of the fact that he played his part against a background of rapid change, East, South, and West.

John Pomfret's career is best seen, in any brief summary, as a kaleidoscope of scenes, making no pretence to the thoroughness of a connected narrative; a quick series of suggestive glimpses. Such a series, however, must begin in Philadelphia, where he was born on September 21, 1898, where his English-born father, an engraver, and his Irish mother, reared him, and where in the University of Pennsylvania he sought his higher education.

I

"Life has a lilt," John Pomfret liked to say when he specially relished any of its phases, and it is with a lilt that the first scene opens.

A group of students, one day in 1922, when Pomfret had begun his graduate work, had just poured out of a red brick hall after a stuffy hour under a dull professor. They drew deep breaths of relief as they glanced down toward the Schuylkill. One sturdy youth, full of vivacity, burst into song, trolling out a romantic ballad called "Margie." His *joie de vivre* as he beat time with one hand and strode away to lunch was so infectious that forty years later a friend recalled the scene; Richard H. Shryock saw himself again a student in his late twenties listening to the tenor notes of his slightly younger associate Jack Pomfret. Pomfret did not sing after every class. Like Shryock, he had moments when his doctoral thesis seemed too grim for human endurance; when the visage of even the amiable, much-loved William E. Lingelbach, one of the men guiding his studies, took on a tyrannous hue; and when he thought rebelliously about Provost Edgar Fahs Smith, so eminent in electrochemical analysis and so distant from humanistic pursuits.

Eminent teachers the University had, like E. P. Cheyney in history, and Arthur Hobson Quinn in literature. Cheyney, whose two volumes on *Elizabeth from the Great Armada* possess enduring qualities, oversaw Pomfret's dissertation on Irish land reform. These were the last years in which John Bach McMaster was seen about the campus, for he passed seventy in 1922. Pomfret had taken an undergraduate course in American history with him, and always recalled the experience vividly. McMaster lectured earnestly, disconnectedly, and inaudibly. Five graduate students in the first row paid close attention but heard him badly. Twenty-five undergraduates behind them paid no attention. Happily, each week he handed out a short résumé of his lectures. They were founded on his huge eight-volume history; all students saved them; and they made it possible to pass the course.

Once later, in graduate student days, Pomfret induced McMaster to give a talk to a history club, and presided in a room at the Penn Club which they filled. The famous historian began with reminiscences and anecdotes that engrossed them all. Unfortunately, he went on for two hours, until weary students began creeping out of a back door on hands and knees. The problem of stopping him became urgent. Finally, Pomfret took advantage of a pause by Mc-

Master for breath, and leaping to his feet, cut him short by vociferating, "We thank you warmly, Mr. McMaster, for the wonderful evening you have given us!" As they went home, McMaster rumbled, uneasily: "It must be late; I should have been in bed an hour ago."

But Pomfret never forgot McMaster, nor the salty observations of Lingelbach and Cheyney, nor their Maryland associate named St. George L. Sioussat who came to Pennsylvania to teach American history in the 1920s and 1930s. He heard echoes of the Scott Nearing case, involving questions of academic freedom in the university's difficulties with a radical faculty member. For the first time he observed how painfully an institution can be limited by financial straits. The University of Pennsylvania had only begun to compete with State College and Pittsburgh for public funds. Meanwhile it got too little private largesse for its needs, even with the aid of such gifted wheedlers of the rich as Provost Edgar Fahs Smith, his predecessor C. C. Harrison, and the influential trustee George Wharton Pepper. Both Smith and Pomfret could count 1920 as a landmark; that year Smith retired, and Pomfret got his second B.A.—the first having nominally been conferred by Central High School. A Master's Degree followed in 1922.

The ambitious young graduate had to solve the problem of self-support by teaching in the best institution that would receive him; in this instance the University of South Carolina, to which he journeyed in the fall of 1924. It was a pleasant, easygoing little institution in the fast-growing town of Columbia. He liked the winter climate, the magnolias, and the azaleas. He relished glimpses of post-Tillman politics in the gray granite State House where a colonial mace, made in London, an oil portrait of Calhoun, a Confederate flag, and a piece of statuary broken by Sherman's men, were reminders of history. He enjoyed the august traditions which had been clustering about college halls from the days when the eminent Thomas Cooper, W. C. Preston, Robert Barnwell, and Augustus Baldwin Longstreet had been presidents. John and Joseph LeConte had been faculty members, and after the war, Lee's chief of artillery, General E.P. Alexander, had taught engineering and mathematics. Particularly did Pomfret like the beautiful university library, with four stately stone columns supporting an impressive portico. Its collections included books bought by Francis Lieber when this learned veteran of Waterloo was professor of history and political economy, and by the versatile Stephen Elliott, botanist, banker, and founder of the *Southern Review*. And John Pomfret admired the southern girls—one in particular.

In fact, South Carolina offered him a liberal new education. He learned how to teach youths who met the standard Carolina specifications: fire in the head, comfort in the belly, and a little lead in the feet. More importantly, perhaps, he learned to drink juleps, he improved his knowledge of poker and dancing, and he acquired social graces unknown in Quakerish Philadelphia. His tuition was crowned when he fell in love with Sara C. Wise, whom he married a little later, on August 28, 1926.

"I well remember," writes one of his friends, "when Jack came back from South Carolina and told my wife and me about Sara. In his description she was a pretty, gentle, completely unformed Southern girl waiting for Jack to shape her personality. When we met Sara we realized how wrong Jack was; as with so many southern girls, there was a lot more than appeared on the surface." To some observers, Jack in early graduate school days had possessed a streak of impetuosity. His wife, whose vivacity equalled, and whose grace much excelled his own, had a wisdom, tact, and patience that steadied him, and that proved simply invaluable in the trials of the years ahead.

II

The scene swiftly changed, after one southern year, to Princeton. The young man who had been associate professor in South Carolina became a mere instructor there, but he and his bride knew that he had taken a step up. They never loved a town more than their new home, or associates better than the other people in the faculty. Princeton had been steeped in conservatism ever since John Grier Hibben was inaugurated president in 1912 to make sure of a subsidence of the emotional upheavals, the social and intellectual antagonisms, that had followed Woodrow Wilson's reforms, and his battle with Dean Andrew F. West. In fact, Hibben had brought peace to the ivied halls with such completeness that some men wondered whether a new idea or an innovation in method would ever percolate into Princeton again. These doubts were overdone. No matter how much the administration might wish to stabilize the university after Wilson's "excesses," it could never put it back into the antiquated mould of James McCosh's day. Since Wilson had put the preceptorial method into operation in 1905, since Grover Cleveland had formally opened the new graduate college in 1906, and since Charles Scribner had given a building and equipment for a university press, currents of change had begun flowing too strong to be checked.

Young and a little shy as he was, John Pomfret in 1925-26 gave one current increased strength. He and Sara were delighted by their new opportunities. With his dissertation on "The Struggle for Land in Ireland" practically completed, his doctorate was ensured. He was made assistant professor, according to expectation, in 1927. Ambitious to strike out on a new line, he found that a course called "Historical Introduction" gave him a chance. It had been conducted by a brilliant but unpredictable teacher who shaped it to cover cultural geography of the Ratzel type rather than history. Freshmen had feared, respected, and denounced its eccentricities. Under Pomfret it became more systematic, rigorous, and historical—and more popular. His class read such texts as Kroeber's *Anthropology* with a feeling that they struck into fresh fields. One able young instructor, Lynn White, who protested that he had absolutely no competence, assisted as preceptor. "I read at night what I taught next morning," he relates, "and was sustained by Pomfret's jovial encouragement." Indeed, Jack's zest in placing history on an anthropological basis changed the whole tendency of Lynn White's studies, and doubtless affected other young men similarly. In time, Pomfret himself got a book out of the course—*The Geographic Pattern of Mankind* (1935).

The Pomfrets were soon among the most popular of the younger faculty in Princeton. They entertained a great deal in a drafty house that the university refused to repair, so that in winter experienced guests learned to preëmpt a chair by the register as the only warm spot. In these prohibition days Jack served the best home-fermented white wine in town, made from his own garden grapes. Sara and he were expert partners at bridge, while with faculty cronies he played a diabolical hand at stud poker, for his impassive face and habitual serenity gave him a great advantage in bluffing. He loved walking trips, tried to save a half day each week for a long excursion into the country, and with Joseph R. Strayer, a young Marylander who had come out of Harvard and the University of Paris to teach medieval history, sometimes made ten or twelve-mile forays. At first he strode along even when it rained. But it was not only the younger staff that he and Sara found congenial. They became close friends of Thomas

J. Wertenbaker, who had been teaching at Princeton since 1910, and who did more than anybody else to divert Pomfret from British to American history. Dana Carlton Munro, the senior member of the department, was particularly fond of them both, so that they became intimate with the whole Munro family, including the son Dana Gardner, a scholar of Latin-American bent much Jack's own age.

Throughout the Princeton community the Wilson-West differences had developed abrasive frictions that still required an emollient touch. As they had been visible among the history teachers, Jack's kindly temper and Sara's tact were especially valuable. At an early date he was put on the examination committee of the department with two other mild-mannered men, for the convincing reason that one professor succinctly stated:

"They're the only three men in the department who won't fight."

Nobody was astonished when, after becoming associate professor in 1933, Jack was raised to an assistant deanship the following year. In a nest of quarreling birds he was a quiet dove; in a prickly-tempered community he got on with all sorts and conditions of men, except pedants and pomposities. He showed more patience and geniality every year, and realized full well that in working for an improvement it was always wise to help some other man claim the idea and the credit. Whenever anybody thwarted him he was too good-natured to sulk, and when he made a blunder he was happy if he could point out that it was a whopper. Stories went around of his helpfulness to youngsters. His protests that he did not like being dean never cloaked a really intense interest in the workings of the university machinery, a subject he better liked to discuss than baseball or politics. His view of Princeton was admiring and his reverence for intellectual pursuits was intense. Yet he was a realist; he surveyed colleagues with shrewd detachment, and sometimes spoke of university ways and the whole academic crew with sharp-edged irony. The critical nature of his gaze did not escape detection.

"I think," writes his colleague Raymond J. Sontag, "a good number of people sensed this refusal to accept the academician at his own valuation and resented it." If so, the knowledge was good for them.

And while still Princeton dean he undertook other duties that broadened his interests. His friend Shryock, who had also attended the Central High School in Philadelphia, and had completed graduate work while Jack was still immersed in it, had become fellowship secretary of the Social Science Research Council. Then, in 1936, he decided to go to Duke University. At his suggestion, Pomfret took over the position. It was a far from inspiring post. Jack had to give rather more time to passing judgment on fledgling scholars and their ambitions than was worth while. However, he threw himself into the task with his usual enthusiasm, travelled a good deal to meet its duties, and learned much.

Meanwhile, another friend joined Wertenbaker in deepening Jack Pomfret's interest in American history. Julian P. Boyd, a gifted southerner, had enrolled in the University of Pennsylvania graduate courses shortly after Pomfret began teaching at Princeton. After several years of study and teaching, he had become assistant librarian of the venerable Historical Society of Pennsylvania. Ambitious, energetic, imaginative, he began revolutionizing the musty place. It had been too much a gentleman's club. Boyd threw open its doors and facilities, beckoned eager scholars in, and established rules to keep it an inviting seat of research. At the same time, he gave its quarterly review, the oldest of the kind in America, fresh vitality and interest. This *Pennsylvania Magazine of History and Biography,* too long of more interest to genealogists and local annalists than to students of broad interests, became valuable to true historians.

For the first time the library grew into a lively center of study, where young men toiled raptly over manuscripts, meanwhile debating furiously, criticizing and encouraging each other, and indulging in competitive jest and horseplay. In summer it was almost a branch graduate school. Scholars boasted of their discoveries, traded ideas for contributions to knowledge, and exchanged erudite gossip.

Although Boyd was the principal leader in all this, Pomfret gave him indefatigable support. They were pioneers in a revival of Pennsylvania historical learning. When Pomfret began his studies in the history of the Quaker colony of West Jersey, which was established four years before the settlement of Pennsylvania, he made almost weekly what he and others thought exciting discoveries. He lighted upon Thomas Budd's "true and perfect account" of the disposal of a hundred shares in the new colony, published in a narrative of which only one badly defaced copy survived; and perfecting its text, he extracted all its values. Boyd at once persuaded him to edit it for the *Pennsylvania Magazine.* He and other members of the group of young scholars, who included Paul A. W. Wallace, author of a good life of Conrad Weiser, Carl Bridenbaugh, who edited Patrick M'Robert's *Tour Through Part of the Northern Provinces 1774-75,* and Henrietta M. Larsen, already at work on Jay Cooke's career, helped each other in all sorts of innovation. They gave impetus to the library's collection of fresh manuscripts. Exploring the possibility of a sustained monograph that would unite the talents of the whole group, they held several seminars for the purpose—quite inconclusively. With enthusiasm, they decided also upon a sixtieth anniversary issue, for which Jack helped provide the leading article.

The story of this contribution throws light on his historical zeal. Boyd relates that he ran down to Princeton to talk about the issue, finding Jack abed with a transient illness. "I told him that we were publishing a number of important letters from the London printer, William Strahan, to his friend Benjamin Franklin. To my utter astonishment Jack told me that, in that very room, he had a bundle of original letters that Franklin had received from Strahan. . . . You may be sure that I did not leave the room without the precious bundle. The letters were immediately transcribed and edited, and inserted in the magazine along with others which they perfectly complemented."

Boyd also tells us that his innovations, happily supported not only by Pomfret and other Young Turks but by such a veteran historian as Conyers Read, aroused a tempest. Philadelphia conservatism then had an armor heavier than triple brass. Main-line Bourbons of rhinoceros hide connected the changes not only with Kemal Pasha and Stalin, but with the unspeakable crimes of Franklin D. Roosevelt. When the gangsters who had taken over the library boldly used more than a hundred WPA workers to help compile a descriptive catalogue of its manuscript possessions, cramming them into its rooms and corridors, old members tore their hair. News that Carl Bridenbaugh, or some such wild radical, was preparing to put all of Benjamin Franklin's *Pennsylvania Gazette* on microfilm, evoked visions of Robespierre and the French Revolution. Yet in the end the Library outrode the storm unscathed and renovated. Memories of the upheaval gave Pomfret lasting enjoyment, and confirmed his taste for practical activity.

It became plain in these years that he had not only reached a turning-point in his career; he had rounded it. His assistant deanship of the college gave him extra pay, interests, and dignity. He liked administration, and lent it a zeal that neither colonial history nor western history, both urged upon him by Wertenbaker, ever aroused. He became very fond of Dean Christian Gauss. He got along well with Harold W. Dodds, another amiable man who, after some years as professor of politics, became an easy-going president of Princeton in 1933. In the fast-expanding world of higher education, successful deans still in their thirties were likely to get all kinds of invitations to higher posts. Jack's friend Robert G. Albion, for example, for some time assistant dean of the Princeton faculty, got them, but being devoted to research, turned them down. Jack was offered the deanship of the graduate school in Vanderbilt University—and with his last field work for the Social Science Research Council behind him, in 1937 he accepted it. He knew it would probably lead higher.

He was badly needed in Vanderbilt, a struggling little university with fewer than 2,000 students registered in a liberal arts college and a handful of professional schools. Until two years earlier the institution had possessed no graduate school—only a graduate department closely linked with the last two years of undergraduate study, so that Pomfret was also dean of the senior college. A true graduate faculty still had to be established. A great many rules and regulations had to be framed. Fortunately, the new chancellor who came in simultaneously with Pomfret, was an able anthropologist of considerable academic experience, Oliver C. Carmichael—a former Rhodes scholar; fortunately too, the faculty contained along with a good deal of dead wood, for the absence of any retirement rule had permitted old fogies to cling to their jobs, some distinguished teachers like Frank Owsley.

Once more, his geniality and moderation were vital qualities. He had to push some superannuated men, as tactfully as possible, out of the faculty; he had to urge others to show more respect for scholarly standards. In a curious way, Vanderbilt was more stiffly formal than Princeton. Faculty members were more likely to insist on last names with full academic titles. Pomfret characteristically did something to break down the social stiffness. He derided some creaky old university conventions and customs; he scolded teachers and faculty in frank but kindly vein; and he gave his sense of humor and freshness of manner full play. He was taken aback when some of his extemporaneous observations got into the press with results embarrassing to oldsters of James K. Polk conservatism. Before he left Nashville he had not merely given character and standing to the graduate school —"things moved when he got back of them," writes Harriet Owsley— but he had done much to make life at Vanderbilt more agreeable.

In what he did for the unity of faculty and students, however, he made no surrender of honesty. His alertness, and the keenness of his appraisals of men, were refreshing. "He would often come out with a judgment of a younger faculty member or of a mature graduate student," notes Dr. Carmichael, "that was not only surprisingly frank, but most times, at least, surprisingly accurate."

Then, in 1942, still below forty-five, he turned the first page of an eventful new chapter of life; he became president of William and Mary, the second oldest seat of higher education in the country. It had the most venerable college building in the land, it was world famous, it numbered among its former students Jefferson, John Marshall, Monroe, and Tyler; but in some respects it was staggering with weakness, and it faced problems that promised its officers and trustees insomnia if not nervous prostration. Jack Pomfret did not blanch.

III

This was fortunate indeed for William and Mary. One of its faculty, recalling that a Negro cook in his family used to chant "I ain't got no future, but God, God, what a past!," remarks that this might well have been a theme-song for the college until Pomfret appeared. One of his chief accomplishments was to change pride in the past into proud hope for the future; to bring William and Mary into the twentieth century.

In student expansion and physical growth, to be sure, the university showed a recent dynamism. Lyon G. Tyler had resigned in 1919, and the executive who had taken his place, Alvin Chandler, was a man of experience and talent. He had earned a doctorate at Johns Hopkins, written several good historical monographs, and served for ten years as superintendent of the Richmond public schools. By virtue of energy, ability, and the friendship of John D. Rockefeller, Jr., he had given William and Mary an impressive group of new buildings to supplement the colonial edifices gracing the campus since pre-Hanoverian days. Three of the early buildings—one of them bearing authentic evidence of the genius of Christopher Wren —had been restored by Rockefeller funds, under Chandler's oversight, as handsome mementos of the eighteenth century, and useful adjuncts of the busy present. The enrollment had shown a healthy increase. President Chandler, however, had been too busy with expansion to strengthen the faculty properly or lift scholarly standards.

It was with some justification, as also with some exaggeration, that Carl Bridenbaugh spoke of the place as "an intellectual graveyard."

The choice of Pomfret, a scholar of distinction, and an out-of-state educator whose Pennsylvania and New Jersey background was certain to jar upon many Virginians, was the result of happy accidents. William and Mary had been thrown off the accreditation list of universities and colleges by a grade-changing scandal in its Norfolk branch. Through the influence of the Rockefeller group that was remaking Williamsburg, Pomfret's name was placed on the list of nominees for the presidency. The trustees, or "visitors," though generally hostile to any "foreigner," prudently left it there even though a majority planned to end their search by taking a home-nurtured educator linked with the Byrd machine. At the last moment serious blots were discovered on the man's personal escutcheon. He had to be discarded, and to the joy of those who had recognized Pomfret's superiority, Jack was chosen. He took office with liberal Virginians congratulating the college, but with some trustees showing chagrin and irritation. Their resentment, in a state sensitive to taxes and hence inclined toward cheeseparing economies in education, was a distinct handicap to the incoming president. He would need all the political help he could get to lift William and Mary out of its financial slough.

He saw at once that his close election against the opposition of a strong faction of the trustees, the alumni, and various citizens and politicians, made it necessary to walk circumspectly. "It is my understanding," writes an observer in the faculty service who later rose to high professional position in Washington, "that certain members of the board never really forgave him for being elected, and certainly never fully supported him after he was elected." A number of them were smallminded reactionaries greedy for power and privilege.

As he set to work he found other difficulties. One, of course, was the war, which more and more completely disorganized American life, and drained able-bodied young men out of the colleges. One was the fact that the board of trustees or "visitors" was an inharmonious body, some members for personal or political reasons detesting other members. Another difficulty was the tendency of some trustees and many alumni to regard William and Mary as an institution created primarily to achieve glory on the athletic field; they thought the ambition of others to help it gain academic and scholarly fame a little un-American. And of course, underlying all other troubles, was the difficulty of getting proper funds. The war brought drastic changes with an unbalanced registration—at one time about nine girls to each man—and also drastic new demands and costs, hard to meet amid a general clamor for economy.

Pomfret began his ten years' administration determined to make the strengthening of the faculty, and the improvement of scholarly interests and standards, his paramount concern; and from this resolution he never swerved. To get a competent faculty he had to make William and Mary more attractive, and then recruit teachers from outside Virginia and the South. Foremost among the new attractions, of course, were better salaries; and one of the chief accomplishments of the decade was the raising of the top stipends by fifty percent. Another attraction was better library facilities. Although for various reasons Pomfret thought that the time was not ripe for a new library building, he took a keen interest in book-purchasing. Meanwhile, he tried to introduce sabbatical years for professors, and in time persuaded the board to approve them in principle. Unfortunately the principle was never translated into practice. Occasionally, though rarely, he did get a specially deserving teacher a half-year leave with pay; but the Commonwealth of Virginia refused to pay for sabbaticals, and private funds for them were unobtainable. He also regularized the college policies on tenure and promotion, and saw that a firm set of rules was adopted by the trustees on the subject. By establishing the Chancellor Professorships he gave specially distinguished members of the faculty a higher prestige. He instilled into the staff much more esprit de corps, and a greater pride in good work, than had previously existed.

All this meant planning, hard toil, and persistent efforts to raise money. He used to tell the faculty he meant to get an additional $100,000 a year in private income for the college, and ultimately he did. It also took his special virtues of tact and patience. A few impatient faculty members thought that he was too amiable in dealing with hostile elements among the trustees and alumni, and should have shown more fighting temper. But pugnacity was just not in his nature. Struggling against irksome wartime restrictions, against a tendency in Richmond to give the best favors to the University of Virginia and the Virginia Polytechnic Institute, against the duplicity and selfishness of various politicians, and against groups inside and outside the college who wanted to see athletics given first place and scholarship a poor second, his calmness and forbearance were invaluable. Coping later with all the problems involved in the return of veterans, the sudden swelling of enrollment, and the national popularity that Williamsburg rapidly gained as a tourist center, he found that his generous attitudes turned out to be as profitable to him as they were congenial.

He had also to meet a normal array of unpleasant incidents in student life. In general, his relations with undergraduates were of course completely amicable, for though he was firm on essentials of discipline, they appreciated the fact that he was giving the college a quite new intellectual tone, and they liked his attitude of comradeship.

A typical incident illustrates his kindliness. One of the wartime students who earned their way through William and Mary by a work-study program which was instituted under Pomfret in cooperation with the Williamsburg Restoration was returning to his room at dusk the day before Christmas. On the empty campus he encountered the president. "What on earth are you doing here?" asked Pomfret. The student explained. "Good heavens!" exclaimed Pomfret, taken aback, "I didn't realize that our arrangement with the Restoration would mean keeping some of you boys from going home at Christmas." He paused a moment. "When do you finish your work?" he inquired. The student told him about nine o'clock. "All right," he said at once. "You get the boys together then and come to my house. We can't have you going back to a lonely dormitory on Christmas Eve."

A knot of seventeen-year-olds duly arrived at the president's house, nervous and ill-at-ease at first, but happy to be lifted from their loneliness. "Both Dr. and Mrs. Pomfret were magnificent," testifies this witness. "Through some miracle of human companionship they won us completely. They became, for that night, father and mother to each of us. It was a memorable experience."

But a disagreeable teapot-tempest arose when, early in 1945, the student editor of the college weekly, a brave girl from Michigan named Marilyn Kaemmerle, published an editorial entitled "Lincoln's Job Half Done." Denouncing the lack of racial integration in William and Mary, she predicted that some day it would have a full body of Negro students. This was too much for conservative Virginians. They brought pressure on the college authorities to discipline the outspoken editor, and guarantee that such incendiary utterances would not be repeated. Angry citizens wrote letters to newspapers, which began playing up the incident. The student body, partly agreeing and partly disagreeing with the girl, was practically a unit in demanding that its weekly should not be put under censorship. As it held a mass meeting and threatened a student strike, carloads of rowdies from neighboring counties began cruising around the campus and shouting insults. Some ugly incidents occurred. In this crisis, which to Virginians of 1945 seemed far more portentous and alarming than anything of the kind could have appeared twenty years later, Pomfret had to find a road out. The board of trustees or visitors met, heard a motion for expulsion of the girl that failed for want of a second, and voted that the president and faculty take such action as they thought necessary. Pomfret then had the whole problem in his lap; the problem of placating public opinion, satisfying a faculty jealous of its academic freedom, and calming the indignant undergraduates. It bristled with embarrassments.

The faculty was of course amenable to reason. Pomfret, deeply disturbed, showed it a median path characteristic of the man. He read it a statement dropping the editor from her office, which as a senior she would soon lose anyway; protecting her continuance in college; and declaring against censorship of the weekly, but placing it under "advisory" supervision. After heated debate, a motion supporting his position was carried by a heavy majority.

At the same time, he called twenty-five or thirty members of the student government to a meeting in old Phi Beta Kappa Hall. There he explained the latest developments and appealed for their help. The girl, he pointed out, was technically at fault in publishing her editorial without first clearing it through the publications committee, as a long-disused rule demanded. She would soon graduate. He would therefore ask only her relinquishment of the editorship, and if the student body agreed to this, would take no further action against her, and allow no censorship of the weekly. "If you reject this solution," he said, "I must admit to the board of visitors that I cannot handle the affair. I shall have to resign as president of the college." The effect of this statement upon the students was tremendous. Some of the girls were in tears. When he left the room they agreed unanimously and unhesitantly to his decision. The case was closed. Calm returned to the campus, and to the breasts of Virginians not yet ready to face the realities of a new age.

We are left in wonderment that such an episode could disturb people who should have seen how harmonious were Pomfret's relations with both students and faculty, and how steadily he was lifting the eighteenth century institution to late twentieth century standards. He established almost complete unison of purpose with the teaching body. Four predecessors had been non-academic men, and the staff had felt the fact. "Now," writes one of the faculty, "there was never any problem of communication or understanding; he spoke our language and we spoke his." Most of them liked him the better because he was not a political animal; Virginia had too many of that menagerie. They felt confidence in his readiness to defend expressions of conscience—he gave battle in 1944 to super-patriots of the local American Legion post who demanded the dismissal of two conscientious objectors from the faculty—and in his convictions upon academic freedom. They respected his efforts to protect his own time for research and writing, even though he could publish only occasional book reviews and articles. They were grateful for the fact that he quickly learned which faculty members had scholarly talent and literary ability, and saw that funds were ear-marked for their assistance, usually to free them from summer teaching.

Meanwhile, he took a profound satisfaction in the creation in Williamsburg of the Institute of Early American History and Culture. He may well be called its founder, and it remains one of his principal monuments. The date of its birth was 1943. He had seen that as seat of the college and of Colonial Williamsburg, Inc., the town was an ideal place for an organization to fortify research and publication in the field of colonial and early national affairs. He took the initiative; he rallied scholars and Rockefeller executives to the work; and he helped everybody realize how much an institute of the highest standards could enhance the prestige of both the restored capital and the revitalized college. The *William and Mary Quarterly* was then in its second series as a magazine of Virginia history. By firm but tactful action Pomfret took it out of the editorial hands of the venerable and much-respected Dr. E. G. Swem, college librarian, and placed it in those first of Professor Richard L. Morton, and then Professor Douglass Adair. The magazine lost many old subscribers; it gained many new ones, and one of the highest positions in the realm of American scholarship. The awards of the Institute, its many books, ranging from important new volumes like Brook Hindle's *The Pursuit of Science in Revolutionary America* to well-edited reprints like Robert Beverley's *The History and Present State of Virginia,* and the authoritative quality of the articles in its *Quarterly,* gave it a unique place and wide influence.

At the same time, Pomfret assisted other Virginia educators, notably Chancellor William T. Sanger of the Medical College of Virginia and Colonel Herbert W. K. Fitzroy, in establishing on a firm basis the Richmond Area University Center, which did invaluable work in breaking down the academic isolation of its supporting colleges. It grew and flourished. By 1965 the institutions it enlisted numbered twenty-four, and President Fitzroy's headquarters in the Ellen Glasgow House was a buzzing focus of varied activities. The Center developed institutional cooperation with vigor; and the Association of Virginia Colleges, in which Pomfret also had a hand, lent it assistance.

IV

With his faculty growing steadily in strength, with his much-prized institute flourishing, and with his influence in the conservative old Commonwealth healthfully leavening the lump, Pomfret had reason during the post-war years to feel much satisfaction. He was moving the college forward. Outside, he belonged to various national organizations. For a dozen years he was a senator of Phi Beta Kappa, which had been founded in Williamsburg, and he ultimately became vice-president of the united chapters. Yet it could not be said that these were really happy years. Financially, William and Mary remained straitened, moving from one budgetary crisis to another. The relations of the president with the trustees were always uneasy, particularly as the character of the board deteriorated (along with state politics) when peace came. The "visitors," with some creditable exceptions, were a shortsighted and selfish body. Mrs. Pomfret, who was in every way an ideal presidential wife and hostess, later remarked: "I cannot recall that any trustee ever came to offer us a favor; but I recall how often they came to ask one." And the deepseated schism in the college between the friends of scholarship and the friends of athletics grew more and more malignant. When Pomfret had outlined a thoughtful and healthy athletic policy to the faculty in 1944, the board had set it aside.

An alarming portent of future trouble appeared in 1946 when the board administered a sharp defeat to the president. He had nominated a new dean of the faculty; the board rejected the nomination, appointing a committee of three to select a dean; and the result was the choice of a man closely identified with an aggressive athletic policy. Many in the faculty felt that the president should have offered his resignation in order to protect his usefulness. The deanship, however, became vacant again in 1949. By urging the board to appoint a committee to help him fill the place, and by arguing against the choice of a candidate highly acceptable to the big-athletics faction, Pomfret was able to bring about the selection of one of the three men whom he thought most desirable. He had won a momentary victory. But a new conflict was at hand. Its onset is best described in the words of a veteran member of the college faculty who was a close observer of events. He relates:

The real desires of a combined group of board members and alumni had become apparent in 1946 with the conclusion of the war, when a statement of policy was adopted opening the way to a return to an expanded program involving more expenditures for staff and athletic scholarships. Pomfret submitted, apparently hoping that if he conceded on this point he could have his way in other matters. At least this was the opinion which he expressed more than once in private. But this policy of appeasement, if one may call it such, was only partially successful. Pomfret continued to try to apply the brakes, calling attention to athletic deficits and opposing a significant increase in the student athletic fee. By 1950 the situation had reached a point where the chairman of the board committee on athletics read an insulting report chiding the President, demanding closer cooperation between athletic officials and administrative officials, and insisting on the revamping of the faculty committee on athletics under a board-selected chairman.

Then in the spring of 1951 the dean of the faculty reported to the president evidence of alleged tampering with entering students' high school transcripts by athletic officials, and the award of unearned credit to college athletes in courses in physical education controlled by the head coach and athletic director.

As was his wont, Pomfret tried to apply patience and tact to the situation. He showed forbearance toward the grade-changing officers who had betrayed him and the college; forbearance toward even the board when it instituted its own investigation with the patent purpose of protecting itself from any charges of responsibility, and blackening the name of the president and dean in the process. Its official report censured the college administration for not moving with more promptness and decision. Doubtless Pomfret would have acted with less apparent temporizing and more as-

21

perity if he had not underestimated, as liberal men usually do, the amount of baseness and malice at the bottom of the affair. But he was also inhibited by his concern for the fame of William and Mary. When the scandal broke he rejected an attitude that would have hurt the college deeply. Another careful observer from the inside states this forcibly:

If Pomfret had stood up on his hind legs and shouted that he was against sin, that his subordinates had bamboozled him, and that he was going to drive the guilty ones out of the profession, he could have attracted national attention and become the most famous college president of the year, since the country was at that time sensitized by the West Point basketball scandals and others. Thus, he would have had an audience and his stand would have been unassailable as a spokesman for outraged virtue, horrified to discover sin in his backyard. Jack refused to take this position in large part, I am sure, because he felt that if the college could be spared this self-righteous revelation of sin, this was best for the institution. So he arranged for the football coach to continue through the season and resign after the season was over; cleaned up the mess; and reformed procedures to keep it from happening again.

On September 13, 1951, nine years and thirteen days after he had entered on the presidency of William and Mary, Pomfret resigned. Had he remained, the faculty would have stood in practically unbroken ranks beside him to do battle with the board on any material issue of the controversy. As it was, he could leave with a feeling that he had accomplished his main purposes in going to the post. He had transformed a commonplace state-supported college, with commonplace teachers and students, into a distinguished institution full of zeal for lively instruction and sound research. He had enriched Williamsburg and the state with an institute and a magazine at the highest level of scholarship. In a historic old seat of learning he had helped replace lassitude with energy, discouragement with hope, and pride in the past with pride in the present and future. And Sara could feel that where he had left impressions of prosaic bluntness, she had left memories of poetic grace. As an accomplished hostess, whose cheery presence lighted up every room she entered, she had won a place in the hearts of the teaching staff as warm as his own.

Ahead stretched the years of the directorship of the Huntington Library and Art Gallery, a post which he had just accepted; years too close to us as yet to be properly appraised. When his planned history of that particular citadel of culture is written, these years will fall into perspective. We can say only that they have been full of achievement: the staff strengthened, the collections of books, manuscripts, and art enriched, the publishing program invigorated, and the work of inspiring and instructing scholars enlarged. To this statement we can add a comment of special significance. The Pomfret years had imparted to devotees of the Library, as earlier they shed upon students and associates in Princeton, Vanderbilt, and William and Mary, a sense of the values of integrity, serenity, and good will; in short, of Aequanimitas. Large groups in all these places, but perhaps most of all in the Huntington Library, would say as they looked back upon the time of Jack Pomfret's benign preceptorship: "In his own phrase, those were years with a lilt."

Jack Pomfret and the Huntington: A Tribute

BY A. L. ROWSE

A. L. Rowse, a distinguished interpreter of the Elizabethan Age in both England and America, first visited the Huntington Library in 1951 and since 1961 has been a part-time member of its research staff. There he has prepared some of the many books that have earned him an international reputation; books ranging from his early TUDOR CORNWALL *through his monumental* THE ELIZABETHAN AGE *to his recent linked biographical studies of* SHAKESPEARE, MARLOWE, *and* SOUTHAMPTON. *Each year A. L. Rowse spends the winter months at the Huntington Library, the spring at All Souls College in Oxford, and the summer at his home in Cornwall. He brings to the following sketch of "Jack Pomfret and the Huntington" a touch of verbal magic that will allow others less fortunate than himself to sense the excitement of research at the Huntington and the pleasure of joining Jack Pomfret on the daily post-luncheon walk about its landscaped grounds.*

THE FIRST THING to be said about the Huntington Library, though by no means the last, is that in all my lengthening experience of life this is the happiest institution that I have ever known, and with the friendliest, kindliest atmosphere. Some share in the credit for this must fall upon the shoulders of the man who has directed its fortunes for the past fifteen years. As to its objective truth there is evidence from scholars all round the English-speaking world who adore the Huntington, who come back to it with pleasure again and again and who, when absent, keep the image of it in the mind's eye—some of us in the heart—as the pleasantest of places to return to, a paradise for scholars.

Of course, the Huntington has the triple advantage of being not only a library and research center, but there are also the art gallery and the garden: equal powers and no less cherished by the most bookish of researchers—though we may not all be sharp enough to discern the finer points of the cacti. We can and do all enjoy the beauty of the place, however, the green lawns and formal terraces, the separate and successive gardens each with its own idiom and flora, the spreading trees—perhaps especially the most splendid of the native California oaks, still in good heart out there on the walk between the library and art gallery. Often on that walk, on the way to lunch or a lecture, one looks back along the terrace with its fringe of Cornish heath (*erica vagans*) and catches one's breath at the scene, the relation of the place to the amphitheatre of the mountains. *Levavi meos oculos,* I often think: there are the San Gabriel Mountains the mission fathers named, tawny-flanked or lavender-pink, the folds rumpled downwards like some velvet material unfolding; the pine-wooded crest of Mount Wilson with its installations punctuating the skyline. In the east, thirty miles away, there is Mount Baldy with the perfection of its peak white under snow in winter, sometimes pale rose in the afternoon as the sun moves round, but always silent, remote, withdrawn, making its own comment upon our temporary avocations.

Mr. Huntington made no mistake in his choice of site—in that showing the extraordinary flair that marked his spirit no less than in his purchases of books and pictures. I hope that his shade is pleased with the way his plans have worked out, I reflect, as I watch him beaming from his portrait benignly down upon the assembled Friends on Founder's Day, packing the exhibition hall to observe his birthday. Few founders can have had more reason to be pleased; for the triple institution is not only famous all over the English-speaking world for its collections, as he intended—the name itself carried to the uttermost parts of the earth—but it is a creative center in scholarship. In addition to this one must not forget its educational role in the cultural life of state and nation, not only in the school-classes that young people attend in art gallery and garden, but in the pleasure and profit, the renewal of spirit, that thousands of citizens from all over the country enjoy. One has only to overhear occasional comments to know how greatly appreciated, what a national service, it all is. It has become a place of pilgrimage.

Every area of it has its particular appeal, its peculiar atmosphere. I know how romantic I find the wilder parts of the place—the canyon where a last family of native Indians once had their shacks; the lane coming up out of it making straight for the mountains, as if for a legendary pot of gold, and where for some unconscious reason I often think of Robert Louis Stevenson and his Californian days. Or there is the deodar avenue, with its cool green glooms and aromatic scent, the impression of the exotic, to recall Kipling. Or perhaps, best of all, there is the secret meadow gold-carpeted with wild mustard in spring, an occasional burst of dark-red toyon berries or Chinese-blue ceanothus (wild lilac they call it in the South), and the cart-track across which Jack walks, has walked every morning for years, to his work from the charming little southern plantation mansion which is the Director's official residence. I see him swinging his way along now, with the powerful shoulders of the ancient footballer, through the brush and through the wild mustard—as I hope others, our successors, may see him and remember his good work, when we are all gone from these walks.

It was the famous lunch-hour walks that gave us the chance to get to know our colleagues best, when relaxed, unbuttoned, off duty, ready to enjoy ourselves and take the air around the grounds before returning to the afternoon's stint. These were led—or perhaps 'shepherded' is the word— by the indomitable Allan Nevins, ready to rush down any slope at sight, breast any hill, jump any chasm, the rest of us lagging, some of us protesting, though Jack usually managed to keep up at the great man's side. And what good talk the excitement engendered!—any subject under the sun was apt to be canvassed, though usually history, sometimes politics, especially past politics, at any rate public affairs, discussed with public spirit and concern, a sense of responsibility—in that like a cognate institution in former years, All Souls College at Oxford. In any case, the talk was usually about a subject, characteristic masculine discourse.

Sometimes the walk would take us down into the Japanese garden (where the rare cycads grow), up the slope by the sweet-smelling osmanthus or tea-olive, sprinkling its scent upon all the ravine below, through the camellias and pine-shrubbery out upon the high waste-space of the wood-dump. Up there, on the high plateau, one gets the best view of the whole crescent of the San Gabriel Mountains. Over across from there snugly situated is the Director's mansion, Sara's rose-garden, her pride and treasure, on the nearer side (herself an excellent, devoted gardener). On the other side is the curving drive through flowering peach and plum, Sara's well-placed clumps of arums, irises, narcissi in spring, the loaded kumquat by the door which I have often robbed, filling my pockets before speeding off to the spartan delights of my solitary cell in the Athenaeum.

This impressive drive used to give me a never-failing chance to tease the Director when I first came. I would recite:

> God bless the Squire and his relations,
> And keep us in our proper stations—

us, of course, being humble researchers like myself. I could usually get a rise by this innocent tease—such is the extraordinary modesty, the genuinely democratic idiom of feeling among the best Americans, with whom modesty is not merely a foible, but a suit of armour in which they are clad, almost a religion. An Englishman, still less a Cornishman, can hardly understand it—how different a picture from Dickens' view of the Americans, or even James Bryce's impressions of Teddy Roosevelt's era! (Hasn't there been an almighty revolution in this century—Jack's lifetime and mine—the landmarks all altered, the familiar signposts down, one hardly knows one's way any more?)

Nevertheless, this extreme modesty is the clue to Jack Pomfret, what makes it difficult to discover his tracks, to put salt on the tail of this wary old bird, makes it almost impossible to write about him and do him justice—for one would be doing him justice against his will. Perhaps that is why this Cornishman has been called in for this impossible assignment. I realize that I am not qualified to give a proper account of his career and work, I am not sufficiently acquainted with the background in American academic life. But I have been asked to contribute just my impressions, and I count that an honor to have been asked.

For in spite of Jack's self-effacing modesty, his actual dislike of any tributes to him or talk about him, it has not escaped my observation that here we have a man exceptionally wise and exceptionally kind. I know from experience how true that is—but we all have had experience of his kindness, of his care and forethought for us, his consideration and solicitude. It has been something quite new and out of the ordinary to me, used to the English environment, where one does not find such generosity, where such things are rarer or at least more intermittent.

It did not take me long to discover that underneath that placid exterior there was a quiet dynamo working. We shall come to something of what it has achieved in a moment, for the evidences are there. But, first, I should say that I have always been struck by how much he knows of what is going on—he knows *everything* that is going on. How he keeps track of it all I cannot think—it is a mystery to me, who am no administrator at all. Jack Pomfret is an admirable example of that increasingly rare type, the scholar-administrator, with the scholar coming first. But then, again, how he has been able to accomplish so much in the way of scholarship, write a number of research-books, while remaining exposed all the time to the demands and duties of administration, to the solicitations and problems of all of us, is another mystery to me, who can only get my writing done by intense concentration to the exclusion of everything else. Somebody asked him however he managed to cope with all those prima donnas on the second floor (does no other floor have its prima donnas, or possibly its *prime donne?*)—'Oh, I leave them to get on with it themselves,' he said peaceably. I suppose that is half the art; it certainly produces results—no one can say that those particular prima donnas do not produce the goods. But there is a serious point behind the joke: with all the kindness and patience, no one would question the authority. He is a man of instinctive, unquestioned authority—so much so that he does not have to exert it: the sense of it is there unspoken. That is another reason why, under his aegis, however great individualists we may be, with whatever difficulties of temperament (speaking for myself), we work for him and under him with a will, as a team with never a moment's difficulty or a cross word—and that is something remarkable in any institution—a team united in common pride for the Library and its great name, in evident wish to do our best, and in simple affection.

In the achievement of that spirit, Jack Pomfret, without raising a finger or his voice, but only those kindly candid eyes that perceive everything and understand everything, has been the indispensable factor, the mainspring of the action.

Now for a word as to his work.

All too inadequate as I am to describe it, I have gradually come to realize that Jack Pomfret is very much a man of ideas, that he holds staunchly by these ideas, sound and tried in themselves, and that they can be seen to bear fruit consistently at each stage in his career. A native Philadelphian, he did both his undergraduate and graduate work at the University of Pennsylvania, and then was at Princeton as instructor in and professor of history for some eleven years (1925-1936). Going to Vanderbilt University for the next seven years (1936-1942) while there he initiated and built up the publications program of the University, launched it into publishing. There is the scholar essentially, concerned to advance the interests of scholarship, to get good work into print. It is a concern that has continued all through his career, as we shall see.

We find it bearing fruit most notably twenty years later, when he became Director of the Huntington Library and Art Gallery in 1951. He immediately set to work to revive the publications program, which had somewhat fallen by the wayside—with the result that the Library has the excellent list of books under its imprint that it has now. Any institution as small as the library might well be proud of the number, as well as of the variety of subjects and interests covered. For there are not only history and literature, mainly English (with the emphasis on the Renaissance) and American (with an increasing, and appropriate, leaning towards California and the west coast), but also horticultural and gardening publications as well as the fascinating books and brochures coming from the art gallery. As Director, Dr. Pomfret can claim more than an indirect interest in these last two classes of publications, since he himself appointed their two departmental heads and inspirers. Our publications are in themselves a speaking tribute to the spread and variety, the keenness, of his interest in the publishing side of the Library's activities. I know myself that he always has a shrewd eye open for a good book. I was going to say that a first-class publisher was lost when he opted for the academic profession; but no—he was retrieved when he came to the Huntington Library with the publishing possibilities that that opened up.

A comparable opportunity was taken at Williamsburg, during the years when Dr. Pomfret was president of the College of William and Mary, 1942-1951. It occurred to him that the *William and Mary Quarterly*, founded in 1892, might be something more than a genealogical record or even than a magazine of Virginia history. Dr. Pomfret conceived of its being converted into 'a journal of wider scope serving the broad field of American history.'[1] He then took the steps, gathered the support, to bring it into being; he recruited 'a board of editors for a new series of the *Quarterly* under the editorship of Dr. Richard L. Morton, chairman of the college's department of history.' Hence he may be regarded as the creator, or the recreator, of the leading journal we have in this field, with its distinguished record of work encouraged and accomplished, of articles and documents published, the succeeding generations of young scholars who have been given their chance in this way, the academic careers rendered fruitful and fulfilled.

But from the first this was only a part of a larger idea that came to the president of William and Mary in the dark, heroic days of the second World War. The restoration of Colonial Williamsburg was already well advanced, through the imaginative support of John D. Rockefeller, Jr. It was Dr. Pomfret who thought of making this the setting for a center for the study of American colonial history and culture in the old capital of Virginia. What more appropriate? Fortunately, Dr. Kenneth Chorley, then president of Colonial Williamsburg, was equally enthusiastic for the project, and under their joint sponsorship there came into being the Institute of Early American History and Culture.

It is not my place, nor am I qualified, to describe the fine flowering of this plan, the large body of good work achieved, the number of distinguished scholars who have taken part, given of their services in advice and counsel, or received inspiration for their research and writing. Perhaps I may quote from a Report of the Special Committee for appraisal of the Institute's work: 'From the beginning, three activities have been central in the Institute's program: (1) publication of the third series of the *Quarterly*; (2) the publication of books, mostly secondary studies but some of them edited texts; and (3) the guidance provided for resident post-doctoral Fellows.' It is simply the modest truth to say that 'the Institute has played an important role for twenty years in promoting a renaissance in scholarly research and writing in colonial, Revolutionary and early national history.'

Perhaps I may be allowed to record only a visitor's impression— the Institute helps to breathe the spirit of life into the beautiful resuscitation of the past that is Colonial Williamsburg, to provide scholarly standards for guidance to the popular appreciation of the past—in itself wholly desirable and to be encouraged—and to help in the work of national education that the place as a whole, with its adjunct of Jamestown, so signally provides. Altogether it is a wonderful flowering—as perhaps a discerning visitor can usefully testify.

One other beneficent project I can now speak of from personal experience. It was from an idea of Dr. Pomfret's that that admirable concern, the Virginia University Center, sprang. The foremost service that this has been enabled to provide is to have brought some hundreds of scholars and lecturers to speak on the campuses of Virginia universities and colleges, when many of these individually would not have been able to finance them. By pooling their resources in a co-operative effort it is possible to bring a large number of the best speakers and lecturers—and to introduce them to the delights of Virginia. (Once across the Blue Ridge Mountains, I imagine, they all return *aficionados* of Virginia.) Some thirty institutions now share in those two-way benefits, directed by the benevolent autocracy of Colonel Herbert W. K. Fitzroy, from that famous address: Number 2, Main Street, Richmond, Ellen Glasgow's old home, rich with the atmosphere and memories of that Victorian literary lady.

And so back (or on) to the Huntington Library. All this varied and fundamentally creative achievement stems from the fact that at heart Jack Pomfret has always been a scholar. It has long been incomprehensible to me how anyone could carry forward scholarly work, could write anything at all, under the thousand daily solicitations and irritations of administration, frittering away one's time and nervous energy, the perpetual telephone calls. (We in England are nothing like so submissive, or perhaps addicted, to the demands of the telephone as Americans are—have they become somewhat got down by it, the patient, long-suffering creatures?)

And yet, in this last phase at the Huntington, Jack Pomfret has been more prolific of books than in any other. This also is not my subject, but someone else's, yet I cannot but pay tribute to the excellence of the work he has managed to achieve—the standard history of New Jersey in the early colonial period, 1609-1702, in two volumes; the admirable research articles in the *Pennsylvania Magazine of History and Biography*; the edition of narratives of *California Gold Rush Voyages*; the work of synthesis on which he has been latterly engaged, *Founding the American Colonies, 1583-1660*. A happy result of retirement and increased freedom is that we may look forward now to more from his pen, beginning with a history of the Huntington Library and Art Gallery.

Of course, so full and well-rounded a life of achievement would hardly have been possible without the strength and support of a happy family life. For one thing Jack could never have accomplished entertaining on his own, as we bachelors have to do; a very masculine type, I doubt if he could have arranged a home for himself. He was made for family life; and we all recognize that in Sara he found an ideal partner, the director of the Huntington an exemplary hostess. Sara Pomfret has her own immensely high standards, modulated by her inveterate kindness of heart, her inability to refuse help to any stray, human or animal, but particularly cats—all the stray cats make straight up the drive and round to Sara's back door: the word has gone round.

It is wonderful what Sara accomplished with that southern plantation mansion, contributing of her own animation and sparkling vivacity to the social life of the Library, making us strangers feel at home, always a smiling welcome, keeping us together—such diverse elements with ways of our own too—communicating a constant sense of the fun, the interest and adventure of life. It is no secret that something of Jack's exceptional range of reading he owes to Sara, especially in literature; for where he is dominantly historical, her intellectual interests are more literary, with her favorites Jane Austen and Anthony Trollope, though we all know her lively and responsible interest in public affairs too. A woman of intellectual distinction and high principle—but I propose to end on the lower note of creature comforts: shall I ever forget those hospitable meals, the southern chicken and the most delicious *crême brulée* I ever tasted, a work of art in itself?

There we leave them, sadly vacating that so friendly house, the garden Sara tended so devotedly—where I shall always see her smiling a welcome to her guests on front porch or back terrace; but moving not so far away after all, whence we may often hope to see them both, moving only up the lovely Californian coast, carrying with them our love and gratitude.

[1]Quoted from "Twenty Years of Reawakening Interest," *The Alumni Gazette of the College of William and Mary* (May 1964).

A Bibliography of the Writings of John Edwin Pomfret

COMPILED BY JOHN M. STEADMAN

John M. Steadman joined the staff of the Huntington Library in 1962 as Research Associate in English Literature and editor of the Huntington Library Quarterly. *A scholar of note, with numerous articles on Renaissance and medieval literature in journals here and abroad to his credit, he holds the doctorate from Princeton University, has taught at the University of North Carolina and the Georgia School of Technology, and engaged in postdoctoral research at the British Museum and the Bodleian Library. Of his association with John Pomfret and the library John Steadman writes: "Few Miltonists possess the good fortune to live in one Earthy Paradise while writing books about another. The Huntington Library is a Paradise Regained that John Milton somehow overlooked. Less primaeval than its Miltonic counterpart and unmenaced by the presence of a serpent, this suburban Eden resembles its predecessor in combining the pleasures of a botanical garden with those of the contemplative life".*

BOOKS AND MONOGRAPHS

The Struggle for Land in Ireland, 1800-1923. Princeton, 1930. 334 pp.

The Geographic Pattern of Mankind. Century Earth Science Series. New York, 1935. 442 pp.

Editor: *Ten Americans Speak: Facsimiles of Original Editions Selected and Annotated.* Alhambra, 1954. 141 pp.

Editor: *Twelve Americans Speak.* San Marino, 1954. 183 pp.

Editor: *California Gold Rush Voyages, 1848-1849.* San Marino, 1954. 246 pp.

The Province of West New Jersey: A History of the Origins of an American Colony. Princeton, 1956. 298 pp.

The Gift of Talent, William Henry Snyder Lecture, Los Angeles City College. Los Angeles, 1956. 17 pp.

The Province of East New Jersey 1609-1702: The Rebellious Proprietary. Princeton, 1962. 407 pp.

The New Jersey Proprietors and Their Lands, 1664-1776. Princeton, 1964. 135 pp.

Founding the American Colonies, 1583-1660. The New American Nation Series. Harper and Brothers, New York. (In progress.)

ARTICLES AND NOTES

"Student Interests at Brown, 1789-1790," *The New England Quarterly,* V (1932), 135-147.

Editor: "Some Further Letters of William Strahan, Printer," *The Pennsylvania Magazine of History and Biography,* LX (1936), 455-489.

"Edward Byllynge's Proposed Gift of Land to Indigent Friends, 1681," *The Pennsylvania Magazine of History and Biography,* LXI (1937), 88-92.

"Thomas Budd's 'True and Perfect Account' of Byllynge's Proprieties in West New Jersey, 1685," *The Pennsylvania Magazine of History and Biography,* LXI (1937), 325-331.

"The German Lutheran Aid Society of 1790," *The Pennsylvania Magazine of History and Biography, LXIII* (1939), 60-65 (with John G. Frank).

"United States: Graduate Study," in *Educational Yearbook of the International Institute of Teachers College, Columbia University, 1943,* ed. I. L. Kandel (New York, 1943), 256-272.

"College of William and Mary," *The Commonwealth,* X (1943), 7-9.

"Education and Government in the Postwar World," in *Postwar Problems in Business, Education, and Government: Papers Presented at a Conference at Vanderbilt University, March 1-3, 1944* (Nashville, 1944), 25-35.

"Historical News," *The William and Mary Quarterly*, Third Series, I (1944), 91-93.

"Philip Lindsley, Pioneer Educator of the Old Southwest," in *The Lives of Eighteen from Princeton*, ed. Willard Thorp (Princeton, 1946), 158-177.

"The Problem of the West Jersey *Concessions* of 1676/7," *The William and Mary Quarterly*, Third Series, V (1948), 95-105.

"The Province of West New Jersey: A Quaker Commonwealth (1674-1702)," *Proceedings of the New Jersey Historical Society*, LXVIII (1950), 21-39.

"The Proprietors of the Province of West New Jersey, 1674-1702," *The Pennsylvania Magazine of History and Biography*, LXXV (1951), 117-146.

"West New Jersey: A Quaker Society, 1675-1775," *The William and Mary Quarterly*, VIII (1951), 494-519.

"Retrospect and Prospect," *Bulletin of the California Institute of Technology*, LXI (1952), 1-9.

"At the Still Point of Turning World," *The Huntington Library Quarterly*, XV (1952), 311-323.

"Letters of Fred Lockley, Union Soldier, 1864-65," *The Huntington Library Quarterly*, XVI (1952), 75-112.

"Robert Barclay and James II: Barclay's 'Vindication,' 1689," *Bulletin of the Friends Historical Association*, XLII (1953), 33-40.

"The Proprietors of the Province of East New Jersey, 1682-1702," *The Pennsylvania Magazine of History and Biography*, LXXVII (1953), 251-293.

"Biographical Memoir of Douglas Southall Freeman," *American Philosophical Society Year Book, 1953* (Philadelphia, 1954), 350-352.

"Publishing at the Huntington Library," *College and Research Libraries*, XV (1954), 388-392.

"The First Purchasers of Pennsylvania, 1681-1700," *The Pennsylvania Magazine of History and Biography*, LXXX (1956), 137-163.

"Governor Gawen Lawrie's 'Brief Account', 1686," *Proceedings of the New Jersey Historical Society*, LXXV (1957), 96-111.

"The Apologia of Governor Lawrie of East Jersey, 1686," *The William and Mary Quarterly*, XIV (1957), 344-357.

"Note on Robert Ormes Dougan," *College and Research Libraries*, XIX (1958), 334.

"Pasadena," *Encyclopaedia Britannica*. Chicago, 1960.

"Mark Hopkins' Formative Years in California," *The Huntington Library Quarterly*, XXV (1962), 57-90.

"Henry Edwards Huntington," in *Keepers of the Past*, ed. Clifford L. Lord (Chapel Hill, 1965), 169-179.

Book reviews in *The William and Mary Quarterly, The American Historical Review, The Mississippi Valley Historical Review, The Pennsylvania Magazine of History and Biography, Quaker History,* and other journals.

Section II

RECENT INTERPRETATIONS OF EARLY AMERICAN HISTORY

The Historians of Early New England

BY EDMUND S. MORGAN

Few historians can pretend to the thorough knowledge of a significant period of history achieved by Edmund S. Morgan. Since earning his doctorate at Harvard University he has immersed himself in the study of the New England colonies and their people, until he is recognized today as one of the few masters of that subject. Both the breadth and depth of his learning is attested by the procession of books from his pen—THE PURITAN FAMILY, THE GENTLE PURITAN, THE STAMP ACT CRISIS, and many more—all marked by fresh viewpoints and challenging new interpretations no less than by their charming style. His teaching at Brown and Yale universities has been interrupted by occasional research trips to the Huntington Library, where he held a fellowship in 1952-1953. His essay on "The Historians of Early New England" will provide new insights even to those most familiar with the field, and will serve as a guideline to future scholarship in an area that has fascinated scholars since the founding of the Massachusetts Bay Colony.

THE HISTORIOGRAPHY of early New England has reached in the past forty years a level of sophistication unmatched in the study of any other part of American history.[1] The lives of the men and women who settled New England have been traced in more detail, the laws they made, the diaries they kept, the letters they wrote, the sermons they preached have been subjected to closer analysis than the words of any other group of Americans. We know what they thought about God, the world, and the devil almost better than we know what we think about these things ourselves. It could in fact be argued that we already know more about the Puritans than sane men should want to know, that we ought therefore to declare a moratorium on further investigation and turn our attention to less familiar fields.

But the law of diminishing returns does not always operate in scholarship; the rewards often increase instead of diminishing as investigation spreads and deepens. Scholarly interest in early New England, instead of slacking off, appears to be rising. And it is rising precisely because historians already know so much about the subject. Every new study suggests two more, and the most advanced analyses become themselves the subject of analysis. New England historiography has reached the critical point where it generates its own energy. How did it get that way and where is its internal energy taking it?

I

In order to understand how the study of early New England history reached its present position, one must begin with the Puritans themselves. The founders of New England were so filled with a sense of their own historic mission that they were writing the history of their settlement even before they set foot in the New World. Theirs was to be a New Canaan as well as a New England, and they were sure the world would one day wish to know how they had preserved the light of the gospel for posterity. Governor John Winthrop started his running account of the enterprise as soon as he boarded the *Arbella*. And though we usually call that account his "Journal," he wrote most of it in the third person and his editor appropriately labelled it *The History of New England*.[2] The governor of Plymouth left a similar account of his colony, which remains the outstanding piece of historical writing produced in the United States before Francis Parkman.[3]

Winthrop and Bradford were by no means alone in their eagerness to record events. Besides the other formal histories, such as Morton's, Johnson's, and Hubbard's,[4] countless Puritans kept diaries. Some, like Michael Wigglesworth's, were introspective.[5] Others, like Cotton Mather's,[6] recorded the author's piety and benefactions with future publication evidently in mind; and one, Samuel Sewall's, is among those rare diaries that relate the author's thoughts and deeds without betraying a self-conscious motive.[7] All of them help to fill out the record of the Puritan venture.

The urge to record was matched by the urge to preserve; it became a New England trait to save papers. Governor Winthrop, besides writing his history, carefully kept the letters that came to him, and so did many others of his generation and later. It is no accident that the first historical society founded in the United States was the Massachusetts Historical Society, or that it was able to gather the richest store of seventeenth-century family papers in the country. If the history of early New England is known today in greater detail than that of any other region, the reason, in part at least, is because the early New Englanders took pains to make it possible.

Nor did the founders fail to transmit to later, more skeptical New Englanders some of the sense of their own importance. After the religious impulse flagged and men stopped thinking of New England as the spearhead of redemption, they discovered the history of its politics. Governor Thomas Hutchinson, deploring the uncooperative attitudes that his New England ancestors displayed toward imperial authority, recounted them in detail.[8] In the pages of his books, his own political opponents, who were busy dismantling imperial authority, could find precedents for their actions. The New Englanders of the Revolutionary generation paid tribute to their ancestors and themselves simultaneously by identifying their own cause—political and religious liberty—as the one that had animated the founding of New England. The independent attitude of a Winthrop or an Endecott toward England, which won strictures from Hutchinson, became for them a prototype of the resistance of Hancock and the Adamses to Hutchinson's own exercise of royal authority.

Thus reinforced with their ancestors' blessings and their ancestors' sense of mission, the Revolutionary New Englanders were able to claim the new nation as a kind of annex to New England. Although Virginia was older than New England, with an older representative assembly, although that assembly was the first to denounce Parliamentary taxation, although a Virginian wrote the Declaration of Independence, although a Virginian commanded the Revolutionary armies and became the first President of the United States and the foremost national hero ever after, New Englanders captured the nation's past. As W. F. Craven has brilliantly shown, the first New Englanders' sacrifices for principle made them more attractive as ancestors than the first Virginians.[9]

As the "Founding Fathers" of the new nation, the Puritans continued to receive the admiring attention of historians. In the pages of George Bancroft's *History of the United States*,[10] they emerged as champions of political and religious freedom, and John Gorham Palfrey managed in five volumes to justify nearly everything they did.[11] Bancroft and Palfrey, in spite of their partisan interpretations, were thoroughly versed in the sources, and they were only two among many nineteenth-century historians who gave their days and nights to unravelling the details of New England history. Gentlemen scholars at the Massachusetts Historical Society transcribed the difficult texts among their ancestors' papers and wrote biographical sketches and learned articles, which they read to one another over the teacups and published in the Society's *Collections* and *Proceedings.* James Savage, for example, transcribed and published John Winthrop's Journal in a heavily annotated edition and also wrote in four compressed volumes biographies of all the sevententh-century settlers of New England that he could identify.[12]

Not all these efforts exhibited the filial piety of Palfrey or Bancroft. New Englanders of the nineteenth century were sufficiently sure of themselves and their ancestors to enjoy an occasional jab at individuals and actions that they found distasteful. Savage, who devised a system of abbreviations for getting as much information as possible on every line of his dictionary, yet gave up precious pages to diatribes against cant and hypocrisy wherever he found his ancestors exhibiting them. Charles Francis Adams and his brother Brooks denounced the intolerance of the Founding Fathers and poked fun at historians who tried to defend them for hanging Quakers and witches.[13] But the Adamses contributed also to the growing body of scholarship. Charles Francis Adams's *Three Episodes of Massachusetts History,*[14] together with his collection of documents on *Antinomianism in Massachusetts Bay*[15] made him perhaps the outstanding New England historian of the century, surpassing Palfrey in style if not in bulk.

Most of these gentlemen scholars devoted themselves, apart from biography and genealogy, to political history: to the colonies' internal politics, to their relationships with one another and with royal authority, and to the New England town and its town meetings. When historians looked at the New England churches they saw them usually as political institutions, whose congregational organization served as a model for later political decentralization and popular government. Even in discussing Anne Hutchinson's heresies, Charles Francis Adams had more to say about politics than he did about theology, and what he did say about theology was not perceptive.

But the churches were not wholly neglected. While the gentlemen of Boston were exploring New England's political history, two scholars from the hinterlands laid the foundations for the serious study of New England church history. Henry Martyn Dexter, a Massachusetts clergyman with a taste for book collecting, gathered an unparalleled library of sixteenth and seventeenth century Puritan tracts, and from this base produced what remains the best working bibliography of early Puritanism: *The Congregationalism of the Last Three Hundred Years as Seen in its Literature.*[16] Building on Dexter's work, Williston Walker, who taught first at Hartford Theological Seminary and later at Yale (to which Dexter bequeathed his collection), produced what is still the most important source book of New England church history: *The Creeds and Platforms of Congregationalism.*[17]

II

With Walker's work New England history was already being swept into the domain of the academic professionals who have presided over the study of history in America since the end of the nineteenth century. The rise of the professional did not mean the total eclipse of the gentlemen scholars, who continued to fill the pages of the Massachusetts Historical Society *Proceedings* with significant articles and even founded the Colonial Society of Massachusetts in order to foster still more studies. The societies welcomed the professionals (who were also professors) from Harvard and Yale to their ranks, especially if they had the proper pedigrees, but the center of historical research had shifted from the private study to the university. And if this appeared to be only a matter of crossing the Charles River from Boston to Cambridge, the appearance was deceptive. Although Harvard had always had strong ties with Boston, it could not have attained or retained its intellectual prestige if it had been guided by Beacon Hill. Historians at Harvard, like those in other universities, recognized that they must stand or fall by the judgment of their academic peers throughout the country. And among academic historians the production of more studies of early New England did not at first seem the most likely way to win professional standing. Charles Francis Adams, who stayed in Quincy and Boston and remained an amateur, could enjoy himself writing about early

New England; his younger brother Henry, who went to Cambridge and became one of the first professionals, chose to write about Jefferson and Madison.

There was accordingly, for a time at least, a shift of attention away from the study of New England history and a tendency to regard the early New Englanders as a good deal less important than their descendants had always considered them. The professionals prided themselves on their objectivity. They liked to consider themselves as scientific, with all the connotations that that term had acquired, and they proposed a systematic study of the past that would rise above local prejudice and provincialism. As far as the colonial period was concerned, this meant a shift of focus from the New World to the Old. In order to see the colonies objectively, it was necessary to see them as part of the British Empire. And when viewed in this perspective, the early New Englanders appeared to be a prickly and crabbed lot. For the "imperial" historians who dominated the professional study of colonial history during the first quarter of the twentieth century, the principal significance of the Puritan experiment in New England was the trouble it caused to the orderly growth of a sound imperial administration. The most valuable study of New England produced during this period was Viola F. Barnes's *Dominion of New England*,[18] which argued that the Dominion was a wholesome experiment in imperial government and that Edmund Andros, the blackest of tyrants in the eyes of Palfrey, was a good administrator faced with a cantankerous crowd of local oligarchs.

But a wide perspective was not the only goal of the professionals. In the late nineteenth and early twentieth century, anyone living in America was confronted daily with the power of economic forces. "Business" was in the saddle and seemed able to bend government as it pleased. Politicians and statesmen might affirm their independence, their devotion to the public welfare, their integrity, but enterprising journalists showed that the "inside" story was otherwise: politics was window-dressing for economics; political power followed economic power. In this atmosphere it was easy to believe that men seldom mean what they say, so that the historian seeking objective truth must find it in the hidden economic facts that secretly dictate the articulate and seemingly rational statements exposed to public view. Many historians had already begun to think this way when Charles A. Beard produced his stunning *Economic Interpretation of the Constitution*.[19]

Beard's book gave direction to the energies of professional historians for the next thirty or forty years. If, as Beard argued, the makers of the United States Constitution were moved less by altruistic patriotism than by the urge to secure the economic interests of their class, then the wise historian must view with suspicion every declaration of principle or statement of purpose. If the words of a Washington or a Madison could not be taken at face value, then whose words could be? Although Beard's work met a barrage of criticism, most professional historians came to accept at least the assumption on which it was based: that public expressions of principle were not reliable, and that historians must therefore seek the inside story, which was less likely to be found in the books men wrote than in the pocketbooks they carried.

It would be difficult to exaggerate the effects of this attitude. In conjunction with Frederick Jackson Turner's emphasis on the West as a controlling influence in American history, it turned historians away from what men said toward what they did, from politics to economics, from the explicit to the implicit, from the rational to the irrational and subconscious. For a time, as historians explored the possibilities for investigation, the new attitude served as a liberating force. It seemed to promise a depth of understanding denied to the earlier, amateur historians who, since they concerned themselves only with the overt aspects of the record, had been taken in by their ancestors' high-sounding words.

In the long run the effect was and is stifling. The economic interpretation of history became less a spur to investigation of economic history than a way of interpreting the past without investigating it. Such was not, of course, Beard's intention. He based his own conclusions on an investigation which, if inadequate, was at least original and imaginative, and some of his disciples studied the records more assiduously than he and produced studies that are still valuable. Nevertheless, the economic interpretation carried an invitation, too often accepted, to substitute intuition for research. If the written record was a snare for the unwary, if what men said could not be trusted, there was no urgency to study what they said. When you are sure that a man who says x really means y, there is no point in pausing over the value of x.

There is still less point if you feel that the man who is doing the speaking deserves only a small share of your attention anyhow. The purveyors of the economic interpretation often felt that the common man had not been given his due in the pages of history. And since the common man did not often write books or keep records, it was not much use to seek him in them. The alternative was to extrapolate his story from a few hints scattered here and there or from the historian's intuition. The inside story often turned out to be only the story inside the historian.

In the past decade or two the tide has turned against the economic interpretation. Further investigation has shown Beard's own work to be faulty, and much of the work that he inspired has proved on examination to depend more on inspiration than on fact. The economic interpretation of history, at least in the form that Beard gave it, now appears to have been a blind alley. But for generations it guided research in nearly every area of American history except one, and even here it seized possession and held the field for a time.

The first important study of New England history to appear after Beard was *The Founding of New England* by James Truslow Adams (no relation of the other Adamses who had written on the subject), published in 1921.[20] Though Adams was not a professor, he was clearly a professional and a Beardian. His work combined an economic interpretation with an imperial perspective. "The one outstanding fact concerning any American colony in the colonial period," he wrote in the preface, "is that it was a dependency, and formed merely a part of a larger and more comprehensive imperial and economic organization. Consequently, the evolution of such a colony can be viewed correctly only when it is seen against the background of the economic and imperial conditions and theories of the time."

Starting from these premises, Adams did for the Founding Fathers of New England what Beard had done for the fathers of the constitution. Adams did not neglect the records, and parts of his study retain today a usefulness and validity that Beard's has lost. Nevertheless, Adams succumbed to the temptation that vitiated so many products of the economic interpretation. On the basis of statistics compiled by Palfrey for the year 1670, Adams decided that only one out of five of the adult males who settled Massachusetts was a church member. From these figures he concluded that not more than one in five "was sufficiently in sympathy with the religious ideas there prevalent to become a church member, though disfranchised for not doing so."[21] Since the adult males were probably representative of the population as a whole, it appeared that four-fifths of the people of Massachusetts, presumably including the vast majority of the common people, were out of sympathy with Puritanism. What they were in sympathy with, obviously, was economic gain. "It seems probable," said Adams, "that the principal cause that induced such an extraordinary number of people, from the ranks of the lesser gentry and those below them, to make so complete a break in their lives as was implied by leaving all they had ever known for the uncertainties of far-off lands, was economic." And by the next sentence the probability had become a certainty: "They came for the simple reason that they wanted to better their condition."[22]

Further study of the records might have revealed to Adams that failure to be a church member in New England did not necessarily indicate lack of sympathy with the church or with the prevailing religious ideas. But his interpretation made sense to a generation of Americans famous equally for pursuit of the dollar and hatred of Puritanism. The ordinary settler of New England, it seemed, was just like his twentieth-century descendant: he liked economic success and he disliked Puritans.

The Founding of New England was well written. It had, like other expressions of the economic interpretation, an air of cold realism, of urbane scholarship conquering filial piety. It received an enthusiastic reception from the reviewers, and it might well have dominated—or paralysed—New England historiography for as long as the economic interpretation prevailed in other areas of investigation.

III

The first sign that it would not came in 1925 when Kenneth Murdock, a Harvard professor, published a lengthy and learned biography of *Increase Mather*.[23] The subtitle, *Foremost American Puritan,* was itself an ironic challenge to the reigning disdain for the Puritans, a disdain that derived not merely from the scholarship of James Truslow Adams but from the polemics of H. L. Mencken and Van Wyck Brooks. In the preface Murdock paid tribute to Adams's work as "stimulating and useful" and admitted that his own creed was not one of which Mather would have approved. But he wrote with an evident respect for Mather and for Mather's ideas and beliefs. He made no attempt to decipher hidden economic motives behind them. Instead, he stayed with the records and treated Puritanism in its own terms as a serious intellectual force.

It was perhaps no accident that Murdock, besides being a Harvard professor, was a Bostonian and that James Truslow Adams spoke not from Boston but from Bridgehampton, New York. Interest in early New England had not subsided among members of the Colonial Society or the Massachusetts Historical Society; and it may have presented a certain challenge to a man who was both Bostonian and professional to see the domain invaded, indeed conquered, by an outsider. In any case, another Bostonian who was also a professional was the next to respond to Adams.

Samuel Eliot Morison, Murdock's senior by a few years, had been a member of the Massachusetts Historical Society since 1914 and of the Harvard History Department since 1915. He was as professional as they come and the most talented American historian of his generation. Morison, while insisting on the most exhaustive research, differed from many of his professional colleagues in the pains he took never to address himself simply to the brethren. He wrote neither for the gentlemen scholars of the Massachusetts Historical Society nor for the professionals in the American Historical Association, but for the elusive general reader. Never indulging in cant or jargon and never talking down, he tried to recapture the audience that men like Bancroft and Parkman had won for history. In pursuing this goal Morison kept a weather eye on anniversaries because of the opportunity they offer for catching popular interest. At about the time when Murdock's book appeared, he set his sights on 1930, the 300th anniversary of the founding of Massachusetts. When the year arrived he had ready his *Builders of the Bay Colony*, a series of biographical sketches through which he retold the story of the founding and recreated the Puritan leaders as human beings.[24]

The book was a tour de force. Where Adams had invited twentieth-century Americans to sympathize with a presumptive majority of anti-Puritan economic opportunists among the settlers of New England, Morison invited sympathy for a set of men and women who were ready to make sacrifices for principle but who remained warm and attractive as human beings. In telling his story, Morison did not indulge in scholarly controversy. His refutation of the economic interpretation lay primarily in the lives of the people he exhibited to view. But in a witty appendix he tackled Adams head on. Adams's account, he noted, "fits in so neatly with the economic interpretation of history, with the fashionable dislike of what to-day is called puritanism, and with the American love for statistics, that the 'four out of five' unpuritan New Englanders are even getting into the school textbooks, where historical theories seldom penetrate until they are obsolete."[25] After marshaling an array of evidence from the records to demolish both the presumption and the ideas Adams based on it, Morison concluded:

It is quite natural that the religious motives of the founders of New England should be questioned, and replaced by the economic. Material success is a motive which the present age can understand, while the mind of a man willing to sacrifice comfort and security in order to worship in a particular way, is to most people incomprehensible. Similarly, nineteenth-century historians often ascribe the puritan emigration to democracy, republicanism, or political discontent. My own opinion, one arrived at by considerable reading of what the puritans wrote, is that religion, not economics nor politics, was the center and focus of the puritan dissatisfaction with England, and the puritan migration to New England.[26]

Morison's next anniversary was 1936, the tercentenary of Harvard College. To most historians a history of seventeenth-century Harvard would have seemed as unrewarding a topic as could be found anywhere. The most ardent defenders of early New England, however fond of celebrating the nation's first college, had not contended that it was anything more than a divinity school for the training of ministers. When Morison devoted three volumes to Harvard's first seventy years, it seemed that he must have fallen prey to near-sighted antiquarianism.[27] Those three volumes, however, may be his finest work. In them he again took the Puritans seriously and addressed himself to what they said and wrote and read and taught. The result was to discover that Harvard from the beginning offered an education comparable to that available at Oxford and Cambridge, an almost incredible achievement for a handful of pioneers struggling to establish a beachhead in the wilderness. The Puritans did wish to train a ministry, but they thought the best training had to be grounded in the traditional liberal arts. The curriculum at Harvard devoted only one day a week to theology. And though most of the later ministers of seventeenth-century New England were graduates of Harvard, the number of seventeenth-century graduates who entered the ministry was less than a majority.

Morison's study, in which an overwhelming weight of scholarship was lifted by the author's usual wit, was not intended as a manifesto. But the effect of it, in combination with *Builders of the Bay Colony* and Murdock's *Mather,* was to reopen Puritanism as a field demanding the attention of intellectual historians. As noted earlier, nineteenth-century scholars had devoted themselves primarily to political history and had often translated the contests and discussions of the seventeenth century into political terms, much as Adams had translated them into economic ones. Perhaps for the first time since the colonial period, the Puritans had been approached on their own terms.

Meanwhile an excited young man from Chicago, who had arrived in Cambridge to sit at the feet of Murdock and Morison, was already well launched into a study of Puritan ideas, a study that was to become at once the most imaginative and the most exhaustive piece of intellectual history that America has produced. Perry Miller was an atheist, and in his tastes he was far from what is usually called Puritan. But he shared with the seventeenth-century New Englanders a respect for theology as an intellectual discipline, and he brought to the study of their ideas a mind that was uncannily sensitive to nuance and implication.

Miller's first book, *Orthodoxy in Massachusetts*,[28] published in 1933, carried a foreword in which he admitted, with an air more of triumph than contrition, that he had "attempted to tell the story of a of a great folk movement with an utter disregard of the economic and social factors" and that in so doing he laid himself open "to the charge of being so very naive as to believe that the way men think has some influence upon their actions." In this book Miller did deal with actions as well as ideas, with the actions of the founders of Massachusetts in setting up congregational churches and a civil government. But it was quite clear that he considered the actions of the founders to be the product of their ideas and not vice versa. He related the settlement of New England not to the economic discontents or social ambitions of the emigrants but to the ecclesiastical ideas developed among English Puritans during the preceding fifty years. The result was to place both the ecclesiastical and the political history of New England in the context of intellectual history.

In subsequent books Miller all but ignored political history and treated ecclesiastical history only as it related to the history of ideas. During the 1930's he systematically read everything written by New Englanders in the seventeenth century along with the bulk of writings by English Puritans. On the basis of what he found he published in 1939 *The New England Mind: the Seventeenth Century*,[29] first of a projected series of volumes that was to carry the intellectual history of New England into the nineteenth century. The initial volume made no effort to deal with the chronological development of ideas. In his reading Miller had found "that the first three generations in New England paid almost unbroken allegiance to a unified body of thought,"[30] and his first volume was a topical analysis of that thought, identifying the principal concepts and accounting for their origins, inter-relations, and significance. In immense detail and with no quarter given to the simple-minded, Miller discussed the patristic and scholastic origins of Puritan ideas, the Puritans' cosmology, logic, psychology, and rhetoric, their ideas about the nature of man and God, and the concepts of human relationship that underlay their political, social, and ecclesiastical institutions. At every point he suggested the implications, paradoxes, and tensions, and the way conflicting or diverging ideas were held together in a system that constituted "one of the major expressions of the Western intellect . . . an organized synthesis of concepts which are fundamental to our culture."[31]

The New England Mind was an invitation to understand the past not through its contributions to political liberty, and not through sympathy with common or uncommon men, but through a study of the way men understood themselves. While preparing the second volume of the *New England Mind,* Miller wrote a study of Jonathan Edwards, the most creative eighteenth-century New England thinker in the Puritan tradition.[32] Edwards, Miller showed, recast the Puritan synthesis in the terms of Lockean psychology and Newtonian physics. Edwards was the starting point for the "New Divinity" of the later eighteenth century, but he also served Miller as the terminal point toward which his study of the New England mind must move. In the second volume of the series, subtitled *From Colony to Province,*[33] Miller held up the system he had described in the earlier volume and showed how its inner tensions increased—how it responded to the challenges posed by those who emphasized a particular idea within it to the exclusion of others. In the early years, when an Anne Hutchinson elevated saving grace to the point of annihilating human will, the masters of the system dealt rapidly and effectively with her. But by the end of the century a host of subtler problems was sapping the strength and the confidence of New England. Paradoxes were turning into irreconcilable contradictions, and human pride was rising toward the reverse of the Antinomian heresy, toward the annihilation of saving grace.

Colony to Province follows the involute maneuvering by which the Mathers, Increase and Cotton, struggled to save the system, in which they took so proprietary an interest that their efforts appeared to be only the result of egotism, another manifestation of human pride rising under the mask of humility. The volume closes in 1730 with Jonathan Edwards preparing to ride from Northampton to Boston to deliver the lecture, *God Glorified in the Work of Redemption,* in which Edwards launched his effort to restore the omnipotence of God. Miller had opened his study of Edwards with a discussion of this lecture, so that the two volumes of the *New England Mind* lead directly into the one on Edwards, with *Orthodoxy in Massachusetts* falling somewhere between the first and second volumes. Miller also published an anthology of Puritan writings, a study of Roger Williams,[34] and a series of essays on New England history gathered under the title *Errand into the Wilderness,*[35] but he did not write another volume of the *New England Mind.*

What he did write must stand, with Morison's volumes on Harvard, as the outstanding achievement of the present century in early American history. In exhaustiveness of research, in subtlety of analysis, and in literary craftsmanship the writings of these two men have set standards for the entire profession. As far as New England history is concerned, they have defined the terms of discussion and established the norms by which every subsequent author knows that his work must be measured. Miller and Morison have not only made it necessary to take Puritanism seriously but have compelled discussion of the subject to begin at a level that has scarcely been approached in other areas of intellectual history.

IV

The challenge created simply by the existence of the work of Miller and Morison helps to account for the surge of interest in New England history. Although neither man attracted large numbers of graduate students, although only a few studies of early New England have been written under their guidance or direction, their pages are so suggestive, so resonant with implication that many of their readers have been prompted to further investigation. Articles and books have been generated by the insights in a single paragraph.

This is not to say that the scholarship of New England history since the 1930's has all been inspired by Miller or Morison. Much of it shows no direct relation to their work. But all of it has proceeded with an awareness of the standards they set.

There has been since 1930, and particularly in the past fifteen years an increasing number of scholarly books devoted to the subject. Among the more mature authors three excel: Raymond P. Stearns, Ola E. Winslow, and Clifford K. Shipton. Stearns, a student of Morison, has produced two books that explore the English connections of New England Puritanism. *Congregationalism in the Dutch Netherlands*[36] discusses the experience of English Puritans in founding and running congregational churches in Holland before coming to New England. *The Strenuous Puritan*[37] follows one leading Puritan, Hugh Peter, from England to New England and back to England, where he ultimately died on the scaffold as a regicide. Stearns, like Miller, has built on the work of Dexter and Walker and on their English contemporary, Champlin Burrage. There yet remains much work to be done on the relations of English and American Puritanism and particularly on the effect of the latter on the former. These two books of Stearns have charted the way.

Ola Winslow has brought to New England history a unique approach. In her most important book *Meetinghouse Hill*[38] she has discussed what might be called the social history of the churches: the way they were founded, their finances, their discipline of erring members, the disputes that split them and the relations between the laity and the ministry. This aspect of church history Miller had scarcely touched on—he was simply not interested in it. Miss Winslow has treated it in what almost appears to be an act of feminine defiance. She manages to write church history and to write it very well without noticing what the churches were there for. She is concerned only with the way the members dealt with one another, not with the way they dealt with God.

This posture is even more striking in her two biographies of Roger Williams and Jonathan Edwards.[39] It would be difficult to find two men in early American history who were more assiduously devoted to ideas. One would suppose it impossible to make sense out of their lives except in reference to the ideas that guided them and for which they sacrificed comfort and reputation. Miss Winslow does it. Without ever denying the force of ideas, without ever suggesting that ideas were less than paramount for Williams and for Edwards, she has written their lives with scarcely a look at the content of their ideas, yet has managed to convey to the reader an impression of each man's humanity and character, a sense of his greatness. In each case her biography is the best yet written of the man.

The achievement of Clifford K. Shipton is on a grander scale. One of the valuable enterprises of the nineteenth-century scholars had been the tracing of the lives of the early Yale and Harvard graduates. Franklin B. Dexter wrote in six volumes the biographies of all Yale graduates from the first one in 1703 through the class of 1815.[40] John Langdon Sibley began the same task for Harvard but was able to finish only three volumes, covering the classes from 1642 through 1689.[41] Shipton resumed Sibley's work and issued a fourth volume in 1933. Since then he has carried the task through nine more volumes to the class of 1755.[42] Shipton's biographies are distinguished not only by their wit, charm, and unabashed Toryism, but also by the intensity of the research that underlies them. Shipton has pursued his subjects through attics and archives all over the country and has uncovered source materials that will take other historians a generation to encompass. He has not only furnished students with an invaluable reference work but has made available a continuity of detailed information on which a great many different kinds of analyses can ultimately be based.

The most significant initial result of Shipton's work has been to show the variety of New England thought. Miller was concerned with the ideas that New Englanders held in common. In *Orthodoxy in Massachusetts* he showed how they maintained religious uniformity in spite of local Congregational independence. In the *New England Mind: the Seventeenth Century* he warned the reader at the outset that he had "taken the liberty of treating the whole literature as though it were the product of a single intelligence,"[43] and only in the second volume, *From Colony to Province,* did he enter into the transformations and divisions that took place during New England's first century. Even in that volume Miller concerned himself primarily with the larger divisions that time produced within a single system. The result was that many readers received an impression of New England thought as monolithic; and since Miller discussed institutions only as expressions of thought, the impression extended to the towns, churches, counties, and even colonies of New England. Miller did not, of course, suppose that all New Englanders thought alike or lived alike, but in his magnificent synthesis their differences became submerged. Shipton by his painstaking reconstruction of the lives of individuals has exhibited some of the differences.

The discovery of variety in New England thought and institutions, by other scholars as well as by Shipton, is perhaps the salient feature of post-Miller studies. One may predict that further research will reveal further variations from the patterns that Miller described. Although nothing yet written demonstrates that those patterns themselves need serious revision, they will eventually be seen to encompass a greater diversity than most students at first recognized. More biographical studies will doubtless pursue this trend. New biographies of Thomas Clap and of Jonathan Mayhew, two very different individuals, have offered insights into eighteenth-century intellectual developments after the period Miller dealt with, and biographies of seventeenth-century figures have begun to enrich the picture of the earliest years.[44]

Another rewarding approach to the variety of New England life has been local history. Some good local history was written in the nineteenth century, especially in Connecticut by Frances Caulkins and Ellen Larned,[45] but as in the case of biography, the new local historians approach their subject with new questions to ask of the records and more exacting standards. The most notable of the new studies is Sumner Powell's examination of Sudbury, which traces the first settlers to three principal points of origin in England: the open-field village of Weyhill, Hampshire, the market town of Berkhamsted, Hertfordshire, and the larger borough of Sudbury, Suffolk.[46] Powell finds that the social and municipal institutions established at Sudbury resembled only remotely what the settlers left behind. Nor did Sudbury closely resemble the conventional historical picture of the New England town: it was a unique creation with a new category of citizen, the "free townsman." Charles Grant, examining an eighteenth-century town, has also found significant variations from the expected pattern and so has Darrett Rutman in a study of Boston's first two decades.[47]

In recent years another method has become available for getting at institutional variations and resemblances. With the aid of computers and exhaustive work on tax lists, voting records, probate records, church records, and other archival materials we can now obtain statistical information on a larger scale than ever before. By using a computer to break down the data in a Boston shipping register for the years 1697-1714, Bernard and Lotte Bailyn have demonstrated the possibility of extracting more detailed and precise information than would have been practicable by older methods.[48] The limits of this type of analysis may be quickly reached, because the fragmentary character of the records makes it impossible to accumulate the necessary data in many areas; but the results, for a time at least, should be rewarding and may hold a few surprises.

Even without benefit of computers Robert E. Brown was able by statistical analysis to upset long held (and evidently still cherished) assumptions about voting in eighteenth-century Massachusetts.[49] By sampling the voting records and tax lists of Massachusetts towns, Brown demonstrated that the vast majority of adult males possessed the requisite property to qualify as voters. Before Brown it had been assumed that the vast majority in all the colonies were unqualified and from this asumption it had been argued that colonial society, including that of Massachusetts, was undemocratic. When Brown maintained as a result of his discoveries that Massachusetts was in fact a "middle-class democracy," his critics shifted the ground of the former argument and replied that democracy was more than a matter of voting. Voting is nevertheless a large element in democracy, and Brown's demonstration that the right to vote was widespread has not been effectively challenged. He has, in fact, made it imperative that discussion of New England political history in the eighteenth century advance to a higher level than it has yet approached.

Political, biographical, local, and statistical studies by no means exhaust the opportunities that scholars have discovered in New England history since the 1930's. The continuing flow of works about different phases of Anglo-colonial relations shows that this vein is far from exhausted.[50] The economic history of New England has scarcely begun to receive the attention it deserves, and will doubtless yield important results from the application of the newer, mathematical methods of economic analysis.[51] Even in intellectual history the opportunities are obvious: Morison gave scant attention to the eighteenth century and Miller very little to the period after Edwards. A number of able scholars have already exploited topics in this large area.[52]

The great opportunity awaiting the modern scholar is the possibility of exploring his subject inside the framework of ideas disclosed by those who have already brought the intellectual history of New England to such an advanced state. Within this larger context many an old and seemingly outworn topic will take on new dimensions: the reconsideration of institutions in the light of ideas that we now know to have accompanied them will surely suggest new insights to every scholar endowed with imagination, for imagination in history as in other fields often consists in perceiving connections not before suspected. Ernest Caulfield may have told us more than any other historian about the Great Awakening simply by pointing out that it followed one of the most deadly epidemics the colonies had ever seen.[53] Carl Bridenbaugh has made sense out of New England's fear of an Anglican bishop, which previously seemed ludicrously exaggerated, by placing it in the context of the revived missionary zeal among Anglicans in the eighteenth century.[54] Alden Vaughan, by considering Anglo-Indian relations in conjunction with Puritan ideas, has reoriented the study of early race relations.[55] Robert Brown has shown us that large numbers of New Englanders were qualified to vote, that they had the power to control their government; but this fact is still seeking its full context, which must be found somewhere among the ideas of the time, ideas about rank, authority, and class, ideas about liberty, power, and popular rights. This kind of study, one that makes the most of the new opportunities, is exemplified by George Haskins' *Law and Authority in Early Massachusetts*,[56] which surveys the history of law in connection with Puritan ideas, with the whole structure of seventeenth-century New England society, and with New England's relations to England.

The reconsideration of institutions will prompt reconsideration of the ideas behind them; an idea seen in its application will sometimes assume a different meaning and origin than was assigned it in the abstract. The web of connections already discerned by scholars is so intricate that every new fact discovered, every new implication perceived can be reason for reassessment not only of ideas but of other facts, events, and institutions. Hence the extraordinary energy of New England historiography. As long as a study proceeds with full awareness of the larger context in which it falls, as long as the student seeks the connections with everything else that was going on, and particularly with the ideas of the time, the topic he chooses may be narrow and detailed, but it will contribute to the understanding not merely of New England, but of human, history.

But if the opportunities are large, so are the dangers. And the dangers lie in neglecting the context that previous scholars have disclosed. Close investigation of a subject—and close investigation is now essential—can induce a myopia that makes the exceptional appear to be the normal. Anyone who studies a part of New England history long enough and hard enough to write a book about it is likely to generalize from what he finds. If New England thought and institutions did exhibit variations, it is easy to argue from the variation either that there was no general pattern or that the variation was general. Similarly when a study of institutions is carried out without reference to ideas, it is easy to jump to the conclusion that the ideas were not there or were unimportant. Sir Lewis Namier's statistical and local study of the structure of British politics in the eighteenth century discredited for a whole generation the role of ideas in British political history,[57] just as Beard discredited the role of ideas in American history. As historians of New England move toward statistical and local history, they will be tempted to repeat the error and to fall at this late date into the trap from which Miller and Morison rescued their subject. Doubtless we should continually reassess the relationship between ideas and institutions. Certainly there is a need to study the institutions themselves and not simply to extrapolate their history from the ideas that accompanied them. But if we dismiss ideas as a mere projection of institutions, in early New England at least, we will be reduced to antiquarianism, if not to eccentricity.

When the statistical studies along with the growing body of biographies and monographs have given us a clearer picture of the richness and diversity of early New England, and of the interplay of ideas, institutions, and events, it will be time to attempt another synthesis of the kind that Miller undertook and to include in it the economic, political, and social developments that he ignored or only lightly brushed. But the prospect sounds a little unrealistic at the moment; men with Perry Miller's gifts do not come along very often, and no one has yet approached his command of the sources. We may have to be contented for some time with a more modest goal: when we have learned a great deal more about early New England, we should be able to learn still more from Miller. Perhaps that will be reward enough.

[1]In this essay I have not considered works dealing with New England after the beginnings of the American Revolution, nor have I considered general works dealing with New England along with the other American colonies or general works dealing with Puritanism.

[2]*The History of New England from 1630 to 1649*, James Savage, ed. (2 vols., Boston, 1853). This is still the best edition.

[3]William Bradford, *The History of Plymouth Plantation 1620-1647* (2 vols., Boston, 1912). This edition, by the editorial committee of the Massachusetts Historical Society, is more fully annotated than any other.

[4]Nathaniel Morton, *New-Englands Memoriall* (Cambridge, 1669; Boston, 1903); Edward Johnson, *A History of New-England. From the English planting in the Yeare 1628* . . . [usually known by running title, *The Wonder-working Providence of Sions Saviour in New England*] (London, 1654; Andover, 1867; New York, 1910); William Hubbard, *A General History of New England from the Discovery to 1680*, second edition, collated with the original manuscript, William T. Harris, ed. (Boston, 1848).

[5]*The Diary of Michael Wigglesworth 1653-1657: The Conscience of a Puritan*, E. S. Morgan, ed. (New York, 1965).

[6] Massachusetts Historical Society, *Collections*, seventh series, vols. VII, VIII (1911, 1912).

[7]Massachusetts Historical Society, *Collections*, fifth series, vols. V-VII (1878-1882).

[8]*The History of the Colony and Province of Massachusetts-Bay*, L. S. Mayo, ed., (3 vols., Cambridge, 1936).

[9]*The Legend of the Founding Fathers* (New York, 1956).

[10](10 vols., Boston, 1834-74).

[11]*History of New England during the Stuart Dynasty* (5 vols., Boston, 1858-90).

[12]*Genealogical Dictionary of the First Settlers of New England* (4 vols., Boston, 1860-62).

[13]Charles Francis Adams, *Massachusetts: Its Historians and its History* (Boston, 1893); Brooks Adams, *The Emancipation of Massachusetts* (Boston, 1887).

[14](2 vols., Boston, 1892).

[15](Boston, 1894).

[16](New York, 1880).

[17](New York, 1893).

[18](New Haven, 1923; New York, 1960).

[19](New York, 1913).

[20](Boston, 1921).

[21]121.

[22]122.

[23](Cambridge, 1925)

[24](Boston, 1930).

[25]340.

[26]346.

[27]*The Founding of Harvard College* (Cambridge, 1935); *Harvard College in the Seventeenth Century* (2 vols., Cambridge, 1936).

[28](Cambridge, 1933).

[29](New York, 1939; Cambridge, 1954).

[30]vii.

[31]viii.

[32]*Jonathan Edwards* (New York, 1949).

[33]*The New England Mind: From Colony to Province* (Cambridge, 1953).

[34]*Roger Williams: His Contribution to the American Tradition* (Indianapolis, 1953).

[35](Cambridge, 1956).

[36](Chicago, 1940).

[37](Urbana, 1954).

[38](New York, 1952). A related study, dealing with church discipline, is Emil Oberholzer, *Delinquent Saints* (New York, 1956).

[39]*Jonathan Edwards* (New York, 1940); *Master Roger Williams* (New York, 1957). Another valuable study of Williams, stressing his political radicalism, is S. H. Brockunier, *The Irrepressible Democrat* (New York, 1940).

[40]*Biographical Sketches of the Graduates of Yale College with Annals of the College History* (6 vols., New York, 1885-1912).

[41]*Biographical Sketches of Graduates of Harvard University* (3 vols., Cambridge, 1873-85).

[42]*Biographical Sketches of Those who Attended Harvard College* (vols. IV-XIII, Boston, 1933-1965).

[43]p. vii.

[44]Among the more notable are L. L. Tucker, *Puritan Protagonist: President Thomas Clap of Yale College* (Chapel Hill, 1962); C. W. Akers, *Called unto Liberty: A Life of Jonathan Mayhew* (Cambridge, 1964); Emery Battis, *Saints and Sectaries: Anne Hutchinson and the Antinomian Controversy in the Massachusetts Bay Colony* (Chapel Hill, 1962); Larzer Zif, *The Career of John Cotton* (Princeton, 1962); Everett Emerson, *John Cotton* (New York, 1965).

[45]Frances M. Caulkins, *History of New London, Connecticut* (New London, 1852); Ellen Larned, *History of Windham County, Connecticut* (2 vols., Worcester, 1874).

[46]*Puritan Village: The Formation of a New England Town* (Middletown, 1963).

[47]C. S. Grant, *Democracy in the Connecticut Frontier Town of Kent* (New York, 1961); D. B. Rutman, *Winthrop's Boston* (Chapel Hill, 1965). For an older study see R. H. Akagi, *The Town Proprietors of the New England Colonies* (Philadelphia, 1924).

[48]*Massachusetts Shipping 1697-1714: A Statistical Study* (Cambridge, 1959).

[49]*Middle-Class Democracy and the Revolution in Massachusetts, 1691-1780* (Ithaca, 1955).

[50]See for example M. G. Hall, *Edward Randolph and the American Colonies, 1676-1703* (Chapel Hill, 1960); R. S. Dunn, *Puritans and Yankees* (Princeton, 1962); and the valuable studies by J. A. Schutz, *Thomas Pownall* (Glendale, 1951) and *William Shirley* (Chapel Hill, 1961).

[51]The old work by W. B. Weeden, *Economic and Social History of New England, 1620-1789* (2 vols., Boston, 1890) contained some useful information but was wholly disorganized. The most valuable recent studies are Bernard Bailyn, *The New England Merchants in the Seventeenth Century* (Cambridge, 1955), and James B. Hedges, *The Browns of Providence Plantations: Colonial Years* (Cambridge, 1952).

52Among the most valuable are Robert Middlekauff, *Ancients and Axioms: Secondary Education in Eighteenth-Century New England* (New Haven, 1963); Joseph Haroutunian, *Piety Versus Moralism: The Passing of the New England Theology* (New York, 1932); Conrad Wright, *The Beginnings of Unitarianism in America* (Boston, 1955); E. S. Gaustad, *The Great Awakening in New England* (New York, 1957); and C. C. Goen, *Revivalism and Separation in New England* (New Haven, 1962). In a related area, Allan I. Ludwig has explored the astonishing symbolic and aesthetic styles of New England gravestone carving in *Graven Images* (Middletown, 1966).

53*A True History of the Terrible Epidemic Vulgarly Called the Throat Distemper* (New Haven, 1939))

54*Mitre and Sceptre: Transatlantic Faiths, Ideas, Personalities, and Politics 1689-1775* (New York, 1962).

55*New England Frontier: Puritans and Indians 1620-1675* (Boston, 1965). For other valuable studies of Puritan-Indian warfare and relationships, see D. E. Leach, *Flintlock and Tomahawk: New England in King Philip's War* (New York, 1959), and *The Northern Colonial Frontier* (New York, 1966).

56(New York, 1960).

57*The Structure of Politics at the Accession of George III* (London, 1928).

The Historians of the Middle Colonies

BY FREDERICK B. TOLLES

Few students of early American history (even the scholar to whom this volume is dedicated) are as familiar with the history of the Middle Colonies as Frederick B. Tolles. The author of such well-known books as Meeting House and Counting House, George Logan of Philadelphia, *and* James Logan and the Culture of Provincial America, *Tolles had shed light on the political, economic, and cultural growth of Pennsylvania and its neighboring colonies. Much of the research necessary for these volumes was done at the Huntington Library, where he served as a member of the research staff between 1951 and 1954. Since that time he has been Jenkins Professor of Quaker History at Swarthmore College. In his essay he not only appraises select histories of the Middle Colonies published in the last quarter-century, but suggests avenues for investigation that should keep scholars occupied for a generation to come.*

"THE FORGOTTEN REGION," Richard H. Shryock had to call the Middle Atlantic area, nearly twenty-five years ago. "There is," he wrote, "no common historical tradition in the Middle Atlantic region."[1] It was not hard in 1943 to show that this was true. It was impossible to refer to more than two or three books that had been written on the area as a distinct region, and the good historical works on any part of it were surprisingly few. A question might even arise in some minds whether there was a Middle Atlantic region in any other sense than that it was what was left over between New England and the South.

This viewpoint has some validity. Much of Long Island belongs historically with New England. Western Pennsylvania lies in the Mississippi Valley. Geographically and economically, western Maryland could be taken as a southward extension of Pennsylvania. And Delaware? Originally called the "lower counties" of Pennsylvania, it occupies a small part of a peninsula which it shares with Maryland and Virginia. If it is part of the Middle Atlantic region, why are not they? Or, since it lies below the Mason-Dixon line, why not call it part of the South?

In sum, there is little or nothing about this area that would lead a geographer, looking at a map, to describe it as a region, save that it does lie between two well-defined regions, each of which produced its own kind of life and culture. Perhaps this is why most historians, desperate to characterize it somehow, can only in the end refer to its "middleness." How many writers, after going in detail into the land systems and local governments of New England and the South, have simply said that in these respects the Middle Colonies could best be described as having a mysterious combination of both. It could be argued that if the Middle Colonies display only a presumably derivative "middleness," they are hardly worthy of serious study. In recent years, however, books have at last been written which clearly show that the Middle Colonies did have exciting, interesting, and important histories, and that colonial life cannot really be understood and appreciated without some knowledge of the colonies that occupied the Hudson and Delaware valleys and extended westward, no one knew how far. Let us, then, in this essay overlook the problem of whether the area was a region or not and consider the trends that have developed in the past quarter-century in historical writing about colonial New York, New Jersey, Pennsylvania, and the Lower Counties, or Delaware.

If there is one subject on which a large amount of productive research has been done, it is the history of the Friends in Pennsylvania and their long control of the province's government. No longer can we dismiss this as the pretty story of a group of idealists who somehow carried on the spirit of William Penn in politics as in their private lives for three-quarters of a century. We have learned something about Penn himself, to begin with—about the intellectual sophistication, the worldly shrewdness, the sometimes incredible financial naiveté that accompanied his undoubted idealism. To the forty or more biographies of Pennsylvania's Founder that had been written before the 'forties have been added two realistic books which pretty adequately take his measure. They understand his sincere religious motivation, but they also recognize that he was a practical-minded colony-promoter who could and would compromise his religious principles when he had to.

William Wistar Comfort's *William Penn: A Tercentenary Estimate*,[2] though written by a Quaker, comes to grips, one feels, with the real William Penn with all the self-contradictions that made him less than a wholly consistent Friend but a great man nevertheless. Catherine Owens Peare in her *Willian Penn*[3] did a great deal to fill out the outlines which Comfort had sketched in and to make him seem like a man who actually lived, not a Sunday-School hero.

These two relatively good biographies make it plain that it would now be possible, as it is surely desirable, for someone at last to write a full-scale scholarly biography of Penn. Most of the facts of his life are known: what we need is a book that will, among other things, recognize that Penn was a man of ideas, able to talk with Algernon Sidney, Robert Boyle, Sir William Petty and the other men of his time who laid the foundations for the English Enlightenment. We need a book which will do justice to the intolerable dilemmas he faced—the religious pacifist who had to agree to serve as Captain-General of the non-existent armed forces of Pennsylvania, the political liberal of the radical Whig variety who could not restrain himself now and then from giving orders to his colony, the landed gentleman who expected to live on the proceeds of his province, which seldom amounted to much, the peaceable Christian who found it necessary to install militant deputy-governors who would do what he could not do.

Perhaps what we need before this can be done is a comprehensive scholarly edition of Penn's writings and of his letters. He wrote nearly a hundred books and pamphlets on many subjects, but there has not been a complete edition of them since 1726 and its texts leave much to be desired. His letters, though often quoted, have never been collected in a single edition. Many years ago, a young man named Albert Cook Myers set about to establish the texts of Penn's writings and to gather information for their annotation. For nearly forty years, he labored on this enterprise, but it finally came to nothing.[4] Certainly now, in the day of the great Franklin, Jefferson, and other editorial projects, is the time for this enterprise to be carried to a completion under scholarly auspices.[5] For with all his faults and inconsistencies, William Penn was a great man, no doubt the most distinguished and interesting of all the colony founders.

William Penn was in his colony for only four years. Much of the credit and blame for the successes and failures of his "holy experiment" belongs to the people. They were devoted to the principles on which Penn had founded his province, but they were often, as Penn once put it, excessively "governmentish" and quarrelsome, and they had little interest in paying the quit rents on which the proprietor hoped to live. Historians have begun at last to study the intricacies of early Pennsylvania politics with these facts clearly in mind. We have in Edwin B. Bronner's *William Penn's "Holy Experiment"*[6] a careful examination of the colony's first two decades. He emerges with the conclusion that the "holy experiment" had clearly failed by 1701. He lays the blame on both the proprietor and the people, but adds that outside forces, especially Pennsylvania's place in the English empire when it was at war with France, had much to do with it.

One is tempted to ask, he says, why anyone thought the "holy experiment" had any chance of survival. The answer is found in the faith and optimism of William Penn and a few like spirits who believed all things possible if man is virtuous and relies on divine assistance. Unfortunately, we will never know whether Penn was right or not, for man failed to keep his half of the bargain and the "holy experiment" failed.[7]

Some people think that the "holy experiment" was not quite dead in 1701, but went on in an increasingly tenuous form until 1756, when the Friends withdrew from control of Pennsylvania's Assembly. About the four decades from 1701 to 1740, however, we are still pretty much in the dark. For this period we have to rely on biographers to tell us what political historians have not told us. Fortunately, biographies of three leading figures of this era have appeared in the last quarter-century. Roy Lokken produced in 1959 a book on David Lloyd,[8] whom historians have for generations been calling either a sly and crafty demagogue or a Jeffersonian republican before his time. We can no longer plead ignorance as a basis for such mislabeling. In 1957 I published a short biography of James Logan,[9] who has usually been dismissed as a black conservative. We know him now as a loyal supporter of the Penn family, an able administrator, a successful fur merchant, and a cultivated gentleman-scholar equally adept at translating Cicero, carrying on botanical experiments, working problems in fluxions, and writing a treatise on natural ethics. And in 1943 Theodore Thayer gave us a biography of Irsael Pemberton,[10] in which he portrayed the leading Friend of the mid-eighteenth century in all his affluence and sometimes misguided good works. The biographers have served us so well that one hopes they will keep on, for there are many more Pennsylvanians who deserve biographies—Andrew Hamilton, the two Isaac Norrises, Joseph Galloway, William Allen, Richard Peters, Owen Biddle.

Only when we come to Theodore Thayer's *Pennsylvania Politics and the Growth of Democracy, 1740-1776*[11] do we come upon another political history of Pennsylvania. Obviously, we need studies of the earlier decades if we are really going to understand how Pennsylvania moved from its allegiance to William Penn to its support of Benjamin Franklin. Two books of non-political history have made some contribution to our understanding of this development. My own *Meeting House and Counting House*[12] was an attempt to comprehend the social and cultural life of the Philadelphia Quaker merchants up to 1763. In the course of describing their growing worldliness, their compromises with their religious principles, I found, I think, a basic reason for their ultimate withdrawal from active politics—the fear that the "world" would overwhelm their religion utterly. Sidney V. James in his study of the Quakers' benevolence in eighteenth-century America, *A People among Peoples*,[13] not only threw a great deal of light on their shift from inward-looking mutual "charity" to an outgoing humanitarianism, but showed also how this shift was accompanied by a change in their attitude towards their own sect: no longer were they a fellowship of the illuminated, concerned chiefly with the welfare of their own members, but a "people among peoples," a group with strict rules for themselves and a duty to help all the unfortunate outside their own number.

Both of these conclusions arose from studies of social, intellectual, and cultural history but had an important bearing on political and institutional history. Does this not suggest that the time is at last coming when we shall no longer regard the various kinds of history—social, economic, political, institutional, cultural, intellectual—as separate ways of approaching the past but shall consider them all as integral parts of the same effort? Will not our political history be richer, more profound, if it absorbs the insights provided by practitioners of other kinds of history? One would have thought that political historians would have recognized this before now, but there is a good deal of evidence that some do not. It is to be hoped that in the future historians of Pennsylvania and all the Middle Colonies will realize that history, like life itself, is one enterprise and that ideas and emotions and habits, social standing and ways of earning a living, religious convictions, political action, and private behavior are all interrelated so that one cannot understand one without understanding all.

There are many things still to be done in Pennsylvania history. We need a thorough study of Penn's ideas on town planning and their influence on American cities. We need studies of the colony's economic life; for instance, a study of the relations between the Philadelphia merchants and the back-country farmers. We need a comprehensive and sensitive account of the Great Awakening in Pennsylvania and all the Middle Colonies to supplement and perhaps replace C. H. Maxson's book, which has done service for many years. We need thorough, professional studies of Middle-Colony architecture to rectify the proportions of such a book as Hugh Morrison's otherwise excellent *Early American Architecture*,[14] in which only two chapters out of seventeen are devoted to that region. We need intensive examinations of Pennsylvania Dutch culture, for which the sources, mostly in German, are waiting, almost untouched, in several Pennsylvania depositories. We have Charles Coleman Sellers' splendid *Charles Willson Peale*,[15] but we have no adequate work on Benjamin West.

Historians of Pennsylvania have done much over the past twenty-five years to reduce our historical ignorance of that colony. Not so with Delaware. One of the mysteries of the American historical profession is: why are there no histories of Delaware? There are a great many questions which one would like to have answered. Who were the people of the Lower Counties? How far back in time does the antagonism of Kent and Sussex counties towards New Castle County go? What indeed happened in the three Lower Counties between 1703 and 1776? We ask, but we get no answer. Hardest of all to understand is the fact that no one has written a biography of John Dickinson since 1891. Dickinson was a moderate, a sedate man as compared with Samuel Adams or Charles Thomson, but he represented nevertheless an important phase in the pre-revolutionary argument, and from 1765 on he was constantly in the service of his state (or states, for he was President of both Delaware and Pennsylvania) and his country. He must be one of the few major figures in our history who has not had a modern scholarly biography.

The situation of New Jersey history is not much better. Richard McCormick has written an admirable *History of Voting in New Jersey*[16] and T. J. Wertenbaker gave us a good history of Princeton University,[17] but beyond that we have little except—and what a big exception it is!—the two books of John E. Pomfret, *The Province of West New Jersey* and *The Province of East New Jersey*.[18] For years, most of us have been a little baffled about the early history of East and West New Jersey. How, we asked, could two such small provinces have compiled such frightfully complex histories in a few years? No one had ever tried to set the stories down in all their intricacy, and some of us, I suspect, tended to skip lightly but guiltily over a third of a century from the British conquest in 1664 to the establishment of a single royal government in 1702. But now John Pomfret has made it easy for us. In his two books he makes his way with superlative ease through the tangled story of East and West Jersey. He has, in a sense, restored the early Jerseys to colonial history, and for this he deserves our thanks.

There is, however, much more that we ought to know about colonial New Jersey. "A keg tapped at both ends," it used to be called, because it had no major seaport and therefore had to rely on New York and Philadelphia. What effect did this unfortunate situation actually have on New Jersey's economic life? We do not know, because no one has ever made a serious study of the colony's economy. Did the same kind of bipolarization apply in New Jersey's cultural life? Again we do not know, for no one has tried to find out. New Jersey is now a highly urban state, but it was once almost completely agricultural; what do we know of its farming practices, its crops, its markets, its prosperity? Very little. What can be said about its social structure? The fact is that the historians in New Jersey seem to have been more interested in other subjects than in their own colony and state. The recent publication of a many-volumed series of books in New Jersey history suggests, however, that an awakening of interest is taking place. Let us hope so.

A fair amount of work has been done recently on New York's colonial history. In 1953 Jerome R. Reich published his *Leisler's Rebellion*. The sub-title of the book, *A Study of Democracy in New York, 1664-1720*,[19] makes it clear what he thought was at issue in the revolt, and several scholars have severely questioned his interpretation. But no one can deny that he gave us, for the first time, a clear narrative of New York politics during a crucial half-century. Lawrence H. Leder in his *Robert Livingston*[20] has written the first full biography of the man who established the Livingston family as a major force in New York politics. He also reviews New York's political history in the early eighteenth century and shows how Livingston finally contrived to reconcile the old Leislerian and anti-Leislerian factions. Obviously, we need similar books on the other families who dominated New York politics—the De Lanceys, Philipses, Van Cortlandts, Van Rensselaers, Schuylers, and the rest. Only then shall we really understand how colonial New York politics and government operated.

One such book has already been written and published under interesting circumstances. Many historians look down their academic noses at genealogists and family historians, to whom, they say, history is nothing but a pattern of births, marriages, and deaths. Sometimes, however, family historians will set an able and well trained writer to work to tell the story in scholarly style. This is what happened when the Beekman Family Association provided funds with which Philip L. White was able to study the voluminous Beekman Papers in the New York Historical Society and produce a splendid book of seven-hundred pages on eight members of this family. In this book, *The Beekman Family of New York in Politics and Commerce, 1647-1877*,[21] he was able to recount much of the colony's political and economic history in the process of dealing with four generations of Beekmans. White was also able to edit and publish three volumes of the Beekman papers, thus making them accessible for research anywhere in this country or abroad.[22]

One important aspect of colonial New York history—its Indian relations—has been given considerable attention over the past twenty-five years. Milton Hamilton in 1962 finally brought to a close the thirteen-volume *Papers of Sir William Johnson*,[23] nearly forty years after this great series had been commenced. On the basis of this fine and comprehensive edition, James T. Flexner was able to write in 1959 a good biography of this superintendent of Indian affairs in the northern colonies.[24] Allen W. Trelease published in 1960 an excellent book called *Indian Affairs in Colonial New York: The Seventeenth Century*,[25] which tells us a great deal about the colony's early relations with the Iroquois, on which the security of many colonists depended.

The Indian relations of a colony often had an important bearing on the safety of another colony, or of all the other colonies. This was so, obviously, of the friendly relations which New York contrived to maintain with the Iroquois, who might otherwise have swept down upon all the seaboard settlers. Certain Pennsylvanians were as deeply involved in dealing with the Six Nations as any New Yorker, and we have lately had good biographies of two of them. Paul A. W. Wallace in his massive *Conrad Weiser: Friend of Colonist and Mohawk*[26] has told us of the many-faceted career of this German frontiersman, who did more than any other person perhaps to keep Pennsylvania at peace with the Indians up to 1756. Nicholas B. Wainwright's *George Croghan: Wilderness Diplomat*[27] told us how a brawny, hard-drinking, extravagant Irishman in the Indian country used his diplomatic skill to preserve the Quaker policy of peace with the Indians. There were other men on the Indian frontier—Christian Frederick Post, Christopher Gist, William Trent—about whom we need to know much more than we now do if we are ever to comprehend all the complexities of Indian relations.

It is not easy to write the biography of an Indian. The written sources usually are few, and almost always they reflect, sometimes unconsciously, the white man's unfriendly attitude. Even the texts of Indian speeches at the council fire are often suspect, for one cannot be certain that the translation is accurate. Anthropologists, however, have their own ways of interpreting the documents in the light of what they know about primitive people. In fact, a new variety of history, called "ethnohistory," has come into being as a result of an interest in history among anthropologists and a willingness among historians to recognize that anthropologists can supply insights that the older techniques of history have never provided. An anthropologist, Anthony F. C. Wallace, has written a biography of Teedyuscung, the troublesome Delaware sachem.[28] It is an excellent example of what can be done by this combination of methods. He uses the anthropologists' "culture-and-personality" approach, and, in so doing, brings new meaning to the fairly extensive documents, which ordinary historians have never, one fears, understood in their full implications. To Wallace Teedyuscung's life is no longer just the story of an arrogant, drunken Indian reaching for what he can get. His tribal culture was fast disintegrating as the white man advanced, and the alternating fits of kindness and violent hatred which dictated his actions simply reflected his bafflement at this in-

73

comprehensible fact. It becomes clear as one reads this book that historians in the past have only half understood Indian relations, that from now on they will need the insights that anthropology can give them. There are surely many other chapters in American Indian-white relations that ought to be so illuminated.

Biographers have been at work in the Middle-Colony area. Page Smith published in 1956 a biography of James Wilson,[29] a too-little-noticed political philosopher of the pre-Revolutionary period. At least two Pennsylvania scientists have at last received their due— David Rittenhouse, astronomer and politician, at the hands of Brooke Hindle, and Dr. John Morgan, founder of the first colonial medical school, from the pen of Whitfield J. Bell, Jr.[30] But no one has yet done justice to the inquiring mind of Cadwallader Colden, who was almost as nearly universal in his intellectual interests as James Logan: besides writing his *History of the Five Indian Nations,* he worked seriously in mathematics, physics, botany, medicine, and philosophy. There are many other persons of importance about whom there has never been a good biography. One thinks of Gilbert Tennent, the revivalist preacher; Gustavus Hesselius, the Swedish painter; Christopher Sower, the influential German printer; John Bartram, the Quaker botanist; Provost William Smith of the College of Philadelphia; Nathaniel Evans, the Philadelphia poet; Dr. John Kearsley, the first great doctor in Philadelphia. The Middle Colonies had some able British governors of whom we should know more than we do: William Burnet of New York and New Jersey, Robert Hunter of New York, James Hamilton of Pennsylvania.

The greatest man in the Middle Colonies, obviously, was Benjamin Franklin. Clearly, he was more than a Philadelphian. He was one of the first real Americans, for he was known and admired in every colony from New Hampshire to Georgia. He was even more than an American: he was a cosmopolitan, better known for his work in electricity in Europe than in America. When he and Voltaire met and embraced at the Academy of Sciences in Paris in 1778, it seemed to the entranced audience to be a symbolic meeting of two heroes of the Enlightenment: it was like a meeting, they said, of Sophocles and Solon. Moreover, Franklin, like Logan and Colden, was a man of manifold gifts, a "harmonious human multitude," as Carl Van Doren put it. Naturally, scholars have produced articles and books on almost every facet of the Franklin personality. In the past quarter-century, we have had studies of Franklin and chess, Franklin as a Freemason, Franklin and the practice of medicine, Franklin's privateers, Franklin and Italy, Franklin as a demographer, Franklin and the Pennsylvania Dutch, and a delightful little book on Franklin's creation of the fecund Polly Baker.

More importantly, we have had from I. Bernard Cohen a fine edition of Franklin's writings on electricity with a long and well-informed introduction, showing clearly how much Franklin contributed to our understanding of it. From the same author we have also had a formidably learned work on Franklin and Sir Isaac Newton.[31] There have been studies of Franklin's political activities in Pennsylvania, of his political ideas, and of his views of foreign policy.[32] Of these the most original and fruitful was Gerald Stourzh's *Benjamin Franklin and American Foreign Policy;* it begins with a keen analysis of Franklin's ideas about reason and power and goes on to deal with aspects of his thought that had previously been given little attention. The ingenuity of scholars will undoubtedly lead to the production of many more monographs on aspects of this endlessly interesting man.

We have not had in recent years a full-scale biography of Franklin, but actually we have not needed one. Carl Van Doren's superb *Benjamin Franklin,* published in 1938, will remain standard for years to come. But we have had in Verner W. Crane's *Benjamin Franklin and a Rising People*[33] a sound and thoughtful short biography. And best of all, we finally have scholarly editions of the most popular and revealing of Franklin's writings, his *Autobiography*. In 1949 appeared Max Farrand's edition of Franklin's "fair copy" with other early versions set in parallel columns.[34] This volume is and always will be a delight to scholars. And in 1964 the Yale University Press published Leonard Labaree's beautifully bound and printed edition of the book with minimal but exceptionally useful annotation.[35] This volume is a delight to anyone who enjoys holding a handsome book in his hands.

The last work to be mentioned in this article is, most appropriately, Leonard Labaree's magnificent edition of Franklin's writings, of which nine volumes have so far appeared in print.[36] I am about to make the sort of remark that no sensible man should ever make, but I shall make it anyway: it is hard to believe that any other edition of Franklin's papers need ever be prepared, except to incorporate such pieces as may come to light after this edition is completed. Mr.

Labaree is a distinguished colonial historian and he has been supported by a staff of extremely able and conscientious assistants. The edition, sponsored by the American Philosophical Society and Yale University, will eventually run to forty (or more) volumes. A new type face, based on the font which Franklin used at Passy during the Revolution, has been used, and the volumes are handsomely bound and well illustrated. Almost everything that Franklin scholars will want will be here—all of Franklin's known letters, all of his essays and other formal writings, all of the state papers in the drawing up of which he had a hand, all of the known letters and other communications addressed to him (some of the latter in abstract), and many of the letters and manuscript essays that were sent to him for his information or action. One can be sure that all the texts are accurate. The annotation and preliminary notes are invariably well done, and moreover, they always have the virtue of brevity. This great edition, when completed, will certainly be regarded as one of the triumphs of scholarship in our age.

What more do we need in Middle-Colony history? I have made some suggestions in the course of this essay. I shall end by making a few more. It would be good to have modern editions of some of the better eighteenth-century histories of the colonies written by colonists—William Smith's *History of the Late Province of New York* (1757), Samuel Smith's *History of the Colony of Nova Caesarea, or New Jersey* (1765), Robert Proud's *History of Pennsylvania* (1797-98). There are a good many colonial diaries still in existence which have never been printed or have been printed only in part. Many of them, if made available, would add color and liveliness to our understanding of colonial history and might well give us important new information. I think immediately, for example, of the extensive diary of John Smith of Burlington and Philadelphia, now in the Library Company of Philadelphia, which has been published only in part; and the even longer diary of Elizabeth Drinker of Philadelphia, of which two volumes of selections have been printed.[37] Both of these diaries, if published in full, would tell us much more than we now know about daily life in pre-Revolutionary Philadelphia.

It would be extremely useful to have a great many more local histories, written by competent scholars, to replace, or supplement, the garrulous, filiopietistic ones published in such great numbers in the 1880's and 1890's, and later. We need to know more than we do about the economy, the social structure, the intellectual life of New

Castle, of Lancaster, of Burlington, of Albany, for example, if we are to understand small-town existence in the Middle Colonies as we are beginning to understand city life in New York and Philadelphia. We have had a good study of New Jersey voting in Richard McCormick's book mentioned above, but we need similar studies of voting in New York, Pennsylvania, and the Lower Counties; such books must be based on intensive study of local records in court houses, town hall basements, local historical societies, and the attics of old houses. Once we know who could and did vote, we may be spared a continuation of ill-informed guesses about the "aristocratic" or "democratic" nature of Middle-Colony politics and society. A study of the roads and waterways in the area would be useful to the economic historian.

One could easily go on enumerating the subjects that still need to be investigated in the history of the Middle Colonies. But let us close by acknowledging that a great deal has been accomplished in the past quarter-century. Even though the Middle Colonies can hardly be called a region, it should be obvious that we know vastly more about the four colonies of New York, New Jersey, Pennsylvania, and Delaware in 1966 than we did twenty-five years ago. And let it be said that the Institute of Early American History and Culture and the Huntington Library have contributed measurably to this advance.

[1]"Historical Traditions in Philadelphia and the Middle Atlantic Area: An Editorial," *Pennsylvania Magazine of History and Biography*, LXVI (1943), 116, 127.

[2]Philadelphia, 1944.

[3]New York, 1958.

[4]Myers's carefully proofread texts and masses of editorial material are now at the Chester County Historical Society at West Chester, Pennsylvania.

[5]It is necessary now to go to the original manuscripts of Penn's letters, when they can be found, and to the first editions of his printed works for accurate texts. For many of his letters we are dependent on Samuel M. Janney's *Life of William Penn;* this excellent book was published in 1852 and alas, followed nineteenth-century standards of editorial accuracy. To cite an example of the poor texts we are forced to use, let me say that not long ago, in editing Penn's *Essay towards the Present and Future Peace of Europe,* I found that almost every one of the many reprints had followed the 1726 edition by rendering the important word *umpire* meaninglessly as *empire*. No doubt, there are many other textual errors in the texts we use.

[6]*William Penn's "Holy Experiment": The Founding of Pennsylvania, 1681-1701* (New York, 1962).

[7]p. 254.

[8]*David Lloyd: Colonial Lawmaker* (Seattle, Washington, 1959).

[9]*James Logan and the Culture of Provincial America* (Boston, 1957).

[10]*Israel Pemberton, King of the Quakers* (Philadelphia, 1943).

[11]Harrisburg, 1954.

[12]*Meeting House and Counting House: The Quaker Merchants of Colonial Philadelphia* (Chapel Hill, 1948).

[13]*A People Among Peoples: Quaker Benevolence in Eighteenth-Century America* (Cambridge, 1963).

[14]*Early American Architecture from the First Colonial Settlements to the National Period* (New York, 1952).

[15]Philadelphia, 1947.

[16]*The History of Voting in New Jersey: A Study of the Development of Election Machinery, 1664-1911* (New Brunswick, 1953).

[17]*Princeton, 1746-1896* (Princeton, 1946).

[18]*The Province of West New Jersey, 1609-1702: A History of the Origins of an American Colony* (Princeton, 1956); *The Province of East New Jersey, 1609-1702: The Rebellious Proprietary* (Princeton, 1962).

[19]New York, 1953.

[20]*Robert Livingston, 1654-1728, and the Politics of Colonial New York* (Chapel Hill, 1961).

[21]New York, 1956.

[22]*The Beekman Mercantile Papers, 1746-1799* (New York, 1956).

[23]Vol. XIII (Albany, 1962).

[24]*Mohawk Baronet: Sir William Johnson of New York* (New York, 1959).

[25] Ithaca, New York, 1960.

[26]Philadelphia, 1945.

[27]Chapel Hill, 1959.

28*King of the Delawares: Teedyuscung, 1700-1763* (Philadelphia, 1949).

29*James Wilson: Founding Father, 1742-1798* (Chapel Hill, 1956).

30Brooke Hindle, *David Rittenhouse* (Princeton, 1964); Whitfield J. Bell, Jr., *John Morgan: Colonial Doctor* (Philadelphia, 1965).

31I. Bernard Cohen, ed., *Benjamin Franklin's Experiments: A New Edition of Franklin's Experiments and Observations on Electricity* (Cambridge, 1941); I. Bernard Cohen, *Franklin and Newton: An Inquiry into Speculative Newtonian Science and Franklin's Work on Electricity as an Example Thereof*, Memoirs of the American Philosophical Society, XLIII (Philadelphia, 1956).

32William S. Hanna, *Benjamin Franklin and Pennsylvania Politics* (Stanford, California, 1964); Paul W. Conner, *Poor Richard's Politicks: Benjamin Franklin and His New American Order* (New York, 1965); Gerald Stourzh, *Benjamin Franklin and American Foreign Policy* (Chicago, 1954).

33Boston, 1954.

34*Benjamin Franklin's Memoirs: Parallel Text Edition* (Berkeley, 1949).

35Leonard W. Labaree, Ralph L. Ketcham, Helen C. Boatfield, and Helene H. Fineman, eds., *The Autobiography of Benjamin Franklin* (New Haven, 1964).

36Leonard W. Labaree et al., eds., *The Papers of Benjamin Franklin* (New Haven, 1959-), Vols. I-IX.

37A small part of John Smith's diary forms the substance of Albert Cook Myers, ed., *Hannah Logan's Courtship* (Philadelphia, 1904); selections from Elizabeth Drinker's diary were published by Henry D. Biddle in *Extracts from the Journal of Elizabeth Drinker, 1759-1807* (Philadelphia, 1889), and further selections appeared in Cecil Drinker, ed., *Not So Long Ago: A Chronicle of Medicine and Doctors in Colonial Philadelphia* (New York, 1937).

Historians and the Southern Colonies

BY CLARENCE L. VER STEEG

The southern colonies, and particularly their development during the eighteenth century, have long been a field of special interest to Clarence L. Ver Steeg, whose exacting research and penetrating insights have added new dimensions to their study. In such respected works as ROBERT MORRIS: REVOLUTIONARY FINANCIER, *the introduction to* A TRUE AND HISTORICAL NARRATIVE OF THE COLONY OF GEORGIA, *and* THE FORMATIVE YEARS, 1607-1763 *he has demonstrated that the boldness of his interpretations are as challenging as the originality of his concepts, qualities that are particularly apparent in the essay that follows. Professsor Ver Steeg has taught at Northwestern University since earning a Columbia doctorate in 1950; in 1954-1955 he served as fellow of the Huntington Library. The tribute that he has prepared for this volume is as notable for its insights as for its searching analysis and criticism of recent historical writing on the southern colonies.*

THE SWEET-SINGING MUSES have drawn scholars in Lorelei fashion to examine those qualities of the South that have made it distinctive, and more often than not the investigators have been shipwrecked and sunk. The legacy of slavery, the peculiar quality of caste and clan, the inbreeding and semi-isolation, the ability under the most unpromising circumstances to produce literary figures of international repute, and the tortuous political configurations are among the hazards and attractions that frighten and fascinate the inquirer. As a result, the South somehow appears greater than life-size. Legend has often over-matched reality, and the consequence has been perverse as well as pervasive.

To untangle legend from fact, the South has been subjected to microscopic examination for more than a century. Each generation of historians, influenced by contemporary ideas and attitudes, has produced "new" interpretations. Learned and frequently emotional debates have focused on such issues as slavery, the profile of antebellum society, the "mind" of the South, reconstruction, the redeemers, populism, and progressivism. Sweeping revision of what is conceived of as the southern experience has given way to still further revisions until finally contemporary scholars have reached some approximation of reality.

In "The Search for Southern Identity," C. Vann Woodward, with his customary grace and perception, sets aside the southern shortcomings and vices—the one-horse farmer, the sharecropper, the Jim Crow car, and the lynching bee—as landmarks of regional identification. Even agrarianism and race consciousness, he reminds us, cannot be said to be enduring or distinguishing characteristics. But Woodward concludes that positive qualities within the South do set it apart, and he discusses at least four of them to differentiate the South from the "American way of life": southern poverty as opposed to American abundance; southern frustration and failures as opposed to American success; southern guilt and pessimism as opposed to American innocence and belief in human perfectability; and, finally, southern identity with place and environment as opposed to American abstraction in the sense of being unable to relate to place and environment.[1]

These distinguishing qualities are not fully applicable to the southern colonies. Poverty existed, but probably in no greater degree than in the other Atlantic seaboard colonies; success rather than frustration or failure was a prominent trait of the southern colonies; perhaps pessimism and an unconscious sense of guilt does describe the southern colonial, but the enlightenment ideas influenced Jefferson while a cynical view of man and his behavior captured the mind of a New England John Adams. The southern colonial definitely identified with his environment, perhaps more than his contemporaries in the northern and eastern colonies, which suggests that this characteristic has the deepest roots and is the most lasting in southern history.

The obvious conclusion, of course, is that "the South" is a nineteenth-century or at least a post-revolutionary creation.[2] Indeed, the southern colonies were never a cohesive section in the same way that New England was. The great diversity of population groups, discussed either in terms of the point of origin or the manner of settlement, the cultural baggage transplanted, and the absence of a hub, a center, discouraged southern sectionalism. No fundamental and embracing commonality—religious, economic, social, or intellectual—existed to overcome these striking differences. Whereas scholars of early American history speak with confidence of a "New England Mind" in the colonial period, which presupposes close connecting links at every level of human activity, no scholar has had the temerity to speak of a "Southern Mind" in the colonial period.[3]

Approaches and points of view generated by discussions of the nineteenth-century South have frequently been read back into the history of the southern colonies, in some cases producing serious distortion or, even more disturbing, snuffing out further inquiry by assuming that what was true of the later period was also true of the seventeenth and eighteenth-century colonies. Under these circumstances, generalizations about southern colonial history were little more than interpretations of the nineteenth-century South superimposed upon the earlier period. Virginia had to be rescued from the Cavaliers,[4] and only recently has the study of the institution of slavery in the southern colonies shown signs of being emancipated from those dated monographs, published when W. A. Dunning's students were "revising" the approach to reconstruction,[5] that are so limited in scope and legalistic in orientation as to divorce statistics from life. Oscar and Mary Handlin, after re-examining the standard materials and statutes and introducing new evidence in evaluating the operation of the statutes as well as placing their investigations within a fresh context, concluded what probably everyone should have known, that the institution of slavery in the southern colonies developed much later than scholars had presumed. Winthrop D. Jordon has challenged the Handlins, and his evidence modifies a part of their work.[6] But the important point is that historians have been unbelievably delinquent, and our knowledge of slavery in the pre-revolutionary southern colonies, as a result, is scanty.

Why, for example, did Negro slavery suddenly emerge as the dominant labor force between 1690-1720? The changing role of the Royal African Company in the slave trade, the expanding operation of the free traders, the altered character of the West Indies, the opening up of the Middle Colonies, the ability of the planters to gain control of land distribution within their respective colonies, the economics of slavery versus indentured servitude—these and many more developments provide ample ingredients for an incisive historical debate, but the debate cannot take place until the issue is brought into better focus.

The lack of focus is characteristic of the scholarship on the southern colonies. New England has its dramatic confrontations—the trial of Anne Hutchinson, the expulsion of Roger Williams, the enactment of the Half Way Covenant, as well as the jeremiads—to light the pathway of scholarship around which historians cluster to discuss and to debate the nature and the course of Puritanism. With the exception of Bacon's Rebellion, key episodes of equal importance do not exist to light the pathway of scholarship for the colonial South. Its society is less well organized, its communication system less sophisticated, and its consciousness of status, at least until the 1680s, less well developed. Historians have not been successful in providing a systematic structure to analyze the southern colonies as a whole, which is another way of saying that the southern colonies, as contrasted with New England, are not a section and do not lend themselves to a uniform discussion, and that a certain alienation exists between the southern colonies and "the South."[7]

The problem of analyzing the newer interpretations for the scholar of the colonial South is filled with hazard. More often than not, fresh insights are in the process of emerging rather than being fully developed and articulated. The consequences for future scholarship of these "newer" interpretations, as they affect the writing of colonial history, southern history, and the mainstream of American historical writing can at best be only suggested rather than precisely determined.

Social institutions and man's relationship to them are being reviewed from a fresh perspective by contemporary historians. The insight of Riesman, Parsons, and Merton has as its counterpart the Handlins, Hofstadter, Woodward, and Potter. Questions are being rephrased. Patterns of behavior and social institutions are being restudied on the basis of man's needs and his methods as well as his options in fulfilling these needs. A new emphasis has been placed upon research on the family, the role of women, the subcultural groups, the significance of status, and the contours and structure of the social system. Research on the southern colonies in this context has been slow to develop, but progress is being made.

A notable illustration is the recent attention devoted to the family. The southern colonies are unusually receptive to such investigation because family and clan have long been recognized as important. The invaluable study of Julia Cherry Spruill, *Women's Life and Work in the Southern Colonies,* as well as Edmund S. Morgan's brief and more popular treatment of Virginia family life provide a reliable base on which to build, as does Bernard Bailyn's essay on education which places primary stress on the family as a key social unit in teaching and learning.[8]

Precise evaluation of the role of each member within the family and causal factors that produced the special characteristics of the family in the southern colonies have come less readily. Placing white women, wives and daughters, on a special pedestal as "protection" in a Negro-dominated plantation family unit, thus introducing a vigorous matriarchal strain into the society, is a persuasive generalization worthy of more profound study than it has received. Dominating personalities at the head of a large family circle producing impotent sons and grandsons, in a managerial and intellectual rather than sexual context, is a second generalization that invites further inquiry, although the Byrds and the Carters in the eighteenth century are fascinating case studies. And what of rivalries within the family, an investigation that has yet to be undertaken?

In view of the emphasis placed upon family by contemporaries and by historians, the absence of intensive research on important family groups is disappointing. Aubrey C. Land's study of the Dulanys of Maryland is, in many respects, the only serious, published recent work on a first-line family.[9] A few dissertations such as that of Maurice Crouse on the Manigaults of South Carolina and that of Emory Evans on the Nelsons of Virginia could represent the beginning of a resurgence of scholarship in conformity with this trend of historical writing, but the general outlook is not promising.[10] Armed with new questions and insights, young scholars can make important contributions to a better understanding of the society of the southern colonies, despite the uneven, limited, and often episodic materials on families at their disposal.

The slave family as a subgroup within the larger plantation family is only beginning to be understood together with its effect upon the non-slave members. On the basis of the current evidence, it is probably a serious mistake to conclude that the suggested ramifications of slavery upon nineteenth and twentieth-century America, namely that the Negro male was robbed of his manhood because of his servile status, thus making the Negro family matriarchal, can be read back into the status of the Negro family in the colonial period. Nor can it be said that the Negro family, at least in the southern colonies, was merely a casual liaison to satisfy the sexual urges of the slave or to breed a labor force for the planter. When more than merely statistical records are available, a student of the period is struck by the recognition of the Negro family as a unit and that the relationships—daughters-in-law, sons-in-law, and grandchildren— are acknowledged even by the white masters.[11] The pattern of Negro family life in Africa, the effect of forced migration upon these patterns, and the adjustments made within the institution of slavery are influences but dimly comprehended.

The social consequences of slavery upon the role of the whites in the southern colonies is related to a more general appraisal of the consciousness of status. The pioneer studies of Philip Bruce, Thomas Wertenbaker, and more recently Louis Wright on Virginia have been invaluable in describing the rise of the planter class, the establishment of the First Families, and the tradition of responsible leadership in the colonial community. Somewhat less familiar is the development of attitudes with regard to rank and to station, not only toward the slave but also toward an acceptable pecking order of planter families, one being more important than the other.

Are new questions being asked about these developments that suggest a reassessment? The historical controversy over the nature of Bacon's Rebellion is a promising point of departure. Thomas J. Wertenbaker in *Torchbearer of American Revolution* sees Bacon as representative of indigenous forces in Virginia challenging British rule as autocratically exercised by Governor Berkeley. In *The Governor and the Rebel* Wilcomb Washburn challenges Wertenbaker's conclusions, and asserts that historians have misread the times and, therefore, the motives animating the participants.[12] In Washburn's account, Governor Berkeley receives much more understanding treatment. These studies have initiated scholarly speculation as to whether the entire episode cannot be better understood in a broader context, specifically that a type of status revolution was underway with the emergence of a native planter group who were eventually to assume the most powerful positions in the colony. The ambition and future of these men were being threatened by the Crown grants in the Northern Neck and the very real prospect that grants equal in size would be made by the Crown throughout Virginia. With their economic future endangered and their political and social gains imperiled, the emerging Virginia gentry, even those of exalted station, experienced a sense of uneasiness that was profound and pervasive.[13]

No crisis of status in the following century equalled that of Bacon's Rebellion. Members of professions, ministers and lawyers, for example, were successful only as they accepted rather than challenged the system. In the eighteenth-century Carolinas, the line between lawyer and planter could scarcely be distinguished, and the merchant families of Charleston—the Wraggs, the Manigaults, and eventually the Laurenses—became planters to achieve acceptable status and power.

The social structure that emerged has been successfully delineated in broad outline by scholars, but recent studies have given it a needed precision and dimension. Among the best is Aubrey C. Land's analysis of the economic base of the social structure in Maryland.[14] By sampling local records, especially the invaluable inventories of estates, Land finds a society of economic competence rather than one of great affluence. His investigation reveals that in the last decade of the seventeenth century 75 per cent of the estates had a value of less than one hundred pounds and that only 1.5 per cent of the estates exceeded one thousand pounds. When it is recalled that a minister's annual salary amounted to no more than 60 to 100 pounds, the economic level of that society can be more readily evaluated. Fifteen pounds income annually represented a good year for a small tobacco planter, and more than one third of the planters were lease-holders. Obviously, the options open to the small planter were limited. If the scholar of the southern colonies recalls that North Carolina was less well off than Maryland and that Georgia experienced even greater hardship, he can scarcely conclude that he is studying a society of extraordinary abundance, despite the significant entrepreneurial spirit manifested by lawyers, middle-sized planters, and merchant groups.

Indeed, scholars studying the southern colonies, and even the South of the nineteenth century, should re-examine the easy generalization of wide currency that asserts that the distinctiveness of America was its break with the feudal legacy of the Old World. Vann Woodward has suggested that "there is still a contribution to be derived from the South's un-American adventure in feudal fantasy," and E. Franklin Frazier's book on the Negro family contains a chapter entitled "Escape from Feudal America."[15] The fact that a man's place in the society was determined by his relationship to the land, that peasants and slaves share certain common characteristics, that the dominant families could control the lives of neighbors for miles around, that feudal trappings such as quit rents yielded a greater return than is customarily suggested should certainly encourage historians to rethink their earlier conclusions. Except for Robert L. Meriwether's exhaustive and reliable investigation in the *Expansion of South Carolina,* scholars know more about the truth as opposed to the mythology of the Homestead Act of 1862 than they do about land holding in the southern colonies.[16]

In political and social-political history, newer interpretations have focused upon three issues: first, the degree of democratization within the colonial governments; second, the systematic effort on the part of the colonial legislatures to model themselves after Parliament by gaining power at the expense of the governor representing the Crown (in a sense the Glorious Revolution transplanted to America); and third, a re-examination of the organization and practice of political life, not merely in theory but in fact.

Democratization, somewhat mistakenly, has centered upon suffrage. Robert E. and B. Katherine Brown, using techniques similar to those applied by the former in investigating eighteenth-century Massachusetts, have assessed the operation of the suffrage requirement in Virginia, the participation of the electorate at the polls, and the results of elections. Their evidence is supplemented by that provided by Lucille Griffith. The conclusions of these studies is unequivocal: that relatively few free white men were deprived of the right to vote, that a respectable percentage participated in elections, and that the small planter controlled the balance of votes in most elections.[17] Similar studies have not been made of Maryland or the Carolinas. There is serious doubt whether adequate source materials exist to make an equivalent investigation for South Carolina; Georgia is so dissimilar to its neighbors during most of the colonial period that it is a case study in itself.

An inevitable question arises in discussing this data: Does provision for voting and representation at the polls lead to the conclusion that political life in the southern colonies, or even in Virginia where the research has been concentrated, was democratic? This question cannot be definitely answered until two historical problems have been thoroughly investigated. One, indigenous to the locale and the period, is the fact that those elected to office, with rare exception, came from the elite groups.[18] Did this occur because men voted in public with all the social pressures this absence of privacy entailed? Or was the expense of being a candidate or of holding a public office so prohibitive that only the elite could afford to serve? Or did the rank and file vote for the elite because these men represented an image of the kind of success everyone desired? Regardless of the answers given these questions, the results tend to support the proposition that voting and office holding in the southern colonies were not vastly different from their exercise in America of the nineteenth and twentieth centuries.

Another problem directly related to democratization could well re-orient the discussion of political organization and operation for all of American history: the realities of local government. Was it, in fact, closest to the people and best representative of their views, a belief held by Jefferson and parroted by a host of scholars? If the answer is negative—and the evidence tends to support this conclusion—the discussion of political life, not only in the southern colonies but also for United States history as a whole, will require major revision in order to be realistic. The scholarship in associated social science disciplines—such as that of V. O. Key, a political scientist, and of John Dollard, a psychologist, to cite but two examples—suggests that a re-thinking of the role of local government in the southern colonies is overdue.[19]

The second major issue—that of transplanting the Glorious Revolution to America during the eighteenth century—is best embodied in Jack P. Greene's *The Quest for Power*. Greene has taken the institutional studies produced under the direction of Herbert Levi Osgood—those of W. Roy Smith for South Carolina, Charles L. Raper for North Carolina, and Percy Scott Flippen for Virginia—introduced new materials from English and American archival sources, and projected the whole to a new level of scholarly and intellectual sophistication. He views the struggle between the colonial legislatures and the authorities representing the Crown from the perspective of America rather than of England, a perspective which disassociates him from the imperial historians; and he is able to make discerning judgments in comparing the initiative and response of one southern colonial assembly as opposed to another.[20]

Greene makes no pretense of discussing the internal struggles for power within the colonies. He sheds little light, therefore, upon the third trend of newer interpretations on southern colonial political life: its organization and practice as expressed in the operation, within each colony, of competing factions, groups, or parties.

To illustrate, the control of the land office does not figure significantly in Greene's work, whereas it becomes a critical issue in studies of political coalitions within individual colonies. D. Alan Williams recognizes the watershed in the evolution of colonial Virginia when the council gains ascendency between 1706-1710.[21] From that date forward control of land distribution became primarily a contest between groups within the colony, and thus an object for an internal struggle for power. Williams also stresses the river systems as the base of significant political coalitions, thus de-emphasizing the stereotypes of frontier vs tidewater, small planter vs large planter, and debtor vs creditor. He receives indirect but powerful support from the findings of the Browns when they discovered that the relative density of slave holding followed the river systems from the tidewater to the mountains, not the seaboard as contrasted with the piedmont. Written but not yet published is a political study of South Carolina by Eugene Sirmans.[22] If the articles he has made available are a test, consensus politics will be underscored in that swiftly developing colony. In these emerging interpretations, it is significant to note that genuine political differences as expressed by internal factions, coalitions, and semi-parties could not assert themselves until the power of the Crown or the proprietor was severely reduced. Indeed, this factor separates seventeenth-century New England from the seventeenth-century Chesapeake colonies.

Recent investigations of colonial governors have been few and disappointing. Those made have failed to view their materials in terms of the newer insights on political organization or of the life-size configurations in the contest for power. Desmond Clarke's biography of Governor Arthur Dobbs of North Carolina all but ignores these themes, although he demonstrates that Dobbs, very much like Francis Nicholson at the end of the seventeenth and beginning of the eighteenth century, was an inter-colonial man. Dobbs' irrational behavior in trying to prove that Hudson Bay led to a Northwest passage reveals a good bit about the man—bigoted, self-righteous, egoistic, and ambitious—but less than we would like to know about North Carolina politics. Scholars must continue to depend upon the substantial contribution of Leonidas Dodson on Alexander Spotswood and the limited and outdated studies of Louis Koontz on Robert Dinwiddie.[23]

Recent scholarship on the organization of economic life in the southern colonies has been alarmingly scanty. This can be explained in part by two factors: first, scholars have assumed that the economic life of the colonial South is self-evident, namely, that after a passing nod in the direction of the fur trader and the producer of forest products, the discussion turns to the development of the planter capitalist who marketed tobacco, rice, and indigo; and second, the evidence on economic life is so scattered and so difficult to analyze that only the most persistent scholar can brave the obstacles.

Tobacco Coast by Arthur Middleton, published almost two decades ago, is, in fact, the only major book to appear on the economic life of the southern colonies.[24] The articles of Jacob Price have revealed the growing importance of Scotland in the tobacco trade, but the southern colonies are still in search of their Richard Pares.[25] Fortunately, several unpublished dissertations promise fresh insights. Robert Thomson has been engaged in a work on Virginia merchants that eventually could tell us much more than we know currently about the organization of trade, the relationship of the changing commercial experience of England to that in the southern colonies, the relative profits, and perhaps even illuminate the relationship between trade, politics, and social behavior.[26] The trade of South Carolina early in the eighteenth century has been analyzed with discrimination by Converse Clowse; using computer techniques, his study has made precise those trends and relationships which heretofore have been impressionistic: the number of vessels engaged in the trade, the quantity and specification of exports, the owners of the vessels, as well as the designated destinations of the cargoes.[27] In a dissertation entitled "Virginia and the English Commercial System, 1689-1733," John Hemphill examines the significant relationship between economic and commercial communities of England and Virginia, so that for the first time the two components are treated as a unit rather than as isolated parts.[28] What these findings will eventually lead to is a matter of conjecture, but the role of the southern colonial economy in the imperial and world setting will be more clearly revealed. In terms of the newer trends of historical writing, scholars should be able to assess with a confidence they now lack the rate of economic growth in the southern colonies and the respective components of that growth.[29] Whether the emerging studies will enable historians to advance a step and relate the development of trade to the status of persons is debatable.

Studies of a second but not unrelated aspect of economic life, the plantation unit producing for market, are slowly building up, sometimes by indirect contributions. Unfortunately, the paucity, if not downright absence, of plantation records for South Carolina and the limited number for North Carolina will always limit any generalizations. County and parish records as well as inventories of estates can yield significant conclusions with respect to the general economic well-being of a designated group—the small planter, the leaseholder, and the like—but they cannot substitute for plantation records in analyzing the character, growth, effectiveness, and development of the plantation as a fundamental unit of production. The indirect evidence supplied by David J. Mays' discriminating study of Edmund Pendleton—who reveals that Speaker Robinson of the House of Burgesses made secret loans of public monies to fellow planters who could not meet their obligations—tells us as much about the value system of the Virginia elite as it does about their financial distress.[30] The evidence is growing to support the conclusion that the southern planter, especially in the eighteenth century, resembled the farmer of the nineteenth in that he depended upon an increase in the value of the land he held for his prosperity rather than upon annual cash returns from crops.

In the 1870s, Sir Leslie Stephen introduced his imperishable inquiry, *History of English Thought in the Eighteenth Century*, with an extensive analysis of "The Philosophical Basis." More recently, Perry Miller's profound and enduring studies on the Puritans were predicated on the presumption that ideas, not necessarily in the abstract but surrounded by the reality and action of life as expressed or rationalized in a systematic fashion, are primary.[31] In contrast, the flourishing scholarship on the social-cultural-intellectual life of the southern colonies reflects the extraordinary influence of the *American Life Series*, which is to say that these investigations have focused upon social-cultural themes rather than upon ideas.

The reason for this pattern is quite obvious. First, the published writing upon which a Perry Miller bases his work simply does not exist for the southern colonies, which means that a different approach is required. Second, the idea-centered intellectual historian cannot successfully fulfill his task until the work of the social-cultural historian has been completed. In this respect, the path-breaking scholarship of men such as Louis Wright and Carl Bridenbaugh has yielded a rich and substantial fare of social-cultural studies, which suggests that the stage is set for the appearance of the idea-centered historian, from whom, it is safe to assume, will eventually emanate a fresh point of view.[32]

Somewhat paradoxically in light of his premise that Americans are not an idea-centered people, Daniel Boorstin has taken a step in this direction.[33] Writing a sociologically-oriented intellectual history Boorstin's aim is to plumb the assumptions of the colonials. In chapters entitled "An American Frame of Mind" and "Culture Without a Capital," Boorstin raises responsible questions about the presumptions, value systems, and cultural priorities of the American colonials. Applying this approach vigorously, imaginatively, and skillfully to the southern colonials, the idea-centered historian will enter into a searching re-examination of the configurations of their intellectual life.

The continuing investigations of many components of cultural-intellectual life—religion, newspapers and other avenues of communication, the arts, writing, and Charleston urban life—have not only reaffirmed its impressive vitality in the southern colonies, but also raised questions about its true place in the value-system of the southern colonials. Generally hardworking and responsible people, the gentry recognized culture as important for "their" country as a civilizing influence, as a necessary ingredient for "completeness" in a gentleman, as an accoutrement that brought prestige, and as a fulfillment of life. But we have long since recognized that the southern colonials did not accept all expressions of culture as an encompassing blanket but discriminated between their various forms.

Affluent southern colonials patronized prestigious dwellings rather than great art.[34] This bias is significantly related to their involvement in family, but it also tells us something about their value system. After thousands of years the world still has magnificent examples of Greek sculpture and Greek public buildings, but the Greek homes were made of highly perishable materials and their clothing, even for the important citizen, was simple. For the Middle Ages, the monument is the cathedral. Just as these facts tell us something about the value system of the people of ancient and medieval times, the relatively numerous southern colonial homes that are reasonably well preserved in contrast to the public buildings that required restoration suggests something about the attitude and values of these Americans. Indeed, later generations have probably invested the public life of the colonial southerners with greater

93

value than they themselves gave it. Or perhaps later generations who made decisions as to what was worthy of preservation are informing us about the value standards of the South rather than those of the southern colonials.

The corroborating evidence is revealing. For all of its personal disclosures, William Byrd II's *Diaries* are deeply disappointing if a scholar is searching for observations on the content of the reading in which he is engaged.[35] Discussions of intellectual or profound political issues find no place in these highly personal documents; the *Diary* is centered on himself or at best the surrounding plantation family. The same generalization can be made of the *Diary* of Landon Carter, so recently and so elegantly published.[36] Carter's principal "ideas" are to be found in his public statements. In his holy of holies, his *Diary*, Carter reflects only the most pedestrian intellectual interest. If a man truly is what he is in his heart, then the public face of many a southern colonial is not a reliable index into his deepest concerns.[37] What is becoming increasingly obvious is that the historians of the colonial South are groping somewhat uneasily to reach a new level of understanding of the southern colonial mind.[38]

Significantly, the principal premise of W. J. Cash's *Mind of the South* is that *the* South developed out of the first American West, or what Frederick Jackson Turner called the Old West. Designated more precisely, the Old West for the southern colonies lay between the lower Piedmont and the Appalachian Mountains. Dismissing the seaboard gentry as the source of the elite group of the Old South, Cash asks: "How account for the ruling class, then? Manifestly, for the great part, by the strong, the pushing, the ambitious, among the old coon-hunting population of the back-country."[39] And where did the rank and file of the Old South originate? From the same area, asserts Cash. The difference in their relative standing rested entirely upon the degree of success or failure in conquering the wilderness of Transappalachia. From the backcountry came the legacy of explosive energy and individualistic behavior, the penchant for violence, the affection for weapons, and the idea that a man solves his problems not by an appeal to the courts or some other system that took time to achieve results but directly, personally, and immediately.

The merit of Cash's arguments—and they are formidable—deserves an essay in itself; for purposes of this essay his suggestions highlight the significance of the historical writing on the eighteenth-century southern frontier. Fortunately, the discussions can rest

94

upon a solid foundation of "classics": Verner Crane's *The Southern Frontier, 1670-1732* and Robert L. Meriwether's unparalleled work of scholarship, *The Expansion of South Carolina, 1729-1765*. More recently, Richard Brown, *The South Carolina Regulators,* the publication of a contemporary account of the backcountry people, written by Charles Woodmason, a psychotic Anglican parson, and David H. Cockran's *The Cherokee Frontier,* continue to build upon this base.[40] Taking proper account of Woodmason's bias, the historian is able to see the backcountry settlers as life-size, while Brown's focus upon the self-regulating aspects of the backcountry people, who found themselves outside the framework of traditional law enforcement, makes Cash's generalization more understandable and acceptable.

The eighteenth-century southern frontier will certainly be the center of emerging new interpretations. It has been suggested that the eighteenth-century frontier served as a genuine safety valve for the settled regions. The subsidy of settlement groups in upcountry South Carolina and the laws that supplied freed indentures with land, livestock, and seed in other colonies were among the factors that enabled the impoverished to move west. The proximity of the frontier, the readiness with which land could be acquired, and the ease of making a living made the eighteenth-century frontier a classic in fact, not merely in theory.[41] The shape of the historical writing that will develop cannot be forecast, but the appearance soon of a volume by W. Stitt Robinson, devoted exclusively to the southern colonial frontier, will certainly enable historians to find a basis for a fresh appraisal. Except for South Carolina, where Meriwether's study makes current assessments reliable, the most serious and most difficult variable to evaluate is land ownership.

Imperial relations between the mother country and the southern colonies, aside from Greene's study, have been confined recently to Lawrence Gipson's magisterial multi-volume investigation of the *British Empire Before the American Revolution.*[42] In terms of the southern colonies, Gipson represents more of a summary than a departure. The Florida frontier, the great Indian nations proximate to the southern colonies, the emergence of the land companies, and the international rivalries focused upon a provincial stage have provided a new appreciation of the fact that the southern colonial, whether in the backcountry or seaboard, whether in Virginia or Georgia, was never allowed to forget his direct tie with the great struggles of Europe. In those struggles, the personal fate of a man was determined, and the fate of "the South" which became English rather than French or Spanish, was decided. These consequences, although obvious, have been given a new urgency as the result of Gipson's sweeping study; in historical terms, therefore, the southern colonial frontier is inextricably linked to imperial as well as to colonial issues.

It is apparent that, regardless of the devoted scholarship directed to a better understanding of the southern colonies, historians have the opportunity still to contribute to a more discriminating, incisive, and imaginative delineation of colonial development. In order to achieve the most illuminating results, the newer tools and approaches available to the profession must be effectively exploited. The writing of American history, of southern history, and of colonial history will benefit. This truly is the lesson.

1C. Vann Woodward, *The Burden of Southern History* (Baton Rouge, 1960) , 3-25.

2See, in this connection, John Alden, *The First South* (Baton Rouge, 1961) .

3The point is made in Clarence L. Ver Steeg, *The Formative Years* (New York, 1964) , 52. The implications of this generalization reappear throughout the volume.

4Thomas J. Wertenbaker, *The Planters of Colonial Virginia* (Princeton, 1922) .

5James A. Ballagh, *A History of Slavery in Virginia* (Baltimore, 1902) , is a representative monograph.

6Oscar and Mary Handlin, "Origins of the Southern Labor System" in the *William and Mary Quarterly*, 3rd Series, VII (1950) , 199-222; Winthrop D. Jordan, "Modern Tensions and the Origins of American Slavery" in the *Journal of Southern History*, XXVIII, (1962) , 18-30.

7This quality is self-evident in the important book of Wesley Frank Craven, *The Southern Colonies in the Seventeenth Century, 1607-1689* (Baton Rouge, 1949. *A History of the South Series*, I. Wendell Stephenson and E. Merton Coulter, eds.)

8Julia Cherry Spruill, *Women's Life and Work in the Southern Colonies* (Chapel Hill, 1938) ; Edmund S. Morgan, *Virginians at Home; Family Life in the Eighteenth Century* (Williamsburg, 1952) ; Bernard Bailyn, *Education in the Forming of American Society; Needs and Opportunities For Study* (Chapel Hill, 1960) .

9Aubrey C. Land, *The Dulanys of Maryland* (Baltimore, 1955) .

10Maurice A. Crouse, "The Manigault Family of South Carolina, 1685-1783" (Unpublished Doctoral Dissertation, Northwestern University, 1964) ; Emory G. Evans, "The Rise and Decline of the Virginia Aristocracy in the Eighteenth Century: The Nelsons" *The Old Dominion; Essays for Thomas P. Abernathy* (Charlottesville, 1964. Darrett B. Rutman ed.) 62-78. A number of the essays in this volume are pertinent to this article.

11Note especially, *The Diary of Landon Carter of Sabine Hall, 1752-1778* (2 vols; Charlottesville, 1965. Ed with an Introduction by Jack P. Greene) 291; and *passim*. E. Franklin Frazier, *The Negro Family in the United States* (New York, 1939; revised, 1948) , does not reach back into the colonial period in a systematic fashion.

12Thomas J. Wertenbaker, *Torchbearer of the American Revolution; The Story of Bacon's Rebellion and Its Leader* (Princeton, 1940) ; Wilcomb Washburn, *The Governor and The Rebel* (Chapel Hill, 1957) . Washburn's first chapter entitled "The Rise of the Democratic Myth" is an excellent historiographical essay on Bacon's Rebellion.

13Bernard Bailyn "Politics and Social Structure in Virginia" in *Seventeenth Century America; Essays in Colonial History* (Chapel Hill, 1959. James M. Smith, ed.) 90-115; see in particular Ver Steeg, *The Formative Years*, 129-51.

14Aubrey C. Land, "Economic Base and Social Structure: The Northern Chesapeake in the Eighteenth Century" *Journal of Economic History*, XXV, (1965) , 639-654.

15Woodward, *The Burden of Southern History*, 22; Frazier, *The Negro Family in the United States*.

16Robert L. Meriwether, *The Expansion of South Carolina, 1729-1765* (Kingsport, 1940) , 34-159.

17Robert E. and B. Katherine Brown, *Virginia, 1705-1786: Democracy or Aristocracy* (East Lansing, 1964) , especially Chapters II, and VI-IX; Lucille Griffith, *Virginia House of Burgesses, 1750-1774* (Northport, 1963) .

18Charles Sydnor, *Gentlemen Freeholders* (Chapel Hill, 1952) . The Browns strongly disagree with certain of Sydnor's views.

19V. O. Key, *Southern Politics in State and Nation* (New York, 1949) ; John Dollard, *Caste and Clan in a Southern Town* (2nd ed. New York, 1949) .

20Jack P. Greene, *The Quest for Power; The Lower Houses of Assembly in the Southern Royal Colonies, 1689-1776* (Chapel Hill, 1963) ; W. Roy Smith, *South Carolina as a Royal Province, 1719-1776* (New York, 1903) ; Charles L. Raper, *North Carolina: A Study in English Colonial Government* (New York, 1904) ; and Percy Scott Flippen, *The Royal Government of Virginia* (New York, 1919) .

21David Alan Williams, "Political Alignments in Colonial Virginia Politics, 1698-1750" (Unpublished Doctoral Dissertation, Northwestern University, 1959) .

22M. Eugene Sirmans, "Masters of Ashley Hall: A Study of the Bull Family in Colonial South Carolina, 1670-1737" (Unpublished Doctoral Dissertation, Princeton, 1959) .

23Desmond Clarke, *Arthur Dobbs Esquire, 1689-1765* (Chapel Hill, 1957) ; Leonidas Dodson, *Alexander Spotswood, Governor of Colonial Virginia, 1710-1722* (Philadelphia, 1932); Louis K. Koontz, *Robert Dinwiddie; His Career in American Colonial Government and Westward Expansion* (Glendale, 1941) . The exception to the generalizations made about recent studies of governors is W. W. Abbot, *The Royal Governors of Georgia, 1754-1775* (Chapel Hill, 1959) . His study illuminates internal politics as well as the struggle between the Crown and the colony, but as the dates suggest, the focus is upon the steps toward separation. Robert L. Morton, *Colonial Virginia* (2 vols. Chapel Hill, 1960) is the best, recent, straightforward, politically-oriented account of a single colony, and it is an invaluable work to consult.

24Arthur Middleton, *Tobacco Coast; a Maritime History of Chesapeake Bay in the Colonial Era* (Newport News, 1953).

25Jacob Price, "The Rise of Glasgow in the Chesapeake Tobacco Trade, 1707-1775," *William and Mary Quarterly*, 3rd Series, XI (1954) .

26Robert P. Thomson, "The Merchant in Virginia, 1700-1775" (Unpublished Doctoral Dissertation, University of Wisconsin, 1955) .

27Converse D. Clowse, "The Charleston Export Trade, 1717-1737" (Unpublished Doctoral Dissertation, Northwestern University, 1963).

28John Hemphill II, "Virginia and the English Commercial System, 1689-1733' (Unpublished Doctoral Dissertation, Princeton University, 1964) .

29See Stuart Bruchey, *The Roots of American Economic Growth, 1607-1861; An Essay in Causation* (New York, 1965) , especially Chapter I.

30David J. Mays, *Edmund Pendleton, 1721-1803* (2 vols., Cambridge, 1952) .

31Leslie Stephen, *History of English Thought in the Eighteenth Century* (Harbinger Edn., 2 vols. New York, 1962), and Perry Miller, *The New England Mind; The Seventeenth Century* (New York, 1939), and *The New England Mind; From Colony to Province* (Cambridge, 1953) have no parallel in the writing of intellectual history in this country.

32Although Louis B. Wright has made his researches available in a number of books, his key study is *The First Gentlemen of Virginia; Intellectual Qualities of the Early Colonial Ruling Class* (San Marino, 1940) . The same comment can be made for Carl Bridenbaugh; his most pertinent study is *Myths and Realities; Societies of the Colonial South* (Baton Rouge, 1952) .

33Daniel Boorstin, *The Americans; Their Colonial Experience* (New York, 1958) .

34The suggestion made is not that southern colonials failed to produce their own artists, which is relatively easy to explain, but that they did not purchase the work of artists of consequence in England, which could be expected of the gentry.

35William Byrd, *Another Secret Diary of William Byrd, 1739-41, with Letters and Literary Exercises, 1696-1726* (Ed. by Maude Woodfin, translated and collated by Marion Tinling. Richmond, 1942); William Byrd, *The Great American Gentleman: William Byrd of Westover in Virginia, his Secret Diary for the Years 1709-12* (Louis Wright and Marion Tinling, eds., New York, 1963); William Byrd, *The London Diary, 1717-1721, and Other Writings* (Louis B. Wright and Marion Tinling, eds., New York, 1958).

36*Diary of Landon Carter, passim.*

37One must concede that to suggest the use of private papers to gain such insight or to make these judgments contradicts the position taken by Perry Miller who asserts the "mind" is the *public* expression of the community. His approach, as suggested earlier, must be modified if it is to be used for the southern colonies. The question is: does this modification alter the result, so that a discussion of the mind of the southern colonials cannot be compared with the New England mind because the end product is based upon different variables? This question opens a serious and unresolved debate.

38What the lack of commonality in assumptions and values can mean in the development of a community or colony can be well illustrated by the first decade or so in the founding of Georgia. See the introduction to *A True and Historical Narrative of the Colony of Georgia; with Comments by the Earl of Egmont* (Clarence L. Ver Steeg, ed., Athens, 1960), ix-xxxi.

39W. J. Cash, *The Mind of the South* (New York, 1941), p. 14.

40Verner W. Crane, *The Southern Frontier, 1670-1732* (Durham, 1928); Richard M. Brown, *The South Carolina Regulators* (Cambridge, 1963); Charles Woodmason, *The Carolina Backcountry on the Eve of the Revolution; The Journal and Other Writings of Charles Woodmason, Anglican Itinerant.* (Richard J. Hooker, ed. Chapel Hill, 1953); David H. Cochran, *The Cherokee Frontier, Conflict and Survival, 1740-62* (Norman, 1962).

41See particularly, Ver Steeg, *The Formative Years*, 152-172.

42Lawrence Gipson, *The British Empire Before the American Revolution* (12 volumes; Caldwell, Idaho, and New York, 1936-1965). The sweep of this work is remarkable. The thirteenth and final volume will be published soon.

Historians and the Nature of the American Revolution

BY MERRILL JENSEN

Among the scholars whose challenging insights forced historians to revise their views on the era of the American Revolution, none played a more prominent role than Merrill Jensen. Two of his several books—THE ARTICLES OF CONFEDERATION and THE NEW NATION—revolutionized thinking on the immediate post-Revolutionary period and touched off a storm of controversy by demonstrating that the Critical Period was far less critical than scholars had assumed. Educated partly in the Pacific Northwest, Profesor Jensen taught for some time at the University of Washington before moving in 1944 to the University of Wisconsin where he has since remained. In 1956-1957 he first used the rich resources of the Huntington Library. In this essay he has brilliantly traced the historiography of the Revolutionary period from its inception to the present, linking the "Patriot" and "Loyalist" traditions of the past with the "Progressive" and "Conservative" interpretations of today.

IN 1813 JOHN ADAMS told a friend that he had been importuned to write a history of the Revolution. His reply was that of the Secretary of the Continental Congress, Charles Thomson, when asked a similar question: "No, my history would so differ from the histories and traditions that I should give offence." Adams went on to say that "I have no great objection to giving offence to people who take offence without just cause; but I have no ambition to be thought a liar by posterity, and I am sure nobody would believe my history who believed any other that I have seen."[1] Two years later he told the Reverend Jedidiah Morse, who had asked Adams' help in writing a history, that he did not know whether to laugh or cry. "If I were to write a history of the last sixty years, as the facts rest in my memory, and according to my judgment . . . a hundred writers in

America, France, England, and Holland would immediately appear, and call me to myself, and before the world, a gross liar and a perjured villain."[2]

A few months later John Adams asked: "Who shall write the history of the American Revolution? Who can write it? Who will ever be able to write it?"[3] Thomas Jefferson replied: "Nobody; except merely its external facts. All its councils, designs and discussions having been conducted by Congress with closed doors, and no member, as far as I know, having even made notes of them, these, which are the life and soul of history must for ever be unknown."[4]

However, the two old men and many others had kept at least partial records that are the "life and soul of history." And despite their conviction that the history of the Revolution could never be written, Americans have been writing histories of it ever since 1775. In that year, the Reverend William Gordon announced that "there have been various special providences in our favor, which I have a design of [writing] down . . . and however these things may be lightly accounted of by the profane, they will excite proper emotions in the breasts of the pious. May there be repeated interpositions of Providence to make the chronicles of the American united colonies the favorite reading of the godly in this new world till the elect shall be gathered in."[5] Two years later, the Reverend Hugh Knox, Alexander Hamilton's sponsor in the West Indies, urged Hamilton to become the "annalist and biographer" of Washington and the "historiographer of the American War."[6] During the same year Arthur Lee, then in Berlin, wrote to George Washington and said that he intended to write "a history of this civil contention" and would need Washington's papers. "Dubious parts of history can be cleared only by such documents; and we shall want every authentic record to vouch against the forgeries which will be offered to the world."[7] Thomas Paine began planning a history of the Revolution as early as 1776 and came back to the idea again[8] and again in the years that followed.[9]

Meanwhile, Europeans began trying to explain the meaning of the Revolution. Americans were scornful. In 1782, John Adams told the Abbé de Mably, in effect, that he was too ignorant to write a history of the Revolution. Adams outlined the intensive research program (as valid today as in 1782) that would be necessary, and said that it would take a lifetime to write a history if one started at age twenty.[10]

That same year another French abbé was taken to task by Thomas Paine. The Abbé Raynal had raised American hackles before the war by contending that plants and animals (including man) degenerated in the New World. In 1781 he published an account of the Revolution which was soon translated into English. Thomas Paine replied in a pamphlet which charged that the foundation of the Abbé's work was wrong and that it was littered with error. "It is yet too soon," said Paine, "to write the history of the Revolution, and whoever attempts it precipitately, will unavoidably mistake characters and circumstances, and involve himself in error and difficulty. Things, like men, are seldom understood rightly at first sight."[11]

At the end of the war in 1783, Thomas Paine, on the advice of Robert Morris, asked Congress to be allowed to present an account of his services to the country.[12] The poverty-stricken Paine did not mention his plan for a history but a committee of Congress reported that "it is indispensably necessary, a just and impartial account of our contest for public freedom and happiness should be handed down to posterity. That this can best be done by a historiographer to the United States of great industry and abilities; by one too, who has been and is governed by the most disinterested principle of public good, totally uninfluenced by party of every kind." The committee then proposed that Thomas Paine be appointed "historiographer to the United States" at an annual salary.[13]

Paine asked the committee to defer action until he could acquaint it with certain matters.[14] He then prepared a long recital of his services to the cause of independence, and made it perfectly clear that he felt that he had never been properly rewarded for what he had done. He told the committee that a history of the Revolution was of fundamental importance and that the writing of one would be a complex and expensive job, and one requiring research in both England and America. Furthermore, "to leave the history of the Revolution to chance, to party, or partiality of any kind, or to be performed as a matter of profit, will subject the character of the present age to various and hazardous representations. . . ." Such a history could not be written without the help of Congress, "yet for Congress to reserve to themselves the least appearance of influence over an historian, by annexing thereto a yearly salary subject to their own control, will endanger the reputation of both the historian and the history." Paine thus set forth the case against "official history" for all time.

Paine concluded bluntly that he would be forced to leave America unless the country made it possible for him to remain independent and a citizen. All he asked for was a reward for his past services. If that were given, and he undertook to write a history of the Revolution, "it will be perfectly voluntary and with freedom to myself, and if Congress pleases to give me the appointment of Historiographer, as honorary, and without salary or conditions, it will facilitate the collection of materials and give the work the foundation of impartiality and clear it of all appearance or suspicion of influence."[15]

Paine was aware that he had political enemies in Congress, and that, despite the support of such friends as Washington, Congress would not agree. "It has ever been my wish and intention," he told James Duane, "to close the scene with a History of the Revolution, but the conduct of Congress puts it out of my power. . . ."[16] His hopes revived briefly in 1784 when some friends suggested that he ask the states for support,[17] but he was soon reduced to begging for a few dollars from Congress, only to be ignored once more. He then turned to an equally futile attempt to get support for building an iron bridge. In despair he left for Europe in 1787 and thus, to the great loss of posterity, the only "history" Tom Paine ever wrote was his reply to the Abbé Raynal.

Among the potential contemporary historians, none was in a better position than Charles Thomson who had been secretary of Congress since its first meeting in 1774. In 1783, John Jay wrote from Paris and urged the one-time "Sam Adams of Philadelphia" to spend one hour in twenty-four writing a "true account" of the American Revolution for posterity. Such a history "need not be burdened with *minute* accounts of battles, sieges, retreats, evacuations, etc—leave those matters to voluminous historians. The *political* story of the Revolution will be most liable to misrepresentation, and future relations of it will probably be replete both with intentional and accidental errors." Jay thought that such a history should remain unpublished during Thomson's lifetime, and that it should not be known that Thomson was at work upon it.[18]

Two years later, Francois Barbé-Marbois, the French consul-general, reported that Thomson had prepared "secret historical memoirs" of everything not published in the printed journals, that he already had more than a thousand pages in folio, and that "it would complete the history of the revolution. . . ." However, Thomson told Marbois that he had taken measures to prevent publication "before the death of those who have taken part in the great events."[19] If there ever was a "history," apart from the original manuscript journals which Thomson kept, it has never been discovered. All that remains in Thomson's handwriting are a few pages called "History of the Confederation" in the Papers of the Continental Congress.[20]

The first participant in the Revolution to publish a history was the Reverend William Gordon. He came to Massachusetts from England in 1770 and was soon a supporter of opposition to Britain. Throughout the war he gossiped, interviewed soldiers and politicians, and read their manuscripts. The parson was a busybody with courage, and he acquired powerful enemies. As an overseer of Harvard he attacked John Hancock's misuse of its funds. In 1779 he outraged Alexander Hamilton by reporting that Hamilton had said that the people should rise and join Washington in throwing out Congress.[21] But there were those who were delighted with Gordon's activities. In 1778, Dr. Benjamin Rush declared that he was impatient to see the history and asked: "How many chapters or volumes have you alloted for the blunders of our Congress and generals? Weak minds begin already to ascribe our deliverance to them. Had not heaven defeated their counsels in a thousand instances, we should have been hewers of wood and drawers of water to the subjects of the King of Britain."[22]

Once the war was over and the history neared completion, newspapers attacked Gordon for his supposed prejudices. He finally gave up hope of publication in America and returned to England in 1786. There, after revision by various people, his work was published in 1788.[23]

The history is cast in the guise of letters, supposedly contemporary with the events they describe. Gordon packs in an amazing amount of material. Quite clearly he had access to the records of the Boston Committee of Correspondence, to at least some of the papers of John Adams, and he used Washington's papers after the end of the war. Gordon has long been ignored, probably because of the old charge that he plagiarized from the *Annual Register*, a curious charge since Gordon, unlike most contemporary historians, admitted in his preface that he had used that publication.

But the important fact about Gordon is not what he copied, but what he had learned as a result of his own intimate experience, especially in Massachusetts. Scattered throughout the volumes are significant bits of information and interpretation. Thus he tells how the Boston merchants were drawn into non-importation in 1768 through their connection with the "politicians" and their "fear of opposing the popular stream," how the signers cheated, and how others were kept in line by the threat of mob action. There is a remarkable account of the background of the Boston Massacre and perhaps a fuller story of the trial of the soldiers than can be found anywhere until the recent publication of the legal papers of John Adams. There are "inside" stories concerning the organization of the Boston Committee of Correspondence and the trick used to publish the Hutchinson-Oliver letters. There is a striking explanation of why the Sons of Liberty in Boston had to send the tea back or destroy it.

Occasionally, too, there are delightful tidbits. Thus Gordon tells of John Hancock and Samuel Adams walking away from Lexington on the morning of April 19, 1775. As they left, Adams remarked: "*'O! what a glorious morning is this!'* in the belief that it would eventually liberate the colony from all subjection to Great Britain." John Hancock "did not penetrate his meaning, and thought the allusion was only to the aspect of the sky."[24]

The second participant in the Revolution to publish a history was Dr. David Ramsay. Born in Pennsylvania, educated at Princeton, and with medical training in Philadelphia, he moved to South Carolina in 1773 where he was soon involved in politics. In 1785 he published a history of South Carolina, and 1789 a history of the American Revolution.[25] Ramsay's history was once thought worthless because he, like Gordon, plagiarized from the *Annual Register*. The other extreme is represented in a recent article praising Ramsay which asserts that "the best interpretation of the causes of the Revolution was made in the decade following the treaty of peace in 1783," and that ever since we have moved "further and further from the truth about our Revolutionary beginnings."[26] Whatever the merits of such an assertion one can still agree that there is much of value in Ramsay. Unlike Gordon he was not concerned with "inside" stories but with broad generalizations, although at least some of these he paraphrased from Gordon's history of the year before.[27]

As Ramsay pictures it, the dispute between Britain and the colonies had economic origins. British enforcement policies after 1763 destroyed trade between the English colonies and the foreign colonies in the West Indies and Spanish America, and convinced Americans that Britain was no longer an "affectionate mother" but an "illiberal step-dame."[28]

Then the issue of the constitutional relationship between Britain and the colonies was raised by Parliament's attempt to tax the colonies. It was useless to appeal to colonial charters for neither the grantor nor the grantees of American territory had anything in mind like "the present state of the two countries." Americans, "intoxicated" by the repeal of the Stamp Act, ignored the assertion of absolute parliamentary authority over them in the Declaratory Act and thus the claims of the two countries were left undecided. After ten years of disputes, "their respective claims had never been compromised on middle ground." The Tea Act of 1773 produced the inevitable result.[29]

A third contemporary history of the Revolution is that of Mercy Otis Warren, completed by the end of the century but not published until 1805.[30] As the sister of James Otis, the wife of James Warren, and the friend and intimate correspondent of such revolutionary leaders as John and Samuel Adams, Mrs. Warren was as much a participant in the Revolution as Gordon and Ramsay. Furthermore, she showed none of their restraint in her pen portraits of individuals.

Aside from her frank and often perceptive analysis of personalities, her view of the Revolution is simple and anticipates in every way the views of the "Whig historians" of the latter part of the nineteenth century. George III was "nurtured in all the inflated ideas of kingly prerogative," was "more obstinate than cruel, rather weak than remarkably wicked," and he considered all opposition "to the mandates of his ministers, as a crime of too daring a nature to hope for the pardon of royalty." His preceptor, Lord Bute, used his influence to "bring over a majority of the house of commons to cooperate with the designs of the crown." Parliament became a "mere creature of administration," and in time "threatened the new world with a yoke unknown to their fathers."

Eventually the connection had to be broken, "the sword drawn, and the scabbard thrown down the gulf of time." Americans had to fight for their freedom, or, as she puts it: "Freedom, long hunted round the globe by a succession of tyrants, appeared at this period, as if about to erect her standard in America; the scimitar was drawn from principles, that held life and property as a feather in a balance against the chains of servitude that clanked in her disgusted ear."[31]

The Patriot historians were not the only people to describe the times in which they lived. There were other native Americans who also wrote histories. Among them were Thomas Hutchinson, the last royal governor of Massachusetts; Joseph Galloway, long a leading political figure in colonial Pennsylvania; Peter Oliver, the last chief justice of the Massachusetts colonial supreme court; and Thomas Jones, a justice of the New York colonial supreme court. These Americans played a far greater role in the history of their native land until 1775 than those who were to write Patriot histories, but they remained loyal to Great Britain, and as Loyalists, their histories have been largely ignored and most of them were not printed until long after the authors' deaths. Joseph Galloway's history was published in 1780,[32] but Hutchinson's was not printed until 1828,[33] Jones's until 1879,[34] and Peter Oliver's until 1961.[35] As a group these Loyalist historians were bitter men and their histories displayed prejudice and a lack of objectivity. But the historian must ask: were the Patriot historians without prejudice, and were they completely objective? The answer is obvious.

The Patriot and Loyalist historians present widely, and even wildly, different interpretations of the motives of political leaders and of the nature of British policies and their impact on the colonies. However, they are in striking agreement on two things. The first is the fundamental importance of the leadership of a few men in the revolutionary movement.

For Mercy Warren, James Otis and Samuel Adams and other patriots were men of principle unselfishly devoted to the defense of American liberty against British tyranny and against the native Americans who abetted the British. Her villain is Thomas Hutchinson. She declared that "few ages have produced a more fit instrument for the purposes of a corrupt court. He was dark, intriguing, insinuating, haughty, ambitious, while the extreme of avarice marked each feature of his character." The "innovating spirit" of the British ministry, she asserted, was "instigated by a few prostitutes of power, nurtured in the lap of America," and the people became suspicious when "they saw some of their fellow-citizens, who did not hesitate at a junction with the accumulated swarms of hirelings, sent from Great Britain to ravish from the colonies the rights they claimed both by nature and by compact." As far as she was concerned, the chief "prostitute of power" in Massachusetts was

Thomas Hutchinson. "Every historical record will doubtless witness that he was the principal author of the sufferings of unhappy Bostonians, previous to the convulsions which produced the revolution."[36]

Peter Oliver offers a stark contrast. Hutchinson was a "gentleman" with an "acumen of genius united with solidity of judgment and great regularity of manners." He worked unceasingly for the good of Massachusetts and was widely applauded. It was his popularity that "roused the envy and malice of the leaders of the faction, who dipped their shafts in more than infernal gall, and made him the butt to level them at. He exerted every nerve to save his country; they were determined to ruin him, though they plunged their country and theirselves too, into absolute destruction."

Oliver described James Otis, John Hancock, Samuel Adams, John Adams, Benjamin Franklin, and others in brilliant, scurrilous character sketches. The Revolution was brought about, he says, "to gratify the pride, ambition, and resentment of a few abandoned demagogues, who were lost to all sense of shame and of humanity. The generality of the people were not of this stamp; but they were weak and unversed in the arts of deception. The leaders of the faction deceived the priests, very few of whom but were as ignorant as the people; and the wheel of enthusiasm was set on going. . . ." The people's brains were set to whirling and "a vacuum was left for Adams, and his posse to crowd in what rubbish would best serve their turn." America, he concluded, had been turned from a land flowing with milk and honey into a wilderness stamped with war, famine, and pestilence "by an Otis, an Adams, a Franklin, and a few others of the most abandoned characters, aided by a set of priests, who are a disgrace to Christianity. . . ." And the rebellion would never have come about if such men in America had not been helped by equally abandoned and selfish characters in England.[37]

Thomas Hutchinson, unlike his friend and political ally, Peter Oliver, was temperate, but he tells essentially the same story. Hutchinson said that there had always been political parties in the colonies as in England. These were the "Ins" and the "Outs," and in Massachusetts the "Outs" used British policies as a screen behind which to attack the governor. He said that it had been the practice in all ages and all countries "to make use of plausible and specious arguments. . . ." In Massachusetts, the people had no cause for alarm but the popular leaders stirred them up by picturing imaginary dangers to their property and freedom. Other means could have been found to "heat the dregs of the people" who were the principal actors, but the more considerate people could not have been persuaded by such means to take an active part.[38]

Thomas Jones's history of New York resembles Peter Oliver's account of Massachusetts in its insistence upon the role of a few unprincipled demagogues. As Jones tells it, a "republican faction" or "republican party," dominated by Presbyterians, was formed as early as 1752. The leaders were William Livingston, William Smith, Jr., and John Morin Scott who "formed themselves into a triumvirate, and determined, if possible, to pull down Church and State, to raise their own government and religion upon its ruins, or to throw the whole province into anarchy and confusion."[39] Their publications were "replete with all kinds of abuse, scurrility, falsehood, fraud, hypocrisy, chicane, sedition, and indeed very little short of treason itself."[40] Jones was convinced that such men were hypocrites whose declamations in behalf of American freedom were sheer bombast to screen their desire for political power.

Jones does not limit his bludgeoning to his fellow Americans. He tells bitter tales of plundering by British soldiers. And one would have to search far and wide to find a more scorching denunciation of the stupidity of British generals, or for a more detailed account of graft and corruption by British army officers. Such graft, he argues, did more to defeat Britain than all the armies in the field. Among the leading grafters was the Boston merchant, Joshua Loring, commissary of prisoners. "In this appointment there was reciprocity. Joshua had a handsome wife. The general, Sir William Howe, was fond of her. Joshua made no objections. He fingered the cash, the general enjoyed madam."[41]

Joseph Galloway agreed with Peter Oliver and Thomas Jones that religion and "republicanism" were forces motivating the Patriot leaders, and he adds an economic motive. In describing the First Continental Congress, he says that it divided at once into two almost equal parties. "The one were men of loyal principles and possessed the greatest fortunes in America; the other were Congregational and Presbyterian republicans, or men of bankrupt fortunes, overwhelmed in debt to the British merchants."[42]

The Loyalist historians' view was that the patriot leaders were "new men" who attacked the old established order in the colonies. David Ramsay is in essential agreement. He says that "old men were seldom warm whigs" and that "few of the very rich were active in forwarding the revolution," especially in the middle and eastern states, although he says that the reverse was true in the southern states. He declares that "the great bulk of those, who were active instruments of carrying on the revolution, were self-made, industrious men" and he goes on to say that "in these times of action, classical education was found of less service than good natural parts, guided by common sense and sound judgment."[43]

In addition to agreeing on the importance of leadership, the Patriot and Loyalist historians also agree on a second important point: that the bulk of the people were indifferent and would not have acted if it had not been for the leadership of the few. Ramsay is explicit in his account of how the other colonies were brought to support Massachusetts after the passage of the Intolerable Acts in 1774. As he puts it, "the patriots who had hitherto guided the helm, knew well, that if the other colonies did not support the people of Boston, they must be crushed," and a precedent dangerous to liberty would be established. It was to the interest of Boston to gain the support of the other colonies but "it was also the interest of the patriots in all the colonies, to bring over the bulk of the people. . . ." To achieve that purpose "much prudence as well as patriotism was necessary. The other provinces were but remotely affected by the fate of Massachusetts. They were happy, and had no cause, on their own account, to oppose the government of Great Britain." Therefore, "to convince the bulk of the people, that they had an interest in foregoing a present good, and submitting to a present evil, in order to obtain a future greater good, and to avoid a future greater evil, was the task assigned to the colonial patriots. But it called for the exertion of their utmost abilities."

How did they exert their abilities? Ramsay says that the leaders effected their purpose "in a great measure, by means of the press. Pamphlets, essays, addresses and newspaper dissertations were daily presented to the public, proving that Massachusetts was suffering in the common cause. . . . It was inculcated on the people, that if the ministerial schemes were suffered to take effect in Massachusetts, the other colonies must expect the loss of their charters, and that a new government would be imposed upon them, like that projected for Quebec." Ramsay states blandly that in the course of this propaganda campaign, the patriot leaders deceived the people. He says: "In order to interest the great body of people, the few who were at the helm, disclaimed anything more decisive, than convening the inhabitants, and taking their sense on what was proper to be done. In the meantime great pains were taken to prepare them for the adoption of vigorous measures."[44]

William Gordon agreed about the importance of the patriot press. "The command, which the sons of liberty have of the press, gives them the superiority in point of influence, over their antagonists in the periodical publications of the day."[45] And in the conclusion of his history, Ramsay paid a final tribute to the role of the press in keeping up the spirit of the people. "In establishing American independence, the pen and the press had merit equal to that of the sword. As the war was the people's war, and was carried on without funds, the exertions of the army would have been insufficient to effect the revolution, unless the great body of the people had been prepared for it, and also kept in constant disposition to oppose Great Britain. To rouse and unite the inhabitants, and to persuade them to patience for several years ... was effected in a great measure by the tongues and pens of the well informed citizens, and on it depended the success of military operations."[46] The Loyalist historians would not have disagreed with this estimate of the power of the press, although they detested the purposes to which that power had been put.

The Patriot and Loyalist historians are also in partial agreement that the idea of independence originated long before 1776. Joseph Galloway asserted that the purpose of a group of men "from the beginning of their opposition to the Stamp Act, was to throw off all subordination and connection with Great Britain; who meant by every fiction, falsehood, and fraud to delude the people from their due allegiance, to throw the subsisting governments into anarchy, to incite the ignorant and vulgar to arms, and with those arms to establish American independence."[47] Peter Oliver scoffed at the idea that Britain forced Americans to declare independence. Independence, he said, "was settled in Boston, in 1768, by Adams and his junto."[48] Thomas Jones believed that the "republican party" in New York had decided upon independence by 1769, and that independence was a logical outcome of their actions ever since 1752.[49]

Gordon and Ramsay tell essentially the same story. "Some of the popular leaders," said Ramsay, "may have secretly wished for independence from the beginning of the controversy, but their number was small and their sentiments were not generally known."[50] Gordon says that in Massachusetts in 1774 there were a few who hankered after independence, and that "at the head of these we must place Mr. Samuel Adams, who has long since said in small confidential companies—'the country shall be independent, and we will be satisfied with nothing short of it'."[51] Furthermore, both Gordon and Ramsay declare that the bulk of the people did not want independence until almost the very end. According to Gordon, the great body of the patriots throughout the colonies in March 1774, even in Massachusetts, wanted no more than a return to conditions before 1763. He says that after the First Continental Congress, the appearance of agreement among Americans was misleading, for "great numbers" in every colony disapproved of its measures. Even in New England "far more than half" the people entitled to attend town and other meetings stayed away, "the popular cry being against them, they have sought personal peace and safety in remaining quiet."[52]

Ramsay is even more specific. He says that Lexington and Concord in April 1775 "abated the original dread" of separation, but for at least twelve months longer "a majority of the colonists" wished for no more than the restoration of ancient rights. "It was not till some time in 1776, that the colonists began to take other ground. . . ."[53] As a result of such British measures as the American Prohibitory Act of December 1775 and the hiring of German troops, Americans were at last forced to decide, and "necessity not choice forced them on the decision." Meanwhile, writers, and above all Thomas Paine in *Common Sense,* convinced thousands. "The multitude was hurried down the stream," although some "worthy men" were still opposed. "The eagerness for independence resulted more from feeling than reasoning," and in the end the "determined resolution of the Mother Country to subdue the colonists" forced Americans to declare independence.

Many Americans in 1776, and the Loyalist historians afterwards, argued that British policies were not a justification for revolt, and that the mass of the people were misled by the few into independence. Ramsay refused to accept either contention, and although he presented evidence to the effect that the people were indifferent and had to be prodded into action by the "Patriot leaders," he insisted that independence "was not forced on the people by ambitious leaders grasping at supreme power, but every measure of it was forced on Congress, by the necessity of the case, and the voice of the people."[54]

Despite their differing interpretations of men and motives, the

Patriot and Loyalist historians were in essential agreement on three fundamental points: (1) the importance of the leadership of the few; (2) the early origin of the idea of independence; (3) the indifference of the mass of the people to independence. The divisions among Americans that the contemporary historians and other participants in the Revolution all recognized, were virtually ignored by George Bancroft who dominated the historiography of the Revolution during the last half of the nineteenth century. His research was prodigious and his account one of the most detailed ever printed, but it was not a tale of a petty squabble between Britain and some of her American colonies. He pictured the Revolution as a great democratic movement by a united people, a movement that had its origins in the "dawn of social being."

According to Bancroft, unity among mankind, aided by the universal religion of Christianity, had been growing steadily for centuries. Simultaneously there had been a continuous evolution of morality, of individual freedom, and above all, of human intelligence and the power of reason. By 1748, "the hour of revolution was at hand, promising freedom to conscience and dominion to intelligence." From the "intelligence that had been slowly ripening in the mind of cultivated humanity sprung the American Revolution, which organized social union through the establishment of personal freedom, and emancipated the nations from all authority not flowing from themselves." The American Revolution, moreover, "was most radical in its character, yet achieved with such benign tranquility that even conservatism hesitated to censure." It was a civil war waged for "the advancement of the principles of everlasting peace and universal brotherhood" and the result was that "a plebeian democracy took its place by the side of the proudest empires." Those empires were doomed, said Bancroft, yet they sent their representatives "to act as the peers of plebeians," and they were "wonderfully swayed to open the gates of futurity to the new empire of democracy: so that, in human affairs, God never showed more visibly his gracious providence and love."[55]

Occasionally Bancroft is more concrete. He entitles one chapter "The Acts of Trade Provoke Revolution," and says that the trouble began in Massachusetts in 1761-1762 because of the enforcement of the acts of trade by the vice-admiralty court. "The people," he concluded, "were impatient of the restrictions on their trade," and began to talk of "procuring themselves justice." In another place he writes that "American independence, like the great rivers of the country, had many sources; but the head-spring which colored all the stream was the colonial mercantile system."[56]

But such statements are incidental if not irrelevant to Bancroft's explanation of the Revolution. By 1774, liberty had been destroyed throughout Europe, and Britain, "allured by a phantom of absolute authority over the colonies, made war on human freedom." He asks: if Britain established its boundless authority over America, "where shall humanity find an asylum?" He answers: "but this decay of the old forms of liberty was the forerunner of a new creation. The knell of the ages of servitude and inequality was rung; those of equality and brotherhood were to come in."[57] As for America, "the hour of the American revolution was come. The people of the continent obeyed one general impulse, as the earth in spring listens to the command of nature and without the appearance of effort bursts into life."[58]

By the end of the nineteenth century a group of English "Whig" historians had taken a place beside George Bancroft as interpreters, with Sir George Otto Trevelyan in the forefront. His account of the Revolution begins abruptly with the year 1766. The chief villain is George III who never forgave the Rockingham Whigs for repealing the Stamp Act. A lesser villain is Charles Townshend, "master of the revels," who secured passage of the Revenue Act of 1767, including the tax on tea. "The Boston Massacre; the horrors of Indian warfare; the mutual cruelties of partisans in the Carolinas; Saratoga and Yorktown; the French war; the Spanish war; the wholesale ruin of the American loyalists; the animosity towards Great Britain which for so long afterwards colored the foreign policy of the United States; all flowed in direct and inevitable sequence from that fatal escapade."

Above all, George III was engaged in subverting the English constitution: "a despotism of a subtle and insidious texture was being swiftly and deftly interwoven into the entire fabric of the Constitution." If George III had only listened to true Whigs like William Pitt and Edmund Burke, all would have been well, but they were borne down by the corrupt forces of the king, and America was lost.[59]

In America, the Whig interpretation was summed up best of all by C. H. Van Tyne when he wrote that "it was the failure of a Parliament, corrupted by George III, to heed the warning of England's greatest living statesmen, Burke and Pitt and Fox and Camden and Barré, that brought about the rending of the Empire." It was doomed to be broken apart "by the insistent demand of Englishmen in America for the full enjoyment of those liberties which England had fostered beyond any other country of the world."[60]

At the very time that Van Tyne was writing, the Whig interpretation was under attack. C. W. Alvord in America, and a little later, Sir Lewis Namier in England, studied the realities of English politics and demonstrated rather conclusively that the Whig version of the Revolution was written in terms of nineteenth-century Whig liberalism, not in terms of eighteenth-century Whig behavior.[61]

Despite attacks upon it, the political-constitutional interpretation of the Patriot historians, Bancroft, and the English Whigs has remained a basic approach in the twentieth century. Charles M. Andrews summed it up in 1925 when he declared that "primarily, the American Revolution was a political and constitutional movement," and only secondarily was it financial, commercial, or social. The fundamental issue was the political independence of the colonies, and in the last analysis the conflict lay between the British Parliament and the colonial assemblies.[62] This is a view that continues to be supported, one of the most notable recent examples being found in the work of O. M. Dickerson.[63]

Nevertheless, a large share of twentieth-century writing about the Revolution has stressed two other interpretations. One of these is economic, or rather a series of economic interpretations. "The echoes of the controversy" in Europe over the role of economic factors in history "have scarcely reached our shores," reported E.R.A. Seligman in the introduction to his *Economic Interpretation of History* in 1902.[64] Doubtless some American scholars were aware of the controversy, but Seligman's book presented a balanced and critical account in English. American scholars were quick to seize upon this tool for analysis of the past.

In 1905 G. E. Howard declared that the "primary cause" of the Revolution was "the old colonial system" in which the colonies were looked upon politically as "dependencies" and economically as "possessions" to be exploited for the benefit of Britain.[65] In 1912, Edward Channing was even more specific. "Commercialism, the desire for advantage and profit in trade and industry, was at the bottom of the struggle between England and America; the immutable principles of human association were brought forward to justify colonial resistance to British selfishness. The governing classes of the old country wished to exploit the American colonists for their own use and behoof; the Americans desired to work their lands and carry on their trade for themselves."[66]

The view that English economic regulations were bad and a cause for revolt has been challenged by a number of historians. One has argued that the regulations benefited the colonies as well as England;[67] another that the bungling after 1763 rather than the regulations themselves was a source of discontent,[68] an idea supported heartily by O. M. Dickerson, who denies that the Navigation Acts were a cause of trouble. He argues that it was Britain's decision to tax trade after 1763 rather than to protect and regulate it as in the past that brought on the war, coupled with the activities of "customs racketeers," whom he describes in words reminiscent of Mercy Warren's.[69]

There are other economic interpretations, of course, some dating back to the eighteenth century. Loyalist and English writers accused smugglers of fomenting war. Galloway accused debtors, among others, and in 1783 George Mason reported that some Virginians were asking: why did we fight and win our independence if we now have to pay our debts to British merchants?[70] During the 1790's New England Federalists were prone to accuse Virginia planters of becoming patriots to get out of paying their debts.[71] In 1916, C. W. Alvord suggested that encroachment on Virginia's western land claims drove Virginians almost "unanimously into the party of the American revolutionists."[72] A writer on Virginia loyalism argues that it was both the restriction on western expansion and planter debts that impelled Virginians to revolt.[73] Such interpretations of Virginia's motives have, of course, been denied by Virginia historians.[74]

The concern with economic interpretations in the twentieth century has been matched by an equal concern with what has been called, perhaps inadequately, the "internal revolution." Scholars who have studied individual colonies and states, and groups such as merchants, farmers, artisans, and religious sects, have presented accounts that do not square with the concept of the American Revolution as a conflict between Britain on the one hand, and the colonies as a whole on the other. They have found that American rhetoric about American rights, whether constitutional or economic, very often does not coincide with the political behavior of groups and individuals. They have described political, economic, and social disputes which were the result of internal developments, not the result of British policies, but nevertheless disputes which had an impact on the revolutionary movement before 1776, and the history of the states and the nation afterwards.

Bancroft, who viewed the Revolution in a world-wide setting, virtually ignored such matters, but in 1889 the author of a chapter in Winsor's *Narrative and Critical History* suggested that it was necessary to discriminate between the "local" and the "general" causes of the Revolution. He said that the "local" causes were the British policies after 1763 but that the "general" causes were the "ever present and ever active strife between parties—liberals and conservatives—arising from a diversity of political ideas, and intensified by ambition, interest, and personal animosities."[75]

By 1900, historians were beginning to write the revolutionary history of certain colonies from this point of view. In 1901, Charles H. Lincoln, after describing discontent with Quaker rule in Pennsylvania, concluded that the "colonial revolution in Philadelphia, and in the colony at large, would have occurred had there been no national movement, but the latter uprising furnished the opportunity and suggested the means of accomplishing the change." The people of Pennsylvania "welcomed a national movement under cover of which they might revolutionize their own colonial conditions."[76]

Eight years later Carl Becker published his study of New York. The first chapter opens with the statement that "The American Revolution was the result of two general movements; the contest for home-rule and independence, and the democratization of American politics and society. Of these movements, the latter was fundamental; it began before the contest for home-rule, and was not completed until after the achievement of independence." The chapter concludes with the oft-quoted—and usually misquoted—lines: "From 1765 to 1776, therefore, two questions, about equally prominent, determined party history. The first was whether essential colonial rights should be maintained; the second was by whom and by what methods they should be maintained. The first was the question of home rule; the second was the question, if we may so put it, of who should rule at home."[77]

Instead of concentrating on one colony, Arthur M. Schlesinger, Sr., turned to a study of a group of men to be found in all the colonies: the colonial merchants. He found that after 1763 the merchants sought the support of the "lower orders" to defeat British policies, only to have the resistance movement turned against the merchants themselves and in the direction of independence. Schlesinger concluded that the "disastrous outcome of this unnatural alliance convinced the merchants as a class that their future welfare rested with the maintenance of British authority," and with some exceptions, the merchant class opposed independence. When it came, many of them stayed in America but they did not change their ideas and their worst fears were confirmed after the war. They drew together in an effort to create a government that would protect their interests and "thus, once more united, the mercantile interests became a potent factor in the conservative counter-revolution that led to the establishment of the United States Constitution."[78]

Such historians as Lincoln, Becker, and Schlesinger, and many others who have followed the path they marked out, have presented a far more complex picture of the Revolution than that offered by those who interpret it in either constitutional or economic terms. They have described an undemocratic political society dominated in most colonies by an east coast ruling class made up of merchants, planters, and British-appointed office-holders. Most of the ruling classes opposed British policies after 1763 and at first they used the "lower orders" to give force to their opposition, only to have the "lower orders" turn against their old leaders and demand political and social changes in America that were in fact, if not in name, democratic. This view is much like that of the Loyalist historians, and of the Patriot historians as well, but where the Loyalist historians, and many a patriot leader, were horrified by the rise of popular leaders and democratic ideas and practices, these twentieth-century historians have, in effect, "voted" for them.

The historians who thus interpreted the age of the American Revolution have been labelled "progressive historians" by a number of historians and political scientists, especially since World War II. The assumption is that the so-called "progressive historians" reflected the spirit of the Progressive Era, and even of the New Deal. Their critics, in turn, have been labelled "new conservative," "neo-Whig," and the like, and one recent summary of their efforts was entitled "The Cult of the 'American Consensus': Homogenizing our History."[79] Like all labels these are inadequate and sometimes misleading. Some of the people so labelled are scholars whose conclusions are based on intensive research and whose writings have broadened our knowledge and led to a modification of earlier views. The majority of them, however, have made a variety of assertions about the nature of the Revolution without an examination of the evidence, or even without a careful reading of the historians they have criticized. They declare that the age of the American Revolution was an age of agreement, not disagreement; that there was no "internal revolution"—that is, no conflict over who should "rule at home"; that there was no period of democratic upheaval followed by a "conservative reaction." In short, they have questioned that there was an "American Revolution."

Various arguments have been offered. Thus one historian who showed that far more men could vote in one colony than was once assumed, went on to assert that this proved the existence of a "middle class democracy" before 1776, and that therefore there was no "internal revolution." Instead, the war for independence was fought to save democracy from British attacks upon it.[80] The author suggested that what was "true" for one colony was probably "true" for others. This idea has been widely accepted as demolishing the theory of an "internal revolution." All too few have raised the question: is the right to vote, assuming that it was widespread, all there is to democratic government? Even fewer have bothered to examine the realities of political and social power in colonial America.[81]

The idea that the Revolution was "conservative" was asserted in more general terms. The most peculiar thing about it, declared one writer, was that in a modern European sense "it was hardly a revolution at all." It was one of the "few conservative colonial rebellions of modern times." Furthermore, the "conservatism" of the Revolution is "an illustration of the remarkable continuity of American history."[82] The idea of continuity was supported by a political scientist who gave the title *Consensus and Continuity, 1776-1787* to a series of lectures in which he emphasized agreement among Americans and argued that the Constitution of 1787 did not represent a "conservative reaction."[83] About the same time an historian described the years after Lexington as "the history of the Americans' search for principles. That search brought them to Lexington and war in 1775, but it did not end there. Throughout the years of fighting it continued and finally culminated in the adoption of the federal constitution." This historian, while admitting the existence of internal conflicts, deplored the attention paid to them because "I believe the movement has not been wholly desirable, for it has exaggerated the divisions among Americans during a period in which the most remarkable and exciting fact was union."[84]

The emphasis on the importance of ideas and principles, as contrasted to economic and political issues, has not produced agreement among the critics of the "progressive historians." Thus one of the first to argue that the Revolution was "conservative," and an illustration of the "continuity" of American history, also argued that the Revolutionary era was not a great age of political thought. He asserted that it was a revolution without ideology, that it was a "prudential decision taken by men of principle rather than the affirmation of a theory."[85] The reverse of this argument has been presented by another historian who declares that the American Revolution "was to a remarkable extent an affair of the mind," and that the age was "the most creative period in the history of American political thought."[86]

While there have been many disagreements among this group of historians during the past two decades, most of them have agreed on one thing: that the "progressive historians" were wrong, or at least misguided. In an essay called "The Flight from Determinism" it was asserted that a concern with economic questions "led many scholars of the progressive school to wrench Revolutionary events out of context by superimposing some of the a priori assumptions and tenets of economic determinism." This writer then declared that while the "progressive historians" were influenced by the "spirit" of their times, the "neo-Whigs" were not influenced by the conservative spirit of the 1950's. His rather remarkable assumption was that the "general levelling of society" after World War II "made possible an increasing detachment among historians of the Revolution."[87]

Whatever their defects, the so-called "progressive historians" at least knew the difference between "economic determinism" (i.e. "historical materialism") and the "economic interpretation of politics" as Charles A. Beard made clear in a series of lectures on "the economic basis of politics." And so far as the "progressive historians" used any theoretical tool at all, they rejected "determinism" in favor of "economic interpretation."[88]

Now, in the seventh decade of the century, there are signs that the pendulum is swinging again. Those who have argued that the American Revolution was not a social revolution like the French Revolution, have been told that they must face the fact that five times more people per thousand of population were exiled from

America than from France. They have also been told that almost as much property was confiscated in America as in France, a country ten times as large.[89]

Those who have argued that ideas were not important in the Revolution have been told that ideas were of overwhelming importance, that the men of the age were in fact controlled by ideas they only half understood, and that they were not "conservative" ideas but a group of ideas summed up in the title of a long essay as "The Transforming Radicalism of the American Revolution."[90]

In the most recent of many summaries of the interpretations of the Revolution, the author points out that while the emphasis on the "transforming radicalism" of the ideas of the Revoluton is a "thoroughly idealistic" emphasis, it at the same time represents a "move back to a deterministic approach to the Revolution. . . ." He suggests that the "remarkable revolutionary character" of American thought indicates that something profoundly unsettling was going on in American society. This raises the question, he declares, "as it did for the Progressive historians, why the Americans should have expressed such thoughts," and that while the "Progressive historians" had a crude concept of propaganda, they "at least attempted to grapple with the problem." He concludes his essay with the statement that "Precisely because they sought to understand both the Revolutionary ideas and American society, the behaviorist historians of the Progressive generation, for all their crude conceptualizations, their obsession with 'class' and hidden economic interests, and their treatment of ideas as propaganda, have still offered us an explanation of the Revolutionary era so powerful and so comprehensive that no purely intellectual interpretation will ever replace it."[91]

Thus the pendulum swings back and forth as it has ever since the Patriot and Loyalist historians began writing histories of the Revolution in the eighteenth century. What conclusions can we draw? Can we draw any conclusions about the nature of the American Revolution, or can we only draw conclusions about the nature of historians? I think we can do both.

As for historians, they are not merely blind men trying to describe an elephant, although one is sometimes tempted to think so. They are human beings most of whom are trying to understand and explain one of the great events in history. In the course of their research and their debates with one another they have produced an ever-greater knowledge of the history of the times. The danger that the historian runs is the danger of assuming that there is any simple and single answer, either to the causes or the consequences of the war for independence.

Many of the participants in the Revolution understood how complex and diverse it was. This was one reason why men like John Adams and Jefferson believed that its history could never be written, although Adams did provide a text for those who insist on trying. In 1807 he was outraged when he read what his old friend Mercy Warren had written about him in her history. In the midst of a series of vehement letters defending himself against her charge that he had deserted his principles, he calmed down long enough to make a statement that should always be in the minds of those who try to explain the nature of the American Revolution. He declared:

The principles of the American Revolution may be said to have been as various as the thirteen states that went through it, and in some sense almost as diversified as the individuals who acted in it. In some few principles, or perhaps in one single principle, they all united.[92]

Adams then went on to define his own principles, but wisely he made no attempt to define the principles of other men, nor did he suggest even one principle upon which all Americans agreed. Historians would be equally wise if they followed his example.

*Only examples of various interpretations have been referred to. Hence the titles of many important books and essays have been omitted. In quotations from eighteenth century sources, capitalization and spelling have been modernized, and contractions spelled out.

[1]November 26, 1813, McKean Papers, IV, Historical Society of Pennsylvania.

[2]March 4, 1815, C. F. Adams, ed., *The Works of John Adams* (10 vols., Boston, 1850-1856), X, 133-134.

[3]To Thomas McKean, July 30, 1815, McKean Papers, IV; to Thomas Jefferson, July 30, 1815, Lester Cappon, ed., *The Adams-Jefferson Letters* (2 vols., Chapel Hill, 1959), II, 451.

[4]To John Adams, August 10, 1815, *Adams-Jefferson Letters*, II, 452.

[5]To Mrs. Elizabeth Smith, July 30, 1775. Emmett Collectiton, No. 2847, New York Public Library.

[6]To Hamilton, April 31, 1777, H. C. Syrett and J. E. Cooke, eds., *The Papers of Alexander Hamilton*, I (New York, 1961), 244-245.

[7]June 15, 1777, R. H. Lee, *Memoir of the Life of Richard Henry Lee. . . .* (2 vols., Philadelphia, 1825), I, 207.

[8] Thomas Paine to Benjamin Franklin, June 20, July 9, 1777; May 16, 1778, Philip S. Foner, ed., *The Complete Writings of Thomas Paine* (2 vols., New York, 1945), II, 1133, 1136, 1151.

[9]September 14, 1779, *Ibid.*, I, 1178-1179.

[10]Adams, *Works*, V, 492-496.

[11]"Letter to the Abbé Raynal," *Writings*, II, 212-263.

[12]To Elias Boudinot, President of Congress, June 7; to George Washington, September 21, [1783], *Ibid.*, II, 1217-1218, 1223-1224.

[13]August 18, 1783, *Journals of the Continental Congress* (Library of Congress, edit.), XXIV, 512-513.

[14]To George Washington, September 21, [1783], *Writings*, II, 1223-1224.

[15]To a Committee of the Continental Congress, [Oct. 1783], *Ibid.*, 1226-1242.

[16]December 3, 1783, *Ibid.*, 1244-1245.

[17]April 28, 1784, *Ibid.*, 1248.

[18]July 19, 1783, Charles Thomson Papers, I, Library of Congress.

[19]To Vergennes, February 25, 1785, in George Bancroft, *History of the Formation of the Constitution of the United States of America* (2 vols., New York, 1882-1883), I, 414.

[20]No. 9, Library of Congress.

[21]See Syrett and Cooke, eds., *The Papers of Alexander Hamilton*, II (New York, 1961), passim.

[22]December 10, 1778, in L. H. Butterfield, ed., *Letters of Benjamin Rush* (2 vols., Princeton, 1951), I, 222.

[23]*The History of the Rise, Progress, and Establishment, of the Independence of the United States of America. . . .* (4 vols., London, 1778). On Gordon's plagiarism see O. G. Libby, "A Critical Examination of Gordon's History of the American Revolution," American Historical Association *Annual Report* (1899), I, 367-388.

[24]Gordon, *History*, I, 479.

[25]*The History of the American Revolution* (2 vols., Philadelphia, 1789).

26Page Smith, "David Ramsay and the Causes of the American Revolution," *The William and Mary Quarterly*, 3rd ser., XVII (1960), 51. On Ramsay's plagiarism, see O. G. Libby, "Ramsay as a Plagiarist," *American Historical Review*, VII (1901-1902), 697-703.

27Smith in the article cited above (pages 56-57) quotes Ramsay admiringly concerning the diversity of political opinions in the colonies. Compare the remarkable similarity between Gordon, *History*, I, 378-379, and Ramsay, *History*, I, 125-126.

28Ramsay, I, 44-46.

29*Ibid.*, 54, 55, 74, 93-94.

30*History of the Rise, Progress and Termination of the American Revolution: Interspersed with Biographical, Political and Moral Observations* (3 vols., Boston, 1805).

31*Ibid.*, I, 22-23, 177-178, 229.

32*Historical and Political Reflections on the Rise and Progress of the American Rebellion* (London, 1780).

33*The History of the Colony and Province of Massachusetts Bay* (L. S. Mayo, ed., 3 vols., Cambridge, 1936). Volume III covers the period of the Revolution.

34*History of New York during the Revolutionary War, and of the Leading Events in the Other Colonies at that Period* (W. F. De Lancey, ed., 2 vols., New York, 1879).

35Douglass Adair and John A. Schutz, eds., *Peter Oliver's Origin & Progress of the American Rebellion* (San Marino, 1961).

36Warren, I, 78-80, 37-38, 123-124.

37*American Rebellion*, 29, 35, 145-146, 149.

38Hutchinson, III, 184, 215, 252-253.

39Jones, I, 4-5.

40*Ibid.*, 23.

41*Ibid.*, 351.

42*Historical and Political Reflections*, 66-67.

43Ramsay, II, 314, 316.

44*Ibid.*, I, 112-114.

45Gordon, II, 379.

46Ramsay, II, 319-320.

47*Historical and Political Reflections*, 66-67.

48*American Rebellion*, 148.

49Jones, I, 24.

50Ramsay, I, 337-338.

51Gordon, I, 347-348.

52*Ibid.*, 426-427.

53Ramsay, I, 335-336.

54*Ibid.*, 336-340.

55George Bancroft, *History of the United States of America. . . .* (Author's last revision, 6 vols., New York, 1891), II, 319-327.

56*Ibid.*, II, 546-555; III, 60.

57*Ibid.*, III, 482.

58*Ibid.*, IV, 3.

[59]*The American Revolution* (Revised edition, 4 vols., New York, 1908), I, 5-6, 120. The first volume was published in England in 1899.

[60]*The Causes of the War of Independence* (Boston, 1922), 478.

[61]C. W. Alvord, *The Mississippi Valley in British Politics* (2 vols., Cleveland, 1917); Sir Lewis Namier, *The Structure of Politics at the Accession of George III* (2 vols., London, 1929), and *England in the Age of the American Revolution* (London, 1930).

[62]"The American Revolution: An Interpretation," *The American Historical Review*, XXXI (1925-1926), 230.

[63]*The Navigation Acts and the American Revolution* (Philadelphia, 1951).

[64]E. R. A. Seligman, *The Economic Interpretation of History* (New York, 1902), 3. The citation here is to the 1961 paperback edition.

[65]*Preliminaries of the Revolution, 1763-1775 (American Nation Series*, New York, 1905), 47.

[66]*A History of the United States*, III (New York, 1912), 1-2.

[67]G. L. Beer, *The Origins of the British Colonial System, 1578-1660* (New York, 1908) and *British Colonial Policy, 1754-1765* (New York, 1907).

[68]Lawrence A. Harper, "Mercantilism and the American Revolution," *Canadian Historical Review*, XXIII (1942), 1-15.

[69]*Navigation Acts and the American Revolution*, passim.

[70]To Patrick Henry, May 6, 1783, K. M. Rowland, *The Life of George Mason, 1725-1792* (2 vols., New York, 1892), II, 46.

[71]Oliver Ellsworth to Oliver Wolcott, Sr., April 5, 1794, in George Gibbs, *Memoirs of the Administrations of Washington and John Adams. . . .* (2 vols., New York, 1846), I, 134-135.

[72]"Virginia and the West: an Interpretation," *Mississippi Valley Historical Review*, III (1916-1917), 25.

[73]Isaac S. Harrell, *Loyalism in Virginia. . . .* (Philadelphia, 1926).

[74]H. J. Eckenrode, *The Revolution in Virginia* (New York, 1916); Thomas P. Abernethy, *Western Lands and the American Revolution* (New York, 1937); and most recently, Thad W. Tate, "The Coming of the Revolution in Virginia: Britain's Challenge to Virginia's Ruling Class, 1763-1776," *William and Mary Quarterly*, 3rd ser., XIX (1962), 323-343.

[75]Mellen Chamberlain, "The Revolution Impending," in Justin Winsor, ed., *Narrative and Critical History of America* (8 vols., Boston, 1884-1889), VI, 62.

[76]*The Revolutionary Movement in Pennsylvania, 1760-1776* (Philadelphia, 1901), 96, 54.

[77]*The History of Political Parties in the Province of New York, 1760-1776* (Madison, 1909), 5, 22.

[78]*The Colonial Merchants and the American Revolution, 1763-1776* (New York, 1918), 592, 606.

[79]John Higham, "The Cult of the 'American Consensus': Homogenizing Our History," *Commentary*, XXVII (1959), 93-100.

[80]Robert E. Brown, *Middle Class Democracy and the Revolution in Massachusetts, 1691-1780* (Ithaca, 1955) and "Economic Democracy before the Constitution," *American Quarterly*, VII (1955), 257-274.

[81]Among those who have are Leonard W. Labaree, *Conservatism in Early American History* (New York, 1948) and Charles S. Sydnor, *Gentlemen Freeholders: Political Practices in Washington's Virginia* (Chapel Hill, 1952). The reader is also referred to Mer-

rill Jensen, *The Articles of Confederation: An Interpretation of the Social-Constitutional History of the American Revolution, 1774-1781* (Madison, 1940) and in particular to the preface to the third printing in 1959. Apparently, the book for the first time gave currency to the term "internal revolution." Incidentally, the book is in no way concerned with the "causes" of the American Revolution, despite what critics of the "progressive historians" assume. Its concern is with the "internal" history of the colonies and the impact of that history on the writing of the first constitution of the United States.

82Daniel J. Boorstin, *The Genius of American Politics* (Chicago, 1953), 68, 70, 81.

83Benjamin F. Wright, *Consensus and Continuity, 1776-1787* (Boston, 1958).

84Edmund S. Morgan, *The Birth of the Republic, 1763-1789* (Chicago, 1956), 3, 162-163.

85Boorstin, *Genius of American Politics*, 95.

86Bernard Bailyn, ed., *Pamphlets of the American Revolution, 1750-1776*, I (Cambridge, 1965), 17, 19.

87Jack P. Greene, "The Flight from Determinism: A Review of Recent Literature on the Coming of the American Revolution," *The South Atlantic Quarterly*, LXI (1962), 258.

88Charles A. Beard, *The Economic Basis of Politics* (New York, 1945). The lectures were delivered in 1916 and first published in 1922. It is remarkable that those who use the label "progressive" have never examined the political affiliations of the historians they criticize. Beard, for instance, was a lifelong member of the Republican Party and one of the leading academic opponents of the Progressive politicians and their ideas. In 1912 he published a defense of the Supreme Court in answer to Progressive attacks upon it, and he went on to become one of the sharpest critics of Woodrow Wilson's "New Freedom" and Franklin Roosevelt's "New Deal." See Robert E. Thomas, "A Reappraisal of Charles A. Beard's *An Economic Interpretation of the Constitution of the United States*," *American Historical Review*, LVII (1951-1952), 370-375.

89Robert R. Palmer, *The Age of Democratic Revolution*, I (Princeton, 1959), 188.

90Bernard Bailyn, "The Transforming Radicalism of the American Revolution," *Pamphlets of the American Revolution*, I, 3-202.

91Gordon S. Wood, "Rhetoric and Reality in the American Revolution," *William and Mary Quarterly*, 3rd ser., XXIII (1966), 23, 31, 32.

92John Adams to Mercy Warren, July 7, 1807, Massachusetts Historical Society *Collections*, 5th ser., IV, 338.

"Experience Must be Our Only Guide:" History, Democratic Theory, and the United States Constitution

BY DOUGLASS G. ADAIR

---

*After receiving his doctoral degree at Yale University in 1943
Douglass G. Adair joined the faculty of William and Mary College under the presidency of John E. Pomfret. Recognizing in
Adair a fresh and vigorous mind, Pomfret soon elevated him to
the editorship of the* William and Mary Quarterly *where he
served between 1946 and 1955, endowing that distinguished
journal with a standard of excellence unsurpassed by any other
professional publication. Since 1955 he has been a professor at
the Claremont Graduate School, and a frequent visitor at the
nearby Huntington Library. In the thoughtful essay that follows, he suggests that historians have failed to recognize the extent to which history governed the actions of the framers of the
Constitution, or to appreciate the light that this recognition
throws on their purposes and results.*

'THE HISTORY OF GREECE," John Adams wrote in 1786, "should
be to our countrymen what is called in many families on the
Continent, a *boudoir*, an octagonal apartment in a house,
with a full-length mirror on every side, and another in the ceiling.
The use of it is, when any of the young ladies, or young gentlemen
if you will, are at any time a little out of humour, they may retire
to a place where, in whatever direction they turn their eyes, they
see their own faces and figures multiplied without end. By thus beholding their own beautiful persons, and seeing, at the same time,
the deformity brought upon them by their anger, they may recover
their tempers and their charms together."[1]

Adams' injunction that his countrymen should study the history
of ancient Greece in order to amend their political behavior sug-

gests two points for our consideration. First, John Adams assumed without question that history did offer lessons and precepts which statesmen could use in solving immediate problems. Secondly, Adams urged the study of the classical Greek republics as the particular history especially relevant, most full of useful lessons and precepts for Americans in 1787.

Adams, as is well known, practiced what he preached. Working at high speed between October 1786 and January 1787, in time stolen from his duties as United States Minister to Great Britain, he composed his *Defence of the Constitutions of the United States* —a 300-page book exhibiting for his countrymen the lessons of history. And though he included material from all periods of western civilization, a large part of his data was collected from the classical republics of antiquity.

Nor did his American audience who read Adams' work in the weeks immediately prior to the meeting of the Philadelphia Convention deny his assumptions or purposes in urging them to study the lessons of Greek history. Benjamin Rush, for example, reporting to the Reverend Richard Price in England on the attitude of the Pennsylvania delegation to the Convention, gave Adams' study the highest praise. "Mr. Adams' book," he wrote, "has diffused such excellent principles among us that there is little doubt of our adopting a vigorous and compounded federal legislature. Our illustrious Minister in this gift to his country has done us more service than if he had obtained alliances for us with all the nations of Europe."[2]

Do Adams and Rush in their view on the utility of history for the constitutional reforms of 1787 represent the typical attitude of the members of the Convention? Did the fifty-five men gathered to create a more perfect union consciously turn to past history for lessons and precepts that were generalized into theories about the correct organization of the new government? Did lessons from the antique past, applied to their present situation, concretely affect their actions at Philadelphia? The evidence is overwhelming that they did, although the weight of modern commentary on the Constitution either ignores the Fathers' conscious and deliberate use of history and theory or denies that it played any important part in their deliberations.

Max Farrand, for example, after years of study of the debates in the Convention concluded that the members were anything but historically oriented. Almost all had served (Farrand noted) in the

Continental Congress and had tried to govern under the impotent Articles of Confederation. There is little of importance in the Constitution (Farrand felt) that did not arise from the effort to correct specific defects of the Confederation.

Robert L. Schuyler, an able and careful student of the Constitution, goes even further in denying the Convention's dependence upon history. "The Fathers were practical men. They lived at a time when a decent respect for the proprieties of political discussion required at least occasional reference to Locke and Montesquieu . . . but . . . such excursions into political philosophy as were made are to be regarded rather as purple patches than as integral parts of the proceedings. The scholarly Madison had gone extensively into the subject of Greek federalism . . . but it was his experience in public life and his wide knowledge of the conditions of his day, not his classical lucubrations that bore fruit at Philadelphia. . . . The debate . . . did not proceed along theoretical lines. John Dickinson expressed the prevailing point of view when he said in the Convention: 'Experience must be our only guide. Reason may mislead us.' "[3]

Dickinson's statement on August 13th: "Experience must be our only guide" does indeed express the mood of the delegates; no word was used more often; time after time "experience" was appealed to as the clinching argument for a controverted opinion. But "experience" as used in the Convention, more often than not, referred to the precepts of history. This is Dickinson's sense of the word when he warned the Convention that "reason" might mislead. "It was not reason," Dickinson continued, "that discovered the singular and admirable mechanism of the English Constitution . . . [or the] mode of trial by jury. Accidents probably produced these discoveries, and experience has given a sanction to them." And then Dickinson, turning to James Wilson and Madison who had argued that vesting the power to initiate revenue bills exclusively in the lower house of the Legislature had proved "pregnant with altercation in every [American] State where the [revolutionary] Constitution had established it," denied that the short "experience" of the American States carried as weighty a sanction as the long historic "experience" of the English House of Commons. "Shall we oppose to this long [English] experience," Dickinson asked, "the short experience of 11 years which we had ourselves, on this subject."[4] Dickinson's words actually point to the fact that theories grounded in historical research are indeed integral parts of the debate on the Constitution.

For Dickinson is not alone in using "experience" in this dual fashion to refer both to political wisdom gained by participation in events, and wisdom gained by studying past events. Franklin and Madison, Butler and Mason, Wilson and Hamilton all appeal to historical "experience" in exactly the same way. "Experience shows" or "history proves" are expressions that are used interchangeably throughout the Convention by members from all sections of the United States.[5] Pure reason not verified by history might be a false guide; the mass of mankind might indeed be the slave of passion and unreason, but the fifty-five men who gathered at Philadelphia in 1787 labored in the faith of the enlightenment that experience-as-history provided "the least fallible guide of human opinions,"[6] that historical experience is "the oracle of truth, and where its responses are unequivocal they ought to be conclusive and sacred."[7]

Schuyler's insistence that the Fathers were "practical men" who abhorred theory, associates him with a standard theme of American anti-intellectualism that honors unsystematic "practicality" and distrusts systematic theoretical thought. His argument, undoubtedly too, reflects nineteenth-century theories of "progress-evolution" that assume the quantitative lapse in time between 400 B.C. and 1787 A.D. *a priori* makes the earlier period irrelevant for understanding a modern and different age. And, of course, what came to be called "sound history" after 1880 when the discipline came to roost in academic groves, is quite different itself from the "history" that eighteenth-century statesmen found most significant and useful. Modern historians have tended to insist that the unique and the particular is the essence of "real history"; in contrast the eighteenth-century historian was most concerned and put the highest value on what was universal and constant through time.

Eighteenth-century historians believed "that there is a great uniformity among the actions of men, in all nations and ages, and that human nature remains still the same, in its principles and operations. The same motives always produce the same actions; the same events follow from the same causes. Ambition, avarice, self-love, vanity, friendship, generosity, public spirit; these passions, mixed in various degrees, and distributed through society, have been from the beginning of the world, and still are the source of all the actions and enterprizes, which have ever been observed among mankind. Would you know the sentiments, inclinations, and course of life of the Greeks and Romans? Study well the temper and actions of the

French and English." Thus David Hume, distinguished eighteenth-century historian and philosopher.[8]

The method of eighteenth-century history for those who would gain political wisdom from it followed from this primary assumption—it was historical-comparative synthesis. Again Hume speaks: "Mankind are so much the same, in all times and places, that history informs us of nothing new or strange, in this particular. *Its chief use is only to discover the constant and universal principles of human nature,* by showing men in all varieties of circumstances and situations, and furnishing us with materials, from which we may form our observations and become acquainted with the regular springs of human action and behavior. These records ... are so many collections of experiments, by which the politician or moral philosopher fixes the principles of his science, in the same manner as the physician or natural philosopher becomes acquainted with the nature of plants, minerals, and other external objects, by the experiments which he forms concerning them."

John Adams would echo Hume's argument and use the identical metaphor in the preface to his *Defence*. "The systems of legislators are experiments made on human life, and manners, society and government. Zoroaster, Confucius, Mithras, Odin, Thor, Mohamet, Lycurgus, Solon, Romulus and a thousand others may be compared to philosophers making experiments on the elements." Adams was too discreet to list his own name with the Great Legislators of the past, but in his own mind, we know from his *Diary* and letters to his wife, he identified himself with Moses, Lycurgus, and Solon as the Lawgiver of his state, Massachusetts, whose republican constitution, based on his study of history, he had written almost single-handed in October 1779. Now eight years later his *Defence* both justified the form of government he had prepared for his own state and "fixed the principles"—to use Hume's words—of the science of government that ought to be followed in modeling a more perfect union of the states. Adams' book, in complete accord with eighteenth-century canons, was a comparative-historical survey of constitutions reaching back to Minos, Lycurgus, and Solon.

History proved, Adams felt sure, "that there can be no free government without a democratical branch in the constitution." But he was equally sure that "Democracy, simple democracy, never had a patron among men of letters." Rousseau, indeed, had argued, as Adams pointed out, that "a society of Gods would govern themselves democratically," but this is really an ironic admission by "the eloquent philosopher of Geneva that it is not practicable to govern *Men* in this way." For very short periods of time pure democracy had existed in antiquity, but "from the frightful pictures of a democratical city, drawn by the masterly pencils of ancient philosophers and historians, it may be conjectured that such governments existed in Greece and Italy . . . [only] for short spaces of time."[9] Such is the nature of pure democracy, or simple democracy, that this form of government carries in its very constitution, infirmities and vices that doom it to speedy disaster. Adams agreed completely with Jonathan Swift's pronouncement that if the populace of a country actually attempted to rule and establish a government by the people they would soon become their "own dupe, a mere underworker and a purchaser in trust for some single tyrant whose state and power they advance to their own ruin, with as blind an instinct as those worms that die with weaving magnificent habits for beings of a superior order to their own." It was not surprising then to Adams that when he surveyed contemporary Europe he found no functioning democracy. Indeed, governments that had even the slightest "democratical mixture" in their constitutions "are annihilated all over Europe, except on a barren rock, a paltry fen, an inaccessible mountain, or an impenetrable forest." The one great exception outside of the American states where a democratic element was part of the constitution was Britain, the great monarchical or regal republic. And as Adams contemplated the English Constitution, he felt it to be "the most stupendous fabric of human invention. . . . Not the formation of languages, not the whole art of navigation and shipbuilding does more honor to the human understanding than this system of government."[10]

The problem for Americans in 1787 was to recognize the principles exemplified in Britain, Adams thought, and to frame governments to give the people "a legal, constitutional" *share* in the process of government—it should operate through representation; there should be a balance in the legislature of lower house and upper house; and there should be a total separation of the executive from the legislative power, and of the judicial from both. Above all, if the popular principles of government were to be preserved in America it was necessary to maintain an independent and powerful executive: "If there is one certain truth to be collected from the history of all ages, it is this; that the people's rights and liberties, and the democratical mixture in a constitution, can never be preserved without a strong executive, or, in other words, without separating the executive from the legislative power. If the executive power . . . is left in the hands either of an aristocratical or democratical assembly, it will corrupt the legislature as necessarily as rust corrupts iron, or as arsenic poisons the human body; and when the legislature is corrupted, the people are undone."

And then John Adams took on the role of scientific prophet. If Americans learned the lessons that history taught, their properly limited democratic constitutions would last for ages. Only long in the future when "the present states become . . . rich, powerful, and luxurious, as well as numerous, [will] their . . . good sense . . . dictate to them what to do; they may [then] make transitions to a nearer resemblance of the British constitution," and presumably make their first magistrates and their senators hereditary.

But note the ambiguity which underlies Adams' historical thinking. Science, whether political or natural, traditionally has implied determinism—scientific prediction is possible only because what was, is, and ever shall be. Reason thus might be free to discover the fixed pattern of social phenomena, but the phenomena themselves follow a pre-destined course of development. The seventeenth-century reason of Isaac Newton discovered the laws of the solar system, but no man could change those laws or the pattern of the planets' orbits; Karl Marx might in the nineteenth century discover the scientific laws of economic institutions, but no man could reform them or change the pattern in which the feudal economy inevitably degenerated into bourgeois economy, which in its turn worked inexorably toward its predetermined and proletarian end.

In the same fashion Adams' scientific reading of history committed him and his contemporaries in varying degrees of rigidity to a species of *political determinism*. History showed, so they believed, that there were only three basic types of government: monarchy, aristocracy, and democracy, or government of the one, the few, or the many. Moreover history showed, so they believed, that each of these three types when once established had particular and terrible defects—"mortal diseases," Madison was to call these defects—that made each pure type quickly degenerate: Every monarchy tended to degenerate into a tyranny. Every aristocracy, or government of the few, by its very nature, was predestined to evolve into a corrupt and unjust oligarchy. And the democratic form, as past experience

135

proved, inevitably worked toward anarchy, class-conflict, and social disorder of such virulence that it normally ended in dictatorship.[11]

On this deterministic-theory of a uniform and constant human nature, inevitably operating inside a fixed-pattern of limited political forms, producing a predictable series of evil political results, John Adams based his invitation to Americans to study the classical republics. This assumption of determinism explains the constant and reiterated appeal to Greek and Roman "experience," both during the Philadelphia Convention and in the State ratifying conventions. At the beginning of the Revolution Adams had invited his rebellious compatriots to study English history, for from 1765 to 1776 the immediate and pressing questions of practical politics related to the vices and corruption of the English monarchy.[12] But after 1776 at which time Americans committed their political destinies to thirteen democratic frames of government loosely joined in a Confederation, English monarchical history became temporarily less relevant to American problems. The American States of 1776 in gambling on democratic republics stood alone in the political world. Nowhere in contemporary Europe or Asia could Americans turn for reassuring precedents showing functioning republican government. So, increasingly from 1776 to 1787, as Americans learned in practice the difficulties of making republican systems work, the leaders among the Revolutionary generation turned for counsel to classical history. They were *obliged* to study Greece and Rome if they would gain "experimental" wisdom on the dangers and potentialities of the republican form. Only in classical history could they observe the long-range predictable tendencies of those very "vices" of their democratic Confederacy that they were now enduring day by day.

It was these frightening lessons from classical history added to their own present difficulties under the Confederation that produced the total dimension of the crisis of 1787.[13] Standing, as it were, in John Adams' hall of magic mirrors where past and present merged in a succession of terrifying images, the Founding Fathers could not conceal from themselves that Republicanism in America might already be doomed. Was it indeed possible to maintain stable republican government in any of the thirteen American States? And even if some of the States units could maintain republicanism, could union be maintained in a republican confederation?

The answer of history to both of these questions seemed to be an emphatic "no." As Alexander Hamilton reminded the Convention June 18th and later reminded the country speaking as Publius, "It is impossible to read the history of the petty Republics of Greece and Italy without feeling sensations of horror and disgust at the distractions with which they were continually agitated, and at the rapid succession of revolutions, by which they were kept in a state of perpetual vibration between the extremes of tyranny and anarchy. If they exhibit occasional calms, these only serve as short-lived contrasts to the furious storms that are to succeed. If now and then intervals of felicity open themselves to view, we behold them with a mixture of regret, arising from the reflection, that the pleasing scenes before us are soon to be overwhelmed by the tempestuous waves of sedition and party rage."[14]

Hamilton along with Madison, Adams, Jefferson, and every educated eighteenth-century statesman thus knew from history that the mortal disease of democratical republics was and always would be the class struggle that had eventually destroyed every republican state in hstory.[15] And *now* with the "desperate debtor" Daniel Shays, an American Cataline—an American Alcibiades—proving only ten years after independence, the class struggle was raising monitory death's-heads among the barely united republican States of America. If potential class war was implicit in every republic, so too did war characterize the interstate relations of adjacent republics. The only union that proved adequate to unite Athens and Sparta, Thebes and Corinth in one functioning peaceful whole was the monarchical power of Philip of Macedon; Rome, after conquering her neighbor city states, it is true, had maintained republican liberty for a relatively long period, in spite of internal conflict of plebes and patricians, but when the Empire increased in extent, when her geographical boundaries were enlarged, Roman liberty died and an Emperor displaced the Senate as the center of Roman authority. In 1787 the authority of scholars, philosophers, and statesmen was all but unanimous in arguing (from the experience of history) that no republic ever could be established in a territory as extended as the United States—that even if established for a moment, class war must eventually destroy every democratic republic.[16]

These were the two lessons that Hamilton insisted in his great speech of June 18 the Constitutional Convention must remember. These were the lessons that were stressed in John Adams' morbid anatomy of fifty historic republican constitutions. This was the

137

theme of Madison's arguments (which the Convention accepted) for junking entirely the feeble Articles of the Confederation in favor of a government that would, it was hoped, neutralize interstate conflict and class war. It was because these lessons were accepted by so many educated men in America that the commercial crisis of 1784-5 had become a political crisis by 1786, and a moral crisis by 1787.

Had the Revolution been a mistake from the beginning? Had the blood and treasure of Americans spent in seven years of war against England ironically produced republican systems in which rich and poor New Englanders must engage in bloody class war among themselves? Had independence merely guaranteed a structure in which Virginians and Pennsylvanians would cut each others' throats until one conquered the other or some foreign crown conquered both?[17]

From our perspective, 179 years later, this may appear an hysterical and distorted analysis of the situation of the United States in 1787, but we, of course, are the beneficiaries of the Fathers' practical solution to this problem that *their* reading of history forced upon them. Americans today have the historic experience of living peacefully in the republic stabilized by their Constitution. History has reassured us concerning what only the wisest among them dared to hope in 1787: that the republican form could indeed be adapted to a continental territory. Priestley, a sympathetic friend of the American Revolution was speaking the exact truth in 1791 when he said: "It was taken for granted that the moment America had thrown off the yoke of Great Britain, the different states would go to war among themselves."

When Hamilton presented his analysis of the vices of republicanism to his acceptant audience in Philadelphia, he also offered the traditional remedy which statesmen and philosophers from antiquity on had proposed as the ONLY cure for the evils of the three types of pure government. This remedy was to "mix" or "compound" elements of monarchy, aristocracy, and democracy into one balanced structure.[18] There was, Hamilton reasoned, little danger of class war in a state which had a king vested with more power than the political organs of government representing either the rich or the poor. The "size of the country" and the "amazing turbulence" of American democracy made him despair of republicanism in the United States, without an elective monarch who once in office could not be voted out by majority rule. The people, i.e., the multitudinous poor, would directly elect the lower house of the legislature; a Senate to represent the rich would be elected for life; and to guard against the poison of democracy in the separate States, they would be transformed into administrative districts with their governors appointed by the elected King.

We mistake the significance of Hamilton's proposal of an elective monarch as a solution of the crisis of 1787 if we think of his plan as either *original* or *unrepresentative* of the thought of important segments of American opinion in 1787. The strength of Hamilton's logical position lay in the fact that his proposal was the traditional, the standard, indeed, as history showed the *only* solution for the specific dangers of interclass and interstate conflict that were destroying the imperfect Union. As early as 1776 Carter Braxton had offered almost this identical plan as the ideal constitution for Virginia.[19] In May, 1782, reasoning parallel to Hamilton's had emboldened Colonel Lewis Nicola to invite Washington to use the Army to set himself up as a King.[20] And after Shays' rebellion voices grew louder, particularly in the New England and the Middle States, proposing two cures for the ills of America. One cure was to divide the unwieldy Confederation into two or three small units; the other was the creation of an American throne.[21] We have Washington's word for it that the most alarming feature of this revival of monarchial sentiment was its appearance among staunch "republican characters"—men who like Hamilton had favored independence in 1776 but who had become disillusioned about ever achieving order and security in a republic. Add to this group of new converts the large bloc of old Tories who had never forsaken their allegiance to monarchy, and it is easy to see why Washington, Madison, and other leaders were seriously alarmed that Union would break up and that kings would reappear in the Balkanized segments.

Futhermore, at the very time the Philadelphia Convention was rejecting Hamilton's mixed-monarchy as a present solution for the vices of American democracy, leading members of the Convention most tenacious of republicanism accepted the fact that an American monarchy was inevitable at some future date. As Mr. Williamson of North Carolina remarked, on July 24, "it was pretty certain . . . that we should at some time or other have a king; but he wished no precaution to be omitted that might postpone the event as long as possible."[22] There is a curious statistical study of Madison's which points to his certainty also, along with the precise prophecy that the end of republicanism in the United States would come approximately 142 years after 1787—about the decade of the 1930's.[23] John Adams' *Defence* contains the same sort of prophecy. "In future ages," Adams remarked, "if the present States become great nations, rich, powerful, and luxurious, as well as numerous," the "feelings and good sense" of Americans "will dictate to them" reform of their governments "to a nearer resemblance of the British Constitution," complete with a hereditary king and a hereditary Senate.[24] Gouverneur Morris is reported to have argued during the Convention "we must have a Monarch sooner or later . . . and the sooner we take him while we are able to make a Bargain with him, the better." Nor did the actual functioning of the Constitution during its first decade of existence lighten Morris' pessimism; in 1804 he was arguing that the crisis would come sooner rather than later.[25] Even Franklin, the least doctrinaire of the Fathers—perhaps with Jefferson the most hopeful among the whole Revolutionary generation regarding the potentialities of American democracy—accepted the long-range pessimism of the Hamiltonian analysis. Sadly the aged philosopher noted, June 2, "There is a natural inclination in mankind to kingly government. . . . I am apprehensive, therefore,—perhaps too apprehensive,—that the government of these States may in future times end in monarchy. But this catastrophe, I think may be long delayed. . . ."[26]

The "precious advantage" that the United States had in 1787 that offered hope for a "republican remedy for the diseases most incident to republican government"—the circumstance which would delay the necessity of accepting Hamilton's favored form of mixed monarchy—lay in the predominance of small free-hold farmers among the American population. Since the time of Aristotle, it had been recognized that yeoman farmers—a middle class between the greedy rich and the envious poor—provided the most stable foundation upon which to erect a popular government. This factor, commented on by Madison, Pinckney, Adams and others, helps explain why the Convention did not feel it necessary to sacrifice either majority rule or popular responsibility in their new Constitution.

Of equal importance was the factor of expedience. Less doctrinaire than Alexander Hamilton, the leaders of the Convention realized that a theoretical best—and member after member went on record praising the British Constitution as *the best* ever created by man—a theoretical best might be the enemy of a possible good. As

Pierce Butler insisted, in a different context, "The people will not bear such innovations. . . . Supposing such an establishment to be useful, we must not venture on it. We must follow the example of Solon who gave the Athenians not the best government he could devise, but the best they would receive."[27]

Consequently the Constitution that emerged from the Convention's debates was, as Madison described it a "novelty in the political world"—a "fabric" of government which had "no model on the face of the globe."[28] It was an attempt to approximate in a structure of balanced republican government the advantages of stability that such mixed governments as Great Britain's had derived from hereditary monarchy and a hereditary House of Lords.

It was an "experiment" as members of the Convention frankly admitted, but one about which most of the Fathers could be hopeful because it adapted to the concrete circumstances of the United States of 1787, the experience of mankind through all ages as revealed by history. Driven by the collapse of the Confederation, the depression of 1785-86, and Shays' Rebellion to take stock of their political situation six years after Yorktown had won for Americans the opportunity for self-government, the Fathers had turned to history, especially classical history, to help them analyze their current difficulties. Their reading of history, equally with their immediate experience, defined for them both the short-range and the long-range potentialities for evil inherent in a uniform human nature operating in a republican government. But their reading of history also suggested a specific type of government that would remedy the evils they already knew and those worse evils they expected to come. Utilizing this knowledge, building on the solid core of agreement which historical wisdom had helped supply, they created, by mutual concession and compromise, a governmental structure as nearly like mixed-government as it was possible to approach while maintaining the republican principle of majority rule. And this they offered the American people *hoping* it would be ratified, *hoping* that after ratification their "experiment" with all its compromises of theory and interest would provide a more perfect union.

If there is substance in the argument offered in the foregoing paragraphs, it should throw some light, at least, on the intellectual confusion exhibited during the last half-century by many learned commentators in discussing the nature of our Constitution. This confused and confusing debate has focused in part on the question: "did the Fathers write a 'democratic' Constitution?"[29] The answers given have been almost as "mixed" as the theory to which the Framers subscribed.

Part of the bother lies in the lack of precision with which the word *democracy* was used then, and the even more unprecise way that we use it now. The more a word is used the less exact its meaning becomes, and in our day *democratic/democracy* has been extended to describe art, foreign policy, literature, etc., etc. Thus, from being a somewhat technical word of political discourse, in 1787, it has become a perfect sponge of squashy vagueness. Luckily, the context of formal theory that mixed government did imply in 1787 does allow us to recognize certain rather concrete and specific features usually associated, then, with the democratic form of government. In the first place, the very concept of "mixture" implies a relativism that modern doctrinaire democrats often forget: a political system, in 1787, was thought of as more-or-less democratic, as possessing few or many democratic features. Only in the pure form was democracy an either/or type of polity. In the second place, the simple democratic form was almost always thought of as appropriate only for a tiny territorial area—Madison in *Federalist 10*, for instance, would only equate the word with the direct democracy of the classical city-state. Thirdly, the functional advantages and disadvantages of the pure democratic form of government were almost universally agreed upon. A government *by* the people (so it was thought) always possessed *fidelity* to the common good; it was impossible for a people not to *desire* and to *intend* to promote the general welfare. However, the vices of democracy were that the people, collectively, were not *wise* about the correct measures to serve this great end and that the people could be easily duped by demagogues, who, flattering their good hearts and muddled heads, would worm their way to unlimited power. It was this well-meaning stupidity, the capacity for thoughtless injustice, the fickle instability of the popular will, that led the classical theorists, who the Fathers were familiar with, to designate "pure democracy" as a form doomed to a short existence that tended to eventuate, with a pendulum swing, in the opposite extreme of tyranny and dictatorship.

In dark contrast to this *fidelity* of the democratic many was the vice afflicting both monarchy and aristocracy: an inveterate and incorrigible tendency to use the apparatus of government to serve the special selfish interests of the one or the few. However, the aristocratic form offered, so it was believed, the best possibility of *wisdom*, in planning public measures, while monarchy promised the necessary *energy, secrecy*, and *dispatch* for executing policy.[30]

It is in this ideological context that one can deduce some of the intentions of the authors of our Constitution. It is clear, I think, that the office and power of the President was consciously designed to provide the *energy, secrecy*, and *dispatch* traditionally associated with the monarchical form. Thus Patrick Henry, considering the proposed Chief Executive and recognizing that the President was not unlike an elective king, could cry wth reason that the Constitution "squints toward monarchy." But it was equally possible for Richard Henry Lee, focusing on the Senate, to complain that the document had a "strong tendency to aristocracy." This was said by Lee six months before Madison, in *Federalists 62-63*, explicitly defended the Senate as providing the *wisdom* and the *stability*—"aristocratic virtues"—needed to check the fickle lack of wisdom that Madison predicted would characterize the people's branch of the new government, the Lower House. Nor were there other critics lacking who, recognizing that the Constitution ultimately rested on popular consent, who, seeing that despite the ingenious apparatus designed to temper the popular will by introducing into the compound modified monarchical/aristocratic ingredients, could argue that the new Constitution was too democratic to operate effectively as a national government in a country as large and with a population as heterogeneous as the Americans. One such was William Grayson, who doubted the need of *any* national government, but who felt, if one was to be established, it ought to provide a President and a Senate elected for life terms, these to be balanced by a House of Representatives elected triennially.[31]

It is, thus, significant that if modern scholars are confused and disagreed about the nature of the Constitution today, so, too, in 1787-1788, contemporary observers were also confused and also disagreed as to whether it was monarchical, aristocratic, or democratic in its essence.

My own opinion is that the Constitution of 1787 is probably best described in a term John Adams used in 1806. Writing to Benjamin Rush, September 19, 1806, Adams, disapproving strongly of Jefferson's style as President, bemoaned the fact that Jefferson and his gang had now made the national government "to all intents and purposes, in virtue, spirit, and effect a democracy."—Alas! "I once thought," said Adams, "our Constitution was *quasi* or mixed government,"—but alas![33]

"Quasi," or better still "quasi-mixed"—for, given the American people's antipathy to monarchy after 1776, and given the non-aristocratic nature (in a European sense) of the American upper class of 1787, the Constitution at best, or worst, could only be "*quasi-mixed*,"[34] since there were not "ingredients" available in the United States to compose a genuine mixture in the classic sense. So what the Fathers fashioned was a "quasi-mixed" Constitution that, given the "genius" of the American people, had a strong and inevitable tendency that "squinted" from the very beginning towards the national democracy that would finally develop in the nineteenth century.

[1]John Adams, *Defence of the Constitutions of the United States of America* (1787), in Charles F. Adams, ed., *The Works of John Adams* (10 vols., Boston, 1850-1856), IV, 469. Hereafter cited as *Defence*, IV.

[2]Lyman H. Butterfield, ed., *Letters of Benjamin Rush* (2 vols., Princeton, 1951), I, 418; to Richard Price, Philadelphia, June 2, 1787.

[3]Robert L. Schuyler, *The Constitution of the United States* (New York, 1923), 90-91.

[4]Max Farrand, ed., *Records of the Federal Convention of 1787* (4 vols., New Haven, 1911-1937), II, under date of August 13, 1787. Unless otherwise noted, quotations from the Debates are from Madison's "Notes." Dickinson, in noting that the English Constitution was not the result of "reason" but of "accident," is referring to the commonly held belief in the eighteenth century that the most successful republican constitutions of antiquity had almost without exception been drafted single-handed by a semi-divine legislator at one creative moment in time: Moses, Lycurgus, Minos, Zaleueus. For a discussion of this tradition see *The Federalist*, No. 38. The two striking exceptions of constitutions not born in the brain of one great lawgiver were the English constitution and the Roman. On the latter see Machiavelli's statement in *Discourses on Livy* (which Adams quotes in his *Defence*, IV, 419): "Though that city [Rome] had not a Lycurgus to model its constitution at first . . . yet so many were the accidents which happened in the contests betwixt the patricians and the plebeians, that chance effected what the lawgiver had not provided for."

[5]Farrand, ed., *Records of the Federal Convention*: Franklin, September 7, "Experience shewed"; Mason, June 4, "Experience, the best of all tests"; Hamilton, June 18, "Theory is in this case fully confirmed by experience"; Madison, June 28, "Experience . . . that instinctive monitor"; Butler, June 22 (Yates), "We have no way of judging of mankind but by experience. Look at the history of Great Britain. . . ." H. Trevor Colbourn uses a quotation from Patrick Henry's 1765 oration, "The Lamp of Experience," as the title of his able and suggestive study of the way in which historical interpretation helped transform a three-penny tax on molasses and a two-penny tax on tea into revolutionary constitutional principles that Americans would die to defend. H. Trevor Colbourn, '*The Lamp of Experience!' Whig History and the Intellectual Origins of the American Revolution* (Chapel Hill, 1965).

[6]Alexander Hamilton, *The Federalist*, No. 6.

[7]James Madison, *ibid.*, No. 20.

[8]David Hume, one of the most penetrating intellects of the age and famed as a great contemporary historian, used "experience" in the same fashion as Dickinson, Madison, et al., and offered analytic proof to show why the two kinds of experience together might provide the highest measure of practical wisdom. See Hume's *Inquiry Concerning Human Understanding*, Section VIII, "Of Liberty and Necessity," from which this and the following quotations are taken.

[9]The following quotations, unless otherwise noted, are all from the preface to Adams' *Defence*, IV, 283-298, and Chapter I of "Democratic Republics," IV, 303-327.

[10]Quoted in Adams' *Defence*, IV, 388.

[11]The classification of the three pure forms of government with their corrupt counterparts is a legacy from Greek political theory first stated by Herodotus (c. 495-425 B.C.), which reached its most penetrating and comprehensive statement in Aristotle's (384-322 B.C.) *Politics*. It was Polybius (201-120 B.C.), however, who first froze the earlier flexible analysis into a doctrinaire theory of cyclical change in Book VI of his *History*. This classical theory was "rediscovered" and popularized by various Renaissance thinkers, among them Machiavelli. It became important in English history in the seven-

teenth century when republican thinkers like Harrington, Milton, and Sidney became converts. See Zera Fink, *The Classical Republicans* (Evanston, 1945). Adams' *Defence* reprints Polybius, in Adams, *Works*, IV, 435 ff.

[12]Adams, *Essay on the Federal and Canon Law* (1765), in *Works*, III, 464-465.

[13]American historians have praised one scholarly research memorandum that Madison prepared for use at Philadelphia. This is his study, running to eight printed pages, entitled "Notes on the Confederacy:—April 1787. Vices of the Political System of the United States," in *Letters and Other Writings of James Madison* (4 vols., Philadelphia, 1867), I, 293-328. Historians in contrast have generally ignored the twenty-two page historical research memorandum, "Notes of Ancient and Modern Confederacies, Preparatory to the Federal Convention of 1787," in *ibid.*, I, 293-315, which Madison rated of equal weight in reaching the conclusions that he voiced at Philadelphia. These two memos which provided the theoretical foundation for the Virginia Plan and hence for the completed Constitution are the most strikingly successful examples of the enlightenment ideal of a rational attempt to reduce politics to a science put into practice. See my essay, "'That Politics May be Reduced to a Science:' David Hume, James Madison, and the *Tenth Federalist*," *Huntington Library Quarterly*, XX (1957), 343-360.

[14]Hamilton, *The Federalist*, No. 9.

[15]Major William Pierce, one of the Georgia delegates to the Convention, wrote character sketches of all the delegates. It is significant that he consistently singles out those who have a "compleat classical education" as being particularly well qualified for the role of American Solons and Lycurguses. Note his comments on Baldwin, Dayton, Hamilton, Ingersoll, Johnson, King, Livingston, Madison, G. Morris, Patterson, C. Pinckney, Randolph, Wilson, and Wythe.

[16]One of the chief arguments of the Anti-Federalists against the Constitution was that the country was too large for unified national government which in an extensive area could function efficiently only as a despotism. See the covering letter of Senators R. H. Lee and William Grayson, September 28, 1789, submitting proposed amendments to the Constitution to the Virginia legislature: "We know of no instances in History that shew a people ruled in Freedom when subject to an individual Government, and inhabiting a Territory so extensive as that of the United States." "Agrippa" (*Massachusetts Gazette*, December 3, 1787) along with dozens of other spokesmen had made the same point over and over in 1787-1788: "It is the opinion of the ablest writers on the subject [of government] that no extensive empire can be governed upon republican principles." For a brilliant analysis of the sterile and essentially undemocratic nature of the Anti-Federalist attacks on the Constitution see Cecelia Keyon, "Men of Little Faith: The Anti-Federalists on the Nature of Representative Government," *William and Mary Quarterly*, XII (1955), 3-43, and the introduction to *The Antifederalists* (Indianapolis, 1966).

[17]Note Franklin's speech on the final day of the Convention, September 17, urging all members to sign the Constitution even if they disapproved of parts: "I think it will astonish our enemies, who are waiting with confidence to hear that our counsils are confounded like those of the builders of Babel; and that our States are on the point of separation, only to meet hereafter for the purpose of cutting one another's throats."

[18]For the theory of the ideal mixed or compounded government, sometimes called balanced government, see Stanley Pargellis, "The Theory of Balanced Government," in Conyers Read, *The Constitution Reconsidered* (New York, 1938), 37-49; John Adams, *Defence, passim*; Hamilton, Speech of June 18.

[19]*Address to the Convention . . . of Virginia . . . By a Native of the Colony* (June, 1776), in Peter Force, ed., *American Archives* (Washington, 1837-1853), 4th Ser., 747-754.

20Colonel Lewis Nicola, in *Dictionary of American Biography* (21 vols., New York, 1928-1937), XIII, 509-510.

21Madison to Pendleton, February 24, 1787, in *Letters and Other Writings of James Madison*, I, 280; Louise Dunbar, *A Study of Monarchial Tendencies in the United States from 1776 to 1801* (Urbana, 1922). The latter collects a mass of contemporary material on this topic, including the Braxton pamphlet and the Nicola letter.

22Williamson in the Convention, July 24.

23*Letters and Other Writings of James Madison*, IV, 21, 29-30. The statistical estimate was of probable American population growth which Madison thought, in 1829, would by 1929 be 192,000,000. This would end the nation's "precious advantage" both of wide distribution of landed property and "universal hope of acquiring property." At that time, being "nearly as crowded" as England or France, with a society increasingly polarized between "wealthy capitalists and indigent laborers," Madison feared an amended Constitution more like England's would be required.

24John Adams, *Defence*, IV, 358-359.

25Mason in 1792 reported this remark of Morris quoted in Dunbar, *Monarchial Tendencies*, p. 91. In 1804, writing to Aaron Ogden, Morris, like Adams and Madison, related the appearance of an American monarchy to the growth of population and poverty. Jared Sparks, ed., *The Life of Gouverneur Morris, with Selections from his Correspondence* (3 vols, Boston, 1832), III, 217.

26Franklin, June 2. It should be noted that acceptance of the deterministic theory of the unmixed democratic form swinging inevitably to the opposite extreme of despotism explains the number of prophets—Hamilton, Morris in America; Burke in England—who foretold the eventual advent of Napoleon almost as soon as the French Revolution began.

27Butler in debate on June 5. Compare Bedford of Delaware's use of the same phrase from Plutarch's *Life of Solon* in debate of June 30.

28Madison, *The Federalist*, No. 14.

29In view of the number of able historiographical essays on the recent revisionist literature about the "critical period" and the writing of the Constitution, it seemed superfluous to add merely another. Two pamphlets printed by the Service Center for Teachers of History that survey the current historical literature on the theme, through 1962, are recommended for those who wish to stand in the most modern historiographical *boudoir*—the contemporary historian's hall-of-mirrors. The first, Edmund S. Morgan's *The American Revolution, A Review of Changing Interpretations* (Washington, 1958), relates the monographic studies dealing with the period 1783-1787 to the general problem of interpreting the whole American Revolution; the second, Stanley Elkins and Eric McKitrick's *The Founding Fathers: Young Men of the Revolution* (Washington, 1962), not only surveys critically historians' commentaries on the framing of the Constitution, but also makes the point that the group of young men who worked most intensely to achieve a stronger national government and a more perfect union had staked their political careers on the national rather than the state scene and thus mingled their self-interest in status and power with a patriotic concern for the national welfare.

Two books and two significant essays have also been published, since 1962, that must be considered by any serious student of the "critical period." Forrest McDonald, in *E Pluribus Unum* (Boston, 1965), continues his analysis, begun in *We The People* (Chicago, 1958), of the multiple economic groups and burgeoning local economic appetites that existed in the United States, post 1783. His most persuasive chapters show how selfish regional and state parties and economic groups—in politics these normally became Anti-Federalists in 1787-88—had strained the tenuous Union to the extreme by

1787, so much so, in fact, that the success of the countervailing movement of the men who wrote and got the Constitution ratified was, in McDonald's view, a "miracle." In a ninety-page introduction to an anthology of Anti-Federalist tracts, (see footnote 16 *supra*.), Cecelia M. Kenyon provides the most thorough and wise analysis of the ideological stance of the men who opposed ratification of the Constitution, in 1787-88; and she makes it clear that the Anti-Federalists were not majoritarian "democrats" in any sense of the term.

Finally, two recent important articles in the *William and Mary Quarterly* throw light on the problem of "democracy" and our Revolution. Richard Buel, Jr., "Democracy and the American Revolution: A Frame of Reference," (3rd ser., XXI (1964), 165-190) makes the point that although Whig theory before 1776 in British-America consistently defended the right of the people to share in government, at the same time an unchecked, "simple," or "pure" democracy was uniformly condemned by all American spokesmen. Jackson Turner Main, in an essay in the same journal, "Government by the People: The American Revolution and the Democratization of the Legislatures" (3rd ser., XXIII (1966), 391-407), shows how, after 1776, "two interacting developments occurred simultaneously: ordinary citizens increasingly took part in politics, and American political theorists began to defend popular government [i.e. simple democracy]." As my essay has argued, the Constitutional Convention was dominated by men who rejected the idea that "simple" democracy was either a desirable or a safe form for the American people. To a certain extent their ideas exemplify a limited, but definite, reaction against both the institutional and theoretical "democratic" developments that Professor Main charts. This shift and change in one leader's estimate of "democracy"— a vague and non-critical view of the American peoples' virtue before 1776, a positive praise of this virtue in 1776, and then reservations about the wisdom and virtue of Americans, 1779 ff.—has been ably analyzed by John R. Howe Jr., *The Changing Political Thought of John Adams* (Princeton, 1966).

[30]Most of the modern discussion of the framing of the Constitution has concerned itself with the domestic consequences of ratification. This, I suspect, springs from the century of military security and isolation that so deeply colored American thinking from 1815 to 1940. The dangers of the international jungle we live in, that now makes foreign policy our primary concern, has helped some of us recognize why a statesman like Hamilton was obsessed with the need for a strong chief executive as a prime measure of defense and security in the world of 1787, where foreign policy showed the same jungle characteristics that frighten us.

[31]For convenience of reference, see Kenyon, *The Antifederalists*: Henry, 257; Lee, 205; and Grayson, 282-283.

[32]Madison, in *Federalist 38*, mocked (somewhat unfairly, under the circumstances) the Anti-Federalists for exactly this disagreement and confusion. "This politician," Madison wrote, "discovers in the constitution a direct and irresistible tendency to monarchy [Henry]; that is equally sure it will end in aristocracy [Lee]. Another is puzzled to say which of these shapes it will ultimately assume, but sees clearly it must be one or other of them [George Mason]; whilst a fourth [Grayson] . . . affirms that . . . the weight on that side [i.e., monarchical/aristocratic] will not be sufficient to keep it upright and firm against its opposite [i.e., democratic] tendencies."

[33]John Adams to Benjamin Rush, 19 September 1806. J. A. Schutz and D. Adair, eds., *The Spur of Fame: Dialogues of John Adams and Benjamin Rush, 1805-1813* (San Marino, 1966), 66.

[34]Quasi, [Latin = as if] seemingly, not real(ly), practical(ly), half-, almost. *Concise Oxford Dictionary* (1963).

Section III

APPROACHES TO EARLY AMERICAN HISTORY

Changing Interpretations of Early American Politics

BY JACK P. GREENE

Jack P. Greene typifies the younger generation of historians of early America who are today questioning the sweeping generalizations that were all too common in the past. Educated in the Middle West and England, and with a doctorate from Duke University, he has taught at Michigan State University, the College of William and Mary, Western Reserve University, the University of Michigan, and the Johns Hopkins University. He has also served as visiting editor of the WILLIAM AND MARY QUARTERLY, *and has held research grants from Colonial Williamsburg, Inc., the Social Science Research Council, and in 1962-1963 from the Huntington Library. His first major book,* THE QUEST FOR POWER: THE LOWER HOUSES OF ASSEMBLY IN THE SOUTHERN ROYAL COLONIES, 1689-1776, *demonstrates the effectiveness with which he and his contemporaries are using political analysis to deepen our understanding of colonial history. The essay that follows not only appraises the vast literature of the subject, but suggests a new synthesis of major importance.*

I N MANY RESPECTS, the extraordinary ferment in the study of early American politics over the past two decades seems to have produced at least as much confusion as understanding. Subjecting various portions of the early American political fabric to a thorough and rigorous scrutiny, a variety of scholars have demonstrated that long accepted interpretations and categories simply do not fit their particular objects of study. Unfortunately, the negative thrust of their work, though enormously valuable, has not been matched by an equally vigorous attempt at reconstruction. We now have a rather clear idea of what the nature of early American politics was not, but we are still not very sure about what exactly it was. Moreover, the bewildering mass of data produced by the new studies seems, on the surface, to defy any effort at rational classification and refinement, any attempt to make explicit and conscious the network of unrecognized, inarticulated, and, in many cases, seemingly contradictory assumptions that lie behind their conclusions. The immediate impression is that the politics of every colony was completely idiosyncratic, that there were as many species of political life as there were political environments. Yet one can discern in the literature as a whole a slow and tentative groping toward some common, if still largely implicit, conclusions. To sort out, identify, and classify those conclusions and to put them in the perspective of the historiography of early American politics is the purpose of this essay.

I

The nineteenth-century approach was predominantly whig. That is, it rested upon the standard whig assumptions about the nature of man and the historical process: that man is animated largely by the desire for freedom, that self-government is, therefore, necessarily the central concern of political life, and that history itself, at least in the western European world, is the story of man's inexorable progress toward liberty and democracy. Colonial politics was, then, simply another chapter in the age-old struggle of liberty against tyranny in which liberty-loving colonials from their first landing at Jamestown in 1607 until the successful conclusion of the War for Independence in 1783 had steadily opposed the arbitrary and tyrannical attempts of the English government to interfere in their affairs, to restrict that freedom and self-government to which all men naturally aspired and for which the American environment was itself peculiarly well suited. Writers like George Bancroft, the most prolific and most admired nineteenth-century historian of early America, whose massive *History of the United States* traced the narrative of American development through the adoption of the Constitution and was the standard account of early American political development for over half a century, fitted all political happenings into this mold. The various colonial rebellions, the many manifestations of opposition to the navigation acts, the friction between assemblies and royal and proprietary governors, the resistance to Parliamentary taxation after 1763, the War for Independence itself—all were part of the colonists' relentless striving for self-government and freedom from British control.[1]

Long before Herbert Butterfield wrote his devastating exposé of this approach in 1931[2] early American historians had sensed its many inadequacies. Fiercely partisan to those men and groups who seemed to be aligned on the side of liberty, it was, because it insisted upon reading the past in terms of the present, shot through with anachronisms. Worst of all, it was starkly simplistic. Rarely more than a narrative of consecutive, if often otherwise unrelated, public events, it ignored political divisions within the colonies, made no effort to identify, much less to explain, the intricate and complex interplay of forces that normally determine political events, and failed completely to fit politics into its broad social context, to look at it, in the words of one recent critic, "in conjunction with other elements of social activity."[3]

II

The whig interpretation of early American politics first came under serious attack during the closing years of the nineteenth century when a number of scholarly studies appeared stressing the importance of internal divisions within the colonies in shaping early American political life;[4] but an alternative framework of interpretation, one which attempted to relate politics to social and economic life, emerged only gradually during the first three decades of the twentieth century. The basic structure of the new interpretation was first worked out in detail in two studies of politics in the middle colonies in the years immediately preceding the Declaration of Independence: C. H. Lincoln, *The Revolutionary Movement in Pennsylvania* (1901), and Carl Becker, *History of Political Parties in the Province of New York, 1760-1776* (1909). Lincoln and Becker found that politics in both Pennsylvania and New York was conditioned by deep-seated internal conflicts between rival social groups. In Pennsylvania there were "two opposing forces, one radical," composed of Scotch-Irish Presbyterians and Germans in the west and non-Quaker lower and middle-class Philadelphians in the east, and the other "conservative," consisting of the Quaker mercantile oligarchy in the east. In New York it was the radical unprivileged and unfranchised common freeholders, tenants, mechanics, and artisans against a tightly-knit land-owning and commercial aristocracy. Unleashed by the contest with Britain between 1763 and 1776, this "latent opposition of motives and interests between the priviliged and unprivileged," the struggle of the radicals to push their way into the political arena and to achieve a wider area of economic and social freedom—the fight over "who should rule at home" and the radical demands for the "democratization of . . . politics and society" —and not the debate over Parliamentary authority in the colonies was the central issue in the politics of both colonies in the years immediately preceding the War for Independence.[5]

The striking similarity between developments in Pennsylvania and those in New York strongly suggested that what was true for those colonies was also true for the others, that the debate with Britain had everywhere been accompanied by an internal struggle for democracy between groups representing mutually antagonistic sectional and class interests, and that such a struggle was the distinguishing feature of early American politics. Over the next three decades, a number of scholars pushed this suggestion back into the colonial period and ahead into the years after 1776[6] and it became the central theme of two powerful and vividly written general interpretations of the early American past: Charles and Mary Beard, *The Rise of American Civilization*,[7] and Vernon Louis Parrington, *Main Currents in American Thought: The Colonial Mind*.[8]

By 1940 the study of early American politics had undergone a profound and seemingly permanent transformation. Applied generally to many areas of early American political life, the suggestions of Lincoln and Becker had been converted into dogma. New categories had replaced the old ones completely. Not American patriots and British tyrants, but radicals and conservatives, lower classes and upper classes, democrats and aristocrats, debtors and creditors, westerners and easterners, tenants and landlords, laborers and capitalists had become the principal actors upon the political stage. Politics was no longer an autonomous and disembodied sphere of activity but a reflection of economic and social cleavages within the colonies, and the essence of political activity was economic and social conflict between "natural" rivals: the little men—the yeomen farmers, agricultural tenants, artisans, and town laborers—against aristocratic merchants, landowners and professional men, with the former contending for human rights and democracy—the demand for greater popular participation in politics and a general equality of social and economic condition—and the latter for property rights and the maintenance of special privileges in all areas of early American life for the upper classes. If the categories had changed, however, and if the contours of political life seemed to have been thoroughly altered, the ultimate end of the political process, the standard against which every particular event and development was to be judged, remained essentially the same as it had been in the whig version. For the new historians, as for their nineteenth-century predecessors, the essential meaning of early American politics was to be found in the slow and at times halting advancement toward freedom and democracy that reached its culmination in the halcyon days of Andrew Jackson and the political triumph of the common man. The past continued to be read in terms of the present.

Although there were endless local variations, the broad outlines of early American political development according to the new interpretation seemed reasonably clear. After some early contests between the privileged and unprivileged that culminated in a series of rebellions at the end of the seventeenth century and resulted in some temporary victories for the unprivileged, the privileged, composed of relatively small groups of wealthy men connected by kinship and interest, gained control of the political life of every colony. Although they were everywhere a small minority of the population, they managed to maintain their hold on government by restricting the suffrage to property holders, refusing to extend equitable representation to egalitarian frontier areas, dominating the elective lower houses of assembly, and securing a monopoly on all appointive offices from seats on the royal and proprietary councils down to the lowest administrative posts in towns and counties.[9] Between 1765 and 1776 radical leaders, devoted to the achievement of social democracy if also at times to their own advancement, "seized on British acts as heaven-sent opportunities to attack the local aristocracy . . . under the guise of a patriotic defense of American liberties" and united the unprivileged "in what became as much a war against the colonial aristocracy as a war for independence."[10] The chief significance of the American Revolution was, in fact, not that it brought the colonies their independence but that it provided the opportunity for the unprivileged to score the first great victory for American democracy by driving some of the privileged to become loyalists and compelling others to give the forces of democracy a larger share in the direction of public affairs. Enabled by the pressures of 1774-1776 to wrest the lion's share of political power from the conservatives, the radicals over the next decade pushed through the Declaration of Independence, the embodiment of their ideals, and inaugurated a program of democratic reform that succeeded in the various states according to the strength and determination of the radicals but was checked, if only temporarily, in 1787-1788 by the Constitution and the conservative resurgence it represented.

This version of early American political development—frequently designated as progressive because it was obviously shaped by the rhetoric and assumptions of Progressive politics[11]—was so widely accepted and so integral a part of American historical consciousness that it seemed, even as late as 1950, eternally viable. In a real sense, however, the progressive interpretation of early American politics was the victim of its own success. Its very symmetry and neatness, its apparent comprehensiveness, and its seemingly easy adaptability to almost every situation combined to render it as lifeless and abstract, as little descriptive of the complex and continually changing realities of colonial society and politics, as the old whig interpretation. Although some scholars continued to produce works set within the progressive mold,[12] in the years since World War II study after study investigating a wide range of phenomena has shown that it is inapplicable to many political situations in early America, that it cannot be superimposed upon existing evidence without serious distortion. The resulting erosion, gradual, piecemeal, and still incomplete though it is, now seems to have left the progressive interpretation as little more than a series of cliches, of continuing importance only for what they reveal about the intellectual fashions of the first half of the twentieth century.

III

The most direct assault upon the progressive interpretation of early American politics has come from Robert E. Brown. In *Middle-Class Democracy and the Revolution in Massachusetts, 1691-1780* (1955) he presented a massively documented case for the propositions that Massachusetts throughout the eighteenth century was a "middle-class society in which property was easily acquired and in which a large portion of the people were property-owning farmers," that 95 per cent of the adult males were qualified to vote, that there was virtually no inequality of representation, that the farmers—not the merchant aristocracy—had by virtue of their superior numbers "complete control of the legislature," and that there was no "sharp internal class conflict." Far from being an aristocracy, Massachusetts, Brown concluded, was a middle-class democracy, and the Revolution, instead of being "an internal class conflict designed to achieve political, economic, and social democracy," was in fact a movement "to preserve a social order rather than to change it," to protect the democratic practices which the British government was trying "to curtail . . . as a necessary step toward the recovery of British authority and the prevention of colonial independence."[13]

What "was true in Massachusetts," Brown suggested in a general projection of his findings, was probably also "true in the other colonies,"[14] and he immediately set to work to substantiate this suggestion with a similar investigation of Virginia. Undertaken in collaboration with his wife, B. Katherine Brown, this study was published in 1964 under the title *Virginia 1705-1786: Democracy or Aristocracy?* Based upon an even greater amount of research and more systematic analysis, it demonstrated, at least, that what was true for Massachusetts was almost true for Virginia. The percentage of adult white males who could meet the property requirement for voting was only 85 per cent instead of 95 per cent, but the electorate was still wide, economic opportunity and social mobility were great, class antagonism was slight, representation was fairly equitable throughout the colony, and the only instance of internal social conflict before or during the Revolution occurred after 1740 between a growing group of dissenters and the Anglican establishment over the privileged position of the Anglican church. These findings led the authors to conclude that Virginia society, like Massachusetts society, was "fundamentally middle-class" with a political system that was "a middle class, representative democracy" and that the Revolution in Virginia, as in Massachusetts, was not an internal social upheaval but a conservative protest movement against the attacks of the British government upon Virginia democracy.[15]

A torrent of criticism followed the publication of both of these volumes. Several critics objected that the Browns' definition of democracy as any system in which social and economic opportunity was open to all and a majority of free adult males could vote was both anachronistic and inaccurate. It was anachronistic because it was derived from twentieth-century rather than eighteenth-century conceptions of democracy and inaccurate because almost all public offices—whether appointive or elective—were held by men from upper-class groups.[16] In the most elaborate critique of the Massachusetts volume, John Cary showed that Brown's sampling techniques were faulty, that his statistics were unreliable, and that, at least for certain selected towns, the percentage of qualified voters, though still quite high, was twenty to thirty per cent lower than Brown had originally indicated.[17]

When the smoke cleared, however, two points became clear. The first was that the Browns had not departed very far from the progressive historians they had set out to criticize. So preoccupied were they with demonstrating the factual and interpretive mistakes of the progressive account that they permitted that account to dictate the questions they asked of their materials. Borrowing wholesale their assumptions, categories, and terminology from the earlier interpretation, the Browns, like the progressive historians, were completely committed to a democratic point of view which assumed, among other things, that in any given political situation it is the people in general and what they want that are of primary importance; that the middle and lower classes have strong political interests and aspirations; and that the struggle for democracy—even though it was a struggle to preserve rather than to obtain democracy—was the central issue in early American politics. As the title of the Virginia book indicated, the Browns assumed, as had their progressive progenitors, that colonial society had to be either aristocratic or democratic, that it had to fit into one or the other of two rigid, abstract, largely self-contained, and mutually exclusive political categories. By insisting upon working entirely within two such broad and abstract polar classifications, the Browns did great violence to the diverse tendencies in early American political life and precluded the possibility of developing new and more meaningful categories for describing those tendencies.

The second point that can be made about the Browns' work is more positive. However unscientific their sampling techniques and however inexact their statistics, they established beyond serious doubt two basic facts about the society of Massachusetts and Virginia that necessitate serious modifications in the progressive conception of early American politics. First, by showing that the economic structure was highly fluid, property widely distributed, and lower-class economic and social discontent minimal they made it clear that neither colony was so rigidly stratified as to produce the kind of social conflicts which progressive historians thought were the stuff of colonial politics. Secondly, by showing that the franchise was considerably wider than had previously been supposed, they demonstrated that the predominance of the upper classes in politics did not depend upon a restricted franchise, that they had to have the support of men from all classes to gain elective office. That both of these conclusions are equally applicable to the rest of the colonies is indicated by the findings of a number of recent independent studies. Investigations of voting requirements and voter eligibility in Plymouth, Connecticut, Rhode Island, Virginia, New York, New Jersey, and Pennsylvania have revealed that the franchise in those colonies was also very wide and that the vast majority of free adult males could expect to acquire enough property during their lifetimes to meet the suffrage requirements.[18] Similarly, Jackson Turner Main in a general examination of *The Social Structure of Revolutionary America* has argued that American society in the late eighteenth century was everywhere relatively free from poverty and had, especially by European standards, a high rate of vertical mobility, great social and economic opportunity, and a remarkably supple class structure. This combination of economic abundance and social fluidity, Main has concluded, tended "to minimize those conflicts which might have grown out of the class structure and the concentration of wealth" that was occurring in older settled areas.[19]

IV

Even before the Browns mounted their vigorous assault, a number of other scholars had been busy turning out a series of detailed studies of the political life of individual colonies that had been quietly effecting a major revolution in the interpretation of early American politics. This movement, which is still in progress, was inspired in part by the early works of Lincoln and Becker and in part by the prosopographical studies of eighteenth-century British politics by Sir Lewis Namier and his followers.[20] Like Lincoln and Becker, the authors of these studies have been primarily interested in penetrating behind the formal institutional arrangements, ostensible issues, and dominant rhetoric of political life to the hard, concrete, and underlying realities. In marked contrast to the progressives, however, they have in general found broad economic and social divisions within the colonies to have been less important in determining the nature and form of political activity than the conflicting interests and ambitions of rival groups within the upper strata of society. In imitation of Namier, they have tried to sort out and describe the networks of interest, kinship, religious affiliation, and regional ties that presumably formed the basis for the major political groupings and to show how those networks related to the social and economic structure of the colonies in which they existed. In the process, they have shown how inadequate the old polar categories employed by the progressive historians actually were, how profoundly those categories obscured and distorted the complex and variegated nature of early American politics.

The first of these studies, John Bartlett Brebner's *The Neutral Yankees of Nova Scotia*, appeared as early as 1937. An exhaustive survey of the development of Nova Scotia from 1749, the year the British government inaugurated its program to turn what had previously been no more than a military garrison presiding over an unassimilated French population into a full-fledged British colony, until the conclusion of the War for Independence, this volume showed that the political life of the colony quickly came under the dominance of a powerful "little commercial group" centered in Halifax and headed by Joshua Mauger, the "economic overlord" of the colony who presided over the colony's fortunes from a London base. By virtue of Mauger's influence among imperial officials at Whitehall, members of this group by the 1760s filled most of the public offices in the colony, including the lieutenant governorship and a healthy majority of seats on the royal Council. With such extensive political power they were able to secure a virtual monopoly over both the distilling industry—the chief pillar in Nova Scotia's rudimentary economy—and the colony's London trade and to reap handsome profits from the sale of lands granted to themselves and from manipulating both the public and private debts of the colony. Because of its economic stranglehold over Halifax and because the bulk of the population, widely scattered over the rest of the province and preoccupied with eking out an existence in a new and not always hospitable environment, was politically inarticulate, disorganized, and acquiescent, this "office-holding clique" usually managed even to get its friends elected to a majority of the seats in the lower house of assembly. On the rare occasions when men from outside the clique were able to obtain a majority in the house, they only infrequently acted in concert against the merchant-official oligarchy, and when they did the members of the oligarchy in the Council could always block their efforts. Thus, except for an occasional and usually ineffective challenge from a royal governor or a newly arrived merchant who resented its monopolization of power, office, and economic opportunity, the oligarchy was free to govern Nova Scotia as its interests demanded.

Its tight political control, Brebner concluded, was one of the main factors in Nova Scotia's failure to join the other colonies in the American Revolution.[21]

Brebner's work on Nova Scotia, by the author's own admission a "marginal" and relatively new colony, did not in itself demand a re-examination of the progressive conception of early American politics, but two other volumes on Maryland politics published in the 1940s indicated that that conception clearly did not apply uniformly even to all of the older colonies. After a close look at Maryland society and politics through the middle decades of the eighteenth century, Charles Albro Barker found in *The Background of the Revolution in Maryland* that political divisions in that colony contained no elements of "western populism, or evangelical democracy," or " 'class struggle'." The conflict was not between classes, not between "plebian and patrician," but "within the upper class"—a classic struggle between "country" and "court" in which the "local squirearchy," which dominated "every phase of the growing life of the province" and expressed itself politically through the elective House of Delegates, was aligned against the absentee proprietor and his representatives who monopolized the seats on the proprietary Council and all major public offices.[22] Although individuals sometimes changed sides as the proprietor sought to lure influential members of the gentry into the proprietary camp by appointment to lucrative offices,[23] the issues which divided these two groups—the special privileges, powers, and revenues of the proprietors—remained constant, subtly shaping every political battle in pre-revolutionary Maryland. The "country party" took the lead in the protest against British policy between 1763 and 1776, and, although the increasing incidence of "election pledges, instructions to delegates, mass meetings, committees and associations" during those years tended to give "increasing force, from outside legislative doors, to the politics of protest," it resulted, Barker argued, not in the diminution but the enlargement of the influence of the gentry by bringing its members into "closer connection with the people" and giving "practical . . . meaning to the phrases about popular rights" employed in the revolutionary debate.[24] That the same group—"a relatively small class of planters, lawyers, and merchants"—continued to dominate Maryland politics after 1776 without serious challenge from below was the argument of Philip A. Crowl in *Maryland During and After the Revolution: A Political and Economic Study*, published in 1942 just two years after Barker's volume. Crowl found plenty of political conflict in Maryland, but it was neither class nor sectional in nature. Rather, it took the form of a series of struggles over opposing interests, ideas, and personalities between ad hoc coalitions of rival groups of leading men.[25]

In the years after World War II investigations of segments of the political history of Connecticut, New Jersey, and Rhode Island revealed both their distinctive features and how far the politics of each colony-state departed from the progressive model. In *Connecticut's Years of Controversy, 1750-1776*, published in 1949, Oscar Zeichner showed that the tradition of political tranquility that had earned for Connecticut its reputation as the "land of steady habits" had been shattered by the Great Awakening, which by fragmenting the colony into a variety of religious groups—Separates and New Lights on one hand and Old Lights, Arminians, and Anglicans on the other—paved the way for a succession of "long and bitterly fought factional and party conflicts." Because the eastern half of Connecticut was the main center of New Light strength while the western half was the primary stronghold of the Old Lights and Anglicans, these conflicts were to some extent sectional. But they also came to represent rival economic interests as eastern merchants and lawyers who formed the core of the Susquehannah Company, a speculative enterprise intent upon securing the support of the Connecticut government for its land schemes in Pennsylvania's Wyoming Valley, came into conflict with western leaders who opposed their project. Because the previously dominant western, Old Light, anti-Susquehannah Company group was too moderate in its resistance to the Stamp Act, the eastern, New Light, Susquehannah Company faction was able to gain the ascendancy in 1766 as the imperial question became an important issue in local politics. The New Light faction retained power until 1776, and the Old Light group gradually disintegrated as first the Old Lights and then the Arminians came to support the New Light opposition to British policy leaving only the Anglicans, many of whom subsequently became loyalists, in opposition. As in Maryland, these conflicts were not along class lines. The leaders of both groups were drawn from Connecticut's "ruling aristocracy of magistrates and ministers."[26]

Similarly, Richard P. McCormick in *Experiment in Independence: New Jersey in the Critical Period, 1781-1789*, published in 1950, found that " 'men of interest' " with powerful family connections played the preponderant role in New Jersey politics. On the state-wide level they were loosely organized into two broad sectional factions, the East Jersey and the West Jersey. But this split did not represent the "sectionalism of tidewater against backcountry, of plantation owners against yeomen, of a metropolis against the hinterlands, of a trading region against an agricultural region, or of an over-represented minority against an under-represented majority." Rather it was a sectionalism that was peculiar to New Jersey, one that followed a familiar historical and cultural cleavage that dated from the earliest settlement of the colony and had been intensified during the War for Independence as East Jersey leaders took the lead in prosecuting the war while West Jersey leaders, many of whom were Quakers, adopted "a negative or neutral attitude."[27]

David S. Lovejoy showed in *Rhode Island Politics and the American Revolution, 1760-1776* (1958), that in the decades just before the American Revolution, Rhode Island politics also revolved around sectional and factional disputes. Like the disputes in Connecticut and New Jersey, these were not the result of "the attempt of one class of people to tear down another and broaden the basis of government" but of a "struggle between equals, between people who already enjoyed the right to vote and who fought to control the government for their own ends." In contrast to the New Jersey factions, those in Rhode Island were sharply defined and well organized around two rival leaders—Samuel Ward from Newport and Stephen Hopkins from Providence—and reflected an overt and explicit contest between Newport and Providence for economic and political supremacy within the colony. That personality was of critical importance in the Ward-Hopkins controversy was indicated by the virtual dissolution of the Ward faction after Hopkins' alliance with the Wantons of Newport resulted in a humiliating defeat for Ward in the election of 1770 and his retirement from politics.[28]

Other studies have shown similarly unique political patterns in still other colonies. Between 1741 and 1767 New Hampshire politics closely resembled those of Nova Scotia. A remarkably close-knit oligarchy—centered around Governor Benning Wentworth, bound together by close family, social, and economic ties, and well connected in official circles in London—occupied most of the important appointive offices and dominated the mast and naval stores industries, the disposition of public lands, and the overseas trade—the most lucrative segments of the New Hampshire economy; and by an effective use of the patronage and other varieties of political influence even managed to control the elected lower house. The failure of an early challenge from a rival group of leading men in the 1740s and early 1750s resulted in the disappearance of faction and the total and unchallenged political ascendancy of the Wentworth family, which governed with the support of the "vast majority of provincial inhabitants."[29] In Georgia, which, like Nova Scotia, was comparatively new and underdeveloped throughout the colonial period, there were no significant internal sectional or class conflicts prior to the Revolution, and only on the question of opposition to British policy after 1763 was there any clear political division as Governor James Wright and a small coterie of Crown officers lined up in support of British authority against the vast bulk of the colony's leading men, some of whom occupied seats on the royal Council but most of whom expressed themselves through the elected Commons House of Assembly.[30] A mild form of sectionalism appeared in the 1780s as leaders from the rapidly expanding upcountry began to compete for political prominence with traditional lowcountry leaders, but this split neither resulted in the development of coherent and permanent factions nor determined voting behavior on the major public issues.[31] Politics in Delaware after the Declaration of Independence continued to manifest a long-standing sectional rivalry between the leaders of the two dominant agricultural southern counties and the dynamic Scotch-Irish minority representing the commercial interests of New Castle in the north.[32]

Factional disputes over proprietary powers, religion, and economic interests characterized the politics of both Carolinas during the proprietary period. Under the Crown, however, the old factional disputes subsided in South Carolina after a chaotic battle over paper currency, which in general pitted the Charles Town mercantile community against the planters, had ended in the early 1730s with the stabilization of the colony's paper money system. Thereafter there were no significant political divisions.[33] Even the regulator movement of the late 1760s, a recent writer has found in sharp contrast to the old interpretation, did not reveal or produce any deepseated class or sectional antagonism because the regulators—a combination of small planters and leading men in the backcountry—were primarily concerned with the establishment of law enforcement agencies adequate to deal with the lawless conditions that prevailed in the backcountry and, once effective courts had been secured, laid aside other subsidiary grievances against the eastern government.[34] The foundations for these grievances—a discriminatory tax system and insufficient representation for the backcountry in the legislature —were presumably to a large extent remedied by the new constitution in 1776.[35] By contrast, North Carolina during the royal period continued to be torn by factional strife over the disposition of lands, payment of quit rents, and the unequal representation of the rapidly expanding southern section of the colony in the legislature. After a dramatic attempt by leaders of the southern counties to change the representation system had been squelched by London authorities in the early 1750s, the north-south quarrel gradually subsided, but in the late 1760s and early 1770s the colony was again plagued by sectional antagonisms as western regulators rose in protest against corrupt local administration by "eastern" appointees intent on enriching themselves at the expense of the western inhabitants. This protest, which was eventually put down with force, apparently produced a deep sectional rift that continued to affect North Carolina politics even after the conditions that produced it had disappeared.[36]

That the progressive model is also inapplicable to the politics of the two oldest colonies, Massachusetts and Virginia, can be inferred from a spate of specialized investigations of each. In Massachusetts after the Restoration, the old Puritan leadership, which had previously been able to maintain its political predominance despite occasional challenges from a variety of discontented groups in the colony,[37] began to crack under pressures from both without and within. The external pressures, described by Michael Garibaldi Hall in *Edward Randolph and the American Colonies 1676-1703*,[38] derived from the attempts of the Crown to assert its authority over the colony, and the internal pressures, discussed by Bernard Bailyn in *The New England Merchants in the Seventeenth Century*,[39] largely from a rising group of interrelated merchants, who, though in many cases Puritans themselves, were discontented with orthodox Puritan leadership. Together with other dissatisfied groups the merchants at first cooperated with the Crown in the hope of breaking the power of the Puritans and formed the bulk of the provisional Council which in 1685 and 1686 governed Massachusetts during the interim period between the recall of the charter and the arrival of royal governor Edmund Andros. But this group, too "multifarious" to constitute a party, as Richard S. Dunn has emphasized in an excellent study of the changing political orientation of New England at the end of the seventeenth century and the beginning of the eighteenth century,[40] made common cause with the old Puritan leadership against Andros as soon as it became clear that it could not control the Dominion government. Under the new government established under the Charter of 1691 the Council, Bailyn has argued, became the "political voice of the merchants" who, over the next forty years, used their connections in Great Britain and cooperated with the country party, which represented the lesser property owners in the House of Representatives, to make and break a succession of governors in an attempt to secure their "permanent interests."[41]

This process can be seen in John A. Schutz's account of the intrigues and maneuvers that preceded the removal of Jonathan Belcher and the appointment of William Shirley as governor of Massachusetts in 1741.[42] Though heated political controversies—which, as George Athan Billias has recently shown in connection with the land bank struggle,[43] were usually between rival groups of leading men representing opposing economic interests—occasionally arose thereafter,[44] Shirley's appointment ushered in a period of political stability that lasted until his removal from the governorship in 1756 and was based upon his deft manipulation of the House of Representatives and a clever distribution of patronage that enabled him to draw many of the colony's leading men into his political orbit and to build a powerful political machine around "a solid core of supporters and a shifting number of auxiliaries."[45] By the 1760s resentment against the engrossment of power and office by this "oligarchy" had become widespread among the wealthy and ambitious who were not a part of it, and, when the oligarchy was cautious in opposing British measures after 1763, its opponents seized the opportunity to discredit it and to strip it of some of its power by excluding its members from the royal Council.[46] This internal political battle, which was sharpened by the revolutionary controversy and ended in 1775 with the outbreak of war and the dissolution of the oligarchy, was played out against a backdrop of western agrarian distrust of the commercial East, which though temporarily submerged during the war, openly manifested itself again in the disturbances of the 1780s.[47] Although westerners seem to have taken the revolutionary ideal of popular sovereignty more seriously than easterners, they revealed, just like Massachusetts citizens in the eastern portion of the colony, a pronounced tendency to trust political affairs at every level of government to leading men except in times of extreme economic distress such as those which accompanied Shays' Rebellion.[48]

Virginia politics, like those of Massachusetts, proceeded through several distinct phases. The chaotic factionalism and chronic disarray of the colony's first few decades gave way under the careful efforts of Governor Sir William Berkeley to a more stable political environment after the Restoration. Berkeley, as Bernard Bailyn has shown, gathered around him many of the most successful among a new wave of immigrants who began coming to Virginia in the 1640s. Bound to Berkeley by "ties of kinship and patronage," this group, called the Green Spring faction after Berkeley's plantation, formed "an inner circle of privilege" with a virtual monopoly over the important public offices and the seats on the governor's Council; easy access to the public lands which constituted the chief form of wealth in the colony; and sufficient political influence to dominate the proceedings of the elective House of Burgesses. Bacon's Rebellion, which, as Wilcomb E. Washburn has emphasized, began over a disagreement on Indian policy and had few of the populist-democratic overtones traditionally associated with it,[49] became an occasion for the venting of pent-up resentment among county leaders outside the official group. No sooner was the rebellion over and Berkeley removed from the scene, however, than this bitter rivalry between court and country and the incipient factionalism it represented began to subside as the leading men in both groups united against a series of royal governors who, unlike Berekeley, were not intimately connected through kinship, patronage, or economic interest with the emergent planter group. For thirty-five years after the rebellion the leading planter families—a "league of local oligarchs"—becoming increasingly self-conscious and expressing themselves largely through the Council, drove one governor after another out of office.[50] Not until the end of the second decade of the eighteenth century, when Lieutenant Governor Alexander Spotswood gave up the fight and allied himself with the local leaders, was this pattern broken and the political infighting it had produced stopped. For the most part, Spotswood's successors followed the same course, and Virginia politics through the middle decades of the eighteenth century acquired a degree of stability that was rare in colonial America.[51] Personal rivalries among leading politicians never hardened into factions, and the local oligarchy, dominating the Council, the House of Burgesses, and the county courts, governed, as Charles S. Sydnor has demonstrated, with rare skill and responsibility to the general satisfaction of the entire Virginia political community.[52] Even the apparent challenge by Patrick Henry and the heated political discussions that followed the disclosure in 1766 that a long-time speaker of the House of Burgesses and colony treasurer had loaned large sums of public money to his friends among the gentry did not produce any permanent or significant divisions within the Virginia polity.[53] Not until the war and confederation periods did a serious split, apparently based upon both opposing sectional and economic interests and personal political rivalries, appear.[54]

A number of recent studies suggest that even in Pennsylvania and New York, the prototypes for the progressive model, politics do not fit that model well. Until the mid-1770s Pennsylvania politics seems to have resembled the Maryland pattern more closely. From the first decades of the colony's history there was a more or less continuous struggle between court and country over the distribution of power between the proprietor and the Assembly. During the first quarter of the eighteenth century both the country party and the court party were Quaker, but the country party, led by lawyer David Lloyd and operating primarily through the Assembly, drew its strength mostly from the country, while the court party, "dominated by city merchants under the leadership of the Proprietor's secretary, James Logan," and in complete control of the Council, was most powerful in Philadelphia, the seat of the proprietor's government.[55] Fanned by personal rivalries and ambitions, this bitter party strife temporarily subsided after 1725 as unparalleled commercial prosperity, the tactful administration of Governor Patrick Gordon, and the disappearance of old political issues ushered in an era of good feeling and resulted in the virtual extinction of the old parties.

Political peace proved to be short-lived, however, and with the end of Gordon's administration in 1736 the old wrangling began anew, this time between a united "Quaker party"—composed of remnants from both of the older factions and supported by many non-Quakers—and the "Proprietary party"—consisting of a growing body of Anglicans, proprietary officeholders, and some Presbyterian and German back settlers—over "the authority of the Proprietors and the best means of achieving a *modus vivendi* with the Indians."[56] These two parties continued to be the principal rivals in Pennsylvania politics up through the middle 1770s, although after the exclusion crisis of 1756—after many Quakers had withdrawn from the

Assembly rather than betray their pacifist principles in what, as Ralph Ketcham has recently emphasized, was a move to preserve not to relinquish Quaker political power—many of the leaders of the Quaker party were no longer Quakers.[57] Although the annual election battles between these two parties were occasionally extremely hard fought, especially from 1764 through 1766 as the proprietary party managed to exploit western discontent over the Paxton affair and resentment over the Quaker Party's moderate response to the Stamp Act to secure its only clear victories, and although both parties appealed broadly to the electorate,[58] the conflict, as William S. Hanna has underlined, was largely a mere "jousting at the top among the gentlemen rulers and their factions" with no basic social issues at stake.[59] For reasons not entirely clear, this contest subsided after 1766, and over the next decade the internal politics of Pennsylvania were remarkably smooth. Only in 1776, when the traditional leaders were slow in deciding for independence, did a rival group of radical "independents," composed primarily of men not previously prominent politically, arise to seize control of Pennsylvania government. But this new group, David Hawke has argued in a recent assault upon the earlier interpretation of Lincoln, was not the mouthpiece of the unprivileged West, which, indeed, does not appear to have been the source of any mass discontent, or even of the urban masses of Philadelphia but rather the political arm of a relatively small group of middle-class ideologues intent upon gaining independence and reconstructing the government of Pennsylvania so that the people would have a greater share in it. The trouble was that when they "gave the people democracy" in the constitution of 1776, "the people spurned the gift," still preferring "the elite to run their affairs."[60] Although the nature of the political struggles of the fifteen years after 1776 remains to be re-examined, Hawke's conclusions suggest that they may have been largely between rival political groups with opposing conceptions of the way the polity ought to be organized and may not, therefore, have represented any fundamental divisions within society.[61]

A still different variety of factionalism characterized the politics of New York. Leisler's Rebellion, which was in part a protest against the monopolization of office and economic resources by a small group surrounding the royal governor, and its ruthless suppression inaugurated a thirty-year-long feud between Leislerians and Anti-Leislerians in which the objective was not just political control of the New York government with the economic advantages such control represented but, as Lawrence H. Leder has stressed, the complete extinction of the opposition party. Although Robert Livingston and others helped arrange a political truce during the administration of Governor Robert Hunter between 1710 and 1719 which eventually resulted in the disappearance of the old parties,[62] new factions appeared in the 1720s and remained as a constant part of the political scene. For the most part loose and temporary alliances, these factions were based upon family rivalries, conflicting economic interests, ethnic and national differences, religious tensions, sectional antagonisms, personal ambition, and political alliances with the royal governors. The principals shifted sides with astonishing ease as their interests or inclinations decreed until the 1750s, when factions solidified "around the Livingston and De Lancey families, and it was their political rivalry which underlined the history of New York until the Revolution" and shaped New York's response to British measures between 1763 and 1776.[63] The debate between the Livingston and De Lancey parties, like the debates between the amorphous factions that preceded them, usually centered upon bona fide issues, and the parties vied with each other for support from a wide electorate;[64] but at bottom this contest was primarily an "intra-class wrangle" between rival upper-class groups and never a struggle between aristocracy and democracy as Becker had insisted. Far from being democratic upheavals, the small farmer and tenant uprisings that culminated in the "Great Rebellion of 1766," Milton M. Klein has argued, were essentially non-political in character and concerned largely with such basic economic questions as "land titles, rents, security of tenure, and . . . personal obligations to the manor lord."[65] Even the radical Sons of Liberty, who played so conspicuous a part in New York politics between 1768 and 1776, Roger Champagne has demonstrated, were largely under the control of the Livingston party and, although they held ideas with more radical implications than party leaders, had no democratic program of their own and were so loosely bound together as to be unable to play a significant role in the Livington party's shaping of the new independent state government in 1776.[66]

Although the picture is far from complete, it can be safely inferred from this survey that every colony-state displayed a unique combination of characteristics that produced its own peculiar configuration of politics and that the old progressive conception is either totally inapplicable or seriously distorting at every point for which there has been a detailed study. But the more important question is whether these seemingly disparate, contradictory, perpetually changing, and highly volatile political systems had enough in common to make it possible to construct an alternative framework of interpretation, Although there has been no systematic attempt to deal with this question, certain preliminary conclusions can be drawn on the basis of the findings of the specialized studies published thus far.

Politics everywhere was primarily elitist in nature. Public office—both appointive and elective—and political leadership were securely in the hands of upper-class groups, and, although there were occasional manifestations of social and economic discontent among the lower classes, that discontent never resulted in widespread demands for basic changes in the customary patterns of upper-class leadership. Political divisions were not along class lines. Rather, they revolved around the ambitions of rival factions, each faction drawing support from all segments of a broad electorate. The chaotic and explosive nature of these divisions in many places—the ease with which groups formed, dissolved, and re-formed, leaders appeared "first on one side and then on another," and issues precipitated "formations without apparent relationship to previous or succeeding groupings"[67]—has led Bernard Bailyn to conclude that colonial politics was "a constant broil of petty factions struggling almost formlessly, with little discipline or control, for the benefits of public authority." According to this characterization, the object of these "shifting, transitory, competitive groupings"—the primary and impelling force behind colonial politics—was "the search for wealth, power, and prestige" by the individuals who composed them.[68] "Uncommitted to any broad principle or program," these factions were "preoccupied with immediate concerns," "local questions and selfish interests." Ideas, theories, principles thus become "mere rhetoric," weapons in the factional armory employed to rationalize the conduct of the protagonists and to distract the unwary among the electorate or the unaligned politicians from the "real" objectives in dispute.[69]

That "chaotic factionalism" is an appropriate rubric for large segments of early American politics, that the competition for wealth, power, and prestige was involved to some extent in almost every factional contest, and that ideas were always closely related to the interests of the people who used them seems beyond dispute, but this formulation, recently applied by Forrest MacDonald to the period between 1776 and 1789,[70] is not free from objection. For one thing, it assumes, like the progressive conception, an "extraordinary rationality in the political behavior of men," the ability of politicians to see not only "their interests clearly" but also "precisely how to go about securing them."[71] Secondly, it rests upon a blanket assumption—which is clearly not universally valid—that ideas are always subordinate to some concrete and tangible factors in politics. Thirdly, it does not accurately describe all portions of early American political life. Some factional divisions were extraordinarily stable, and some political environments were free from factionalism altogether. Finally, unless it falls back upon the old progressive formula of repression, manipulation, propaganda, and control, which posits a degree of efficiency and sophistication not easily associated with colonial and revolutionary America, it does not by itself explain why the electorate tolerated such a patently irresponsible brand of politics. To remedy these objections it is necessary to turn to recent writings on the "political culture" of the colonies.

V

As here used the term *political culture* applies to that intellectual and institutional inheritance which inevitably conditions, however slightly in many instances, all—even the most revolutionary and impulsive—political behavior. For early America the most visible elements of that culture—the formal concepts of political thought and the external forms of institutional development—have received a considerable amount of attention from historians during the past seventy-five years.[72] What has been until recently almost completely ignored and what, it now appears, is vastly more important, is that elusive and shadowy cluster of assumptions, traditions, conventions, values, modes of expression, and habits of thought and belief that underlay those visible elements. Although the inquiry into this area has not yet proceeded very far, work already published has yielded some extremely important results.

The findings of one group of independent studies help to resolve a problem that to the progressive historians and the Browns was an incomprehensible paradox: why (in the words of J. R. Pole) "the great mass of the common people might actually have given their consent to concepts of government" that by "systematically" excluding them "from the more responsible positions of political power" restricted "their own participation in ways completely at variance with the principles of modern democracy."[73] What these studies have found through an intensive examination and "imaginative reconstruction of the values and assumptions" of early American political thought is that colonial *and* revolutionary society was essentially what Walter Bagehot called "a deferential society" that operated within an integrated structure of ideas that was fundamentally elitist in nature. That structure of ideas assumed, among other things, that government should be entrusted to men of merit; that merit was very often, though by no means always, associated with wealth and social position; that men of merit were obliged to use their talents for the benefit of the public; and that deference to them was the implicit duty of the rest of society. All society was therefore divided among the rulers and the ruled, and the rulers, including the representatives of the people, were not the tools of the people but their political superiors. "The mass of the people," Richard Buel, Jr., has argued in the most thorough exposition of these ideas, thus "elected representatives not to order them around like lackeys to do the people's bidding, but to reap benefit from the distinguished abilities of the few upon which the safety of society might in large measure depend" and to utilize the "political expertise of the realm in the people's behalf."[74]

Another group of studies has suggested that more than the simple pursuit of wealth, power, and prestige may have been involved in the factional struggles of colonial politics. Works by Perry Miller, Edmund S. Morgan, George Lee Haskins, and others on the Puritans[75] and Frederick B. Tolles on the Quakers[76] have indicated how important the special religious, social, and political ideas of each were in shaping the political behavior of the leaders of early Massachusetts Bay and Pennsylvania. Of vastly more general influence appears to have been the group of ideas analyzed by Z. S. Fink and Caroline Robbins[77] and called by J. G. A. Pocock the "Country ideology." This ideology, which appeared with minor variations and modifications in all parts of the British political world during the seventeenth and eighteenth centuries, shared certain dominant assumptions about human nature and the function and process of government: that men were imperfect creatures, perpetually self-deluded, enslaved by their passions, vanities, and interests, confined in their vision and understanding, and incapable of exercising power over one another without abusing it; that government and constitutions existed to restrain the vicious tendencies of man by checking them against one another; that to fulfill that function each of the elements in the polity had to be balanced against each of the others in such a way as to prevent any of them from gaining ascendancy over the rest; and that history was the record of a continual struggle between liberty and power, purity and corruption. A mixed constitution was the device by which this delicate balance was to be achieved, but the tendency of men in power, especially men connected with the administration (the court), to seek to increase it by corrupting Parliament—the voice of the men of independent property (the country)—was so great that the country members in Parliament had to keep a wary eye on the court to see that it did not succeed in throwing the constitution out of balance or overturning it altogether and establishing an unrestrained executive tyranny that would make free with the liberties and property of the citizenry. It was essential, therefore, both that every seeming abuse of ministerial power be immediately detected and rooted out of the polity and that every representative of the country be constantly on guard lest he somehow be seduced into the conspiracy of power and thereby betray his country and lose his own personal independence, which was regarded as the basis of "all human excellence."[78] This fetish of independence led to the condemnation of *parties,* which perforce were the instruments of *partial* men, and to the idealization of the virtuous patriot, the man of preeminent virtue whose behavior was determined not by self-interest, not by the narrow interests of some group or region with which he was associated, but by nothing less than the welfare of the entire country.[79]

The state of knowledge is still too imperfect for historians to be able to assess with any certainty the importance of the country ideology in giving shape and coherence to the configuration of early American politics. That all of its components including its several stock personae—the court villain, dependent court lackey, independent country patriot—as well as its conventions of behavior, its rhetoric, and its patterns and categories of thought were transferred in toto to the colonies is clear enough from the frequent application of the terms *court* and *country* to colonial politics, the oft expressed dread of arbitrary power and aversion to parties, the extent to which they infused the thought and informed the behavior of individuals,[80] the conscious cultivation of them by colonial leaders through the

middle decades of the eighteenth century, and the more or less continuous efforts of the lower houses of assembly to check the prerogative and undermine executive authority—attempts which persisted
both because and in spite of the factional disputes and internal divisions in colonial politics and resulted in a roughly uniform pattern
of constitutional development in all of the colonies.[81] But it is not
enough to know that the country ideology was an integral part of
early American politics. We need to know as well the precise nature
of its role and its relationship to other elements of political life. That
role and that relationship will, of course, be different for every situation, and any generalization will therefore have to await a series of
detailed investigations similar to the one conducted by Bernard
Bailyn for the pre-revolutionary debate. But Bailyn's study suggests
what those answers may be. He finds that ideas expressed by Americans in the debate, many of which were descended directly and in a
fairly undiluted form from the country ideology, had a dual role.
They were first of all *explanatory* both in the sense that they enabled
the principals to explain to themselves and the world what they were
about and to see themselves in some kind of cosmic, or at least historical, perspective, and in the sense that they revealed "not merely
positions taken but the reasons why positions were taken." Only
through these ideas, only through the beliefs, attitudes, assumptions,
motivations, and professed goals that "lay behind the manifest
events of the time," he insists, can the "contemporary meaning" of
the Revolution be understood. However much those ideas may have
distorted underlying realities, they were always thought by the participants to be true and were, therefore, as Gordon S. Wood has
phrased it, "psychologically true." Because these ideas—these inher-
ited values and habits of thought—also exerted a powerful influence
upon the way Americans perceived reality, shaping into predictable
and familiar patterns their interpretations of and response to imperial actions, they were also in an important and fundamental sense
determinative.[82] Ideas, then, in all of their several forms, operate to
impede men's perception of reality at the same time that they give it
shape and meaning, and in some situations they may even become as
real as the more tangible elements of political life and exercise
greater causative power than the manifest events or the underlying
interests or ambitions they were first called into the political arena
to serve.

VI

Despite the impressive accomplishments of the past three decades, our knowledge is still too fragmentary and the character of the subject too complex to permit any firm or easy generalizations about the nature of early American politics. Out of the overwhelming tangle of interests, ideas, and ambitions that seem, at least on the surface, to make colonial politics incomprehensible, however, emerge certain basic regularities that make it possible to establish at least a rough typology of political forms into which, after the elimination of certain individual variants, most pre-1776 colonial political activity can be fitted.[83] On the basis of present knowledge, this typology would seem to require at least four distinct, if also overlapping, and not necessarily sequential classifications.

For the first, which is probably also the most common, we can use Bailyn's term, *chaotic factionalism*. It involved a ruthless competition for dominance, power, and economic advantage among rival groups of leading men, groups which were largely ad hoc and impermanent, formed as temporary alliances on specific occasions, then dissolving as quickly as they appeared only to have the individuals who had composed them regroup in different combinations in response to later events. This form seems to have been typical of Virginia prior to 1660, Massachusetts from 1684 to 1741, New York from 1720 to 1755, Pennsylvania from 1680 to 1720, Maryland before 1689, South Carolina and New Hampshire prior to 1730, and North Carolina until 1745. To some extent, it was present in every classification, but it was the dominant characteristic only in the first.

The second type may be called *stable factionalism*. It was distinguished by the emergence of two semi-permanent opposing interest groups with relatively stable memberships and representing explicit regional—perhaps a more precise and appropriate term than sectional—economic, religious, or kinship rivalries (occasionally in combination) and, in some cases, standing for rather well-defined sets of principles and beliefs. This type appears to have predominated in Massachusetts from 1760 to 1776, Rhode Island and Connecticut after 1750, New Hampshire in the 1730s and 1740s, New York from 1690 to 1720 and again from 1755 to 1776, in New Jersey, Maryland, and perhaps Delaware through most of the eighteenth century, in Pennsylvania from 1735 to 1776, in North Carolina in the 1740s and 1750s, and in South Carolina from 1720 to 1740.

The third classification may perhaps best be described as *domina-*

tion by a single, unified group. In this type of politics all of the avenues to political power and most of the primary sources of wealth were monopolized by a dominant elite bound together by common economic interests, religious beliefs, patronage and kinship ties, or some combination of these factors. In this system faction was submerged by some form of repression, manipulation, or corruption—in the "country" sense of the term—of potential leaders of opposition elements. Massachusetts Bay prior to 1684 and again from 1741 to 1760, New York before Leisler's Rebellion, Virginia between 1660 and 1720, and New Hampshire and Nova Scotia after 1750 are examples of this type.

The fourth and rarest form was almost wholly *faction free with a maximum dispersal of political opportunity within the dominant group* composed of the elite and potential members of the elite. This type, which appears to have existed over a long period only in Virginia after 1720 and South Carolina after 1740, depended upon a homogeneity of economic interests among all regions and all social groups, a high degree of social integration, and a community of political leaders so large as to make it impossible for any single group to monopolize political power. It was, in a real sense, the epitome of the country ideal of a government composed of independent men and, at least in Virginia, was in part the result of the conscious cultivation of that ideal by the leaders of the polity.

Whatever its defects, however much it stands in need of refinement, clarification, modification, and elaboration, this typology may by providing a general frame of reference at least make it easier to discuss early American politics. Hopefully, it may also be a first step toward the development of new, less abstract categories which will more accurately reflect the political life they seek to describe. Perhaps even, it will serve as a foundation for achieving some understanding of the relationship between these early political forms and the more sophisticated party structure that emerged in the United States after 1790.

[1](10 vols., Boston, 1834-74), *passim.*

[2]*The Whig Interpretation of History* (London, 1931).

[3]Bernard Bailyn, "A Whig Interpretation," *Yale Review,* new ser., L (March 1961), 438-441.

[4]See, e.g., Brooks Adams, *The Emancipation of Massachusetts: The Dream and The Reality* (Boston, 1887).

[5]Lincoln, *Revolutionary Movement,* 3-4, 7, 14, 39, 53-54, 77, 96-98, 150, 189-190; Becker, *History of Political Parties,* 5-24, 27-28, 51-52, 275-276.

[6]Among the more important studies that applied some variant of this interpretation to early American politics are James Truslow Adams, *The Founding of New England* (Boston, 1921), *Revolutionary New England 1691-1776* (Boston, 1923), and *New England in the Republic 1776-1850* (Boston, 1926); Charles A. Beard, *An Economic Interpretation of the Constitution* (New York, 1913); Robert L. Brunhouse, *The Counter-Revolution in Pennsylvania, 1776-1790* (Harrisburg, 1942); H. J. Eckenrode, *The Revolution in Virginia* (Boston, 1916); J. Franklin Jameson, *The American Revolution Considered as a Social Movement* (Princeton, 1926); Merrill Jensen, *The Articles of Confederation; An Interpretation of the Socio-Constitutional History of the American Revolution 1774-1781* (Madison, 1940); Irving Mark, *Agrarian Conflicts in Colonial New York 1711-1775* (New York, 1940); John C. Miller, "Religion, Finance and Democracy in Massachusetts," *New England Quarterly,* VI (1933), 29-58; Allan Nevins, *The American States during and after the Revolution* (New York, 1924); Arthur M. Schlesinger, *The Colonial Merchants and the American Revolution* (New York, 1917); J. Paul Selsam, *The Pennsylvania Constitution of 1776: A Study in Revolutionary Democracy* (Philadelphia, 1936); Ernest W. Spaulding, *New York in the Critical Period, 1783-1789* (New York, 1932); Richard Upton, *Revolutionary New Hampshire: An Account of the Social and Political Forces Underlying the Transition from Royal Province to American Commonwealth* (Hanover, 1936); and Thomas Jefferson Wertenbaker, *Patrician and Plebeian in Virginia* (Charlottesville, 1922), and *Torchbearer of the Revolution, The Story of Bacon's Rebellion and Its Leader* (Princeton, 1940). About the only works published during these years on any aspect of early American politics which did not emphasize the importance of internal class and sectional divisions were those which treated constitutional relations between Great Britain and the colonies and took for their main theme the opposition of colonial lower houses of assembly to royal governors. The most important studies in this category are Charles M. Andrews, *Colonial Background of the American Revolution* (New Haven, 1924), and Leonard W. Labaree, *Royal Government in America* (New Haven, 1930).

[7](New York, 1927).

[8](New York, 1927). A decade later Curtis P. Nettels systematically developed the same theme at greater length in a general textbook on colonial history, *The Roots of American Civilization: A History of American Colonial Life* (New York, 1938).

[9]For a capsule statement of this view see Merrill Jensen, "Democracy and the American Revolution," *Huntington Library Quarterly,* XX (1957), 321-341.

[10]Jensen, *Articles of Confederation,* 11.

[11]See Charles Crowe, "The Emergence of Progressive History," *Journal of the History of Ideas,* XXVII (1966), 109-124; Richard Hofstadter, "Beard and the Constitution, History of an Idea," *American Quarterly,* II (1950), 195-213; Douglass Adair, "The Tenth Federalist Revisited," *William and Mary Quarterly,* 3d ser., VIII (1951), 48-67; and Cecelia M. Kenyon, " 'An Economic Interpretation of the Constitution' After Fifty Years," *Centennial Review,* VII (1963), 327-352.

12The most important are Merrill Jensen, *The New Nation* (New York, 1950); Jerome R. Reich, *Leisler's Rebellion: A Study of Democracy in New York 1664-1720* (Chicago, 1953); Elisha P. Douglass, *Rebels and Democrats: The Struggle for Equal Political Rights and Majority Rule during the American Revolution* (Chapel Hill, 1955); Richard Walsh, *Charleston's Sons of Liberty: A Study of the Artisans 1763-1789* (Columbia, 1959); Jackson Turner Main, *The Anti-Federalists: Critics of the Constitution, 1781-1788* (Chapel Hill, 1961); Staughton Lynd, *Anti-Federalism in Dutchess County, New York: A Study of Democracy and Class Conflict in the Revolutionary Era* (Chicago, 1962); the Lynd portion of Staughton Lynd and Alfred Young, "After Carl Becker: The Mechanics and New York City Politics, 1774-1801," *Labor History*, V (1964), 215-276; and Bernard Friedman, "The New York Assembly Elections of 1768 and 1769: The Disruption of Family Politics," *New York History*, XLVI (1965), 3-24.

13pp. 401-408.

14"Reinterpretation of the Revolution and Constitution," *Social Education*, XXI (1957), 103.

15(East Lansing, 1964), *passim.*

16Among the most searching reviews of the Massachusetts volume were those by Robert J. Taylor, *Mississippi Valley Historical Review*, XLIII (1956), 111-113, and Clifford K. Shipton, *Political Science Quarterly*, LXXI (1956), 306-308, while David Alan Williams, *William and Mary Quarterly*, 3d ser., XXII (1965), 149-152, is perhaps the best review of the Virginia volume. Other, more extended criticisms of the Browns' assumptions, use of terms, and conclusions may be found in Jensen, "Democracy and the American Revolution"; Roy N. Lokken, "The Concept of Democracy in Colonial Political Thought," *William and Mary Quarterly*, 3d ser., XVI (1959), 568-580; J. R. Pole, "Historians and the Problem of Early American Democracy," *American Historical Review*, LXVII (1962), 626-646; and John M. Murrin, "The Myths of Colonial Democracy and Royal Decline in Eighteenth-Century America: A Review Essay," *Cithara*, V (1965), 53-69.

17"Statistical Method and the Brown Thesis on Colonial Democracy," *William and Mary Quarterly*, 3d ser., XX (1963), 251-264. See also the rebuttal by Brown in *Ibid.*, 265-276.

18See George D. Langdon, Jr., "The Franchise and Political Democracy in Plymouth Colony," *Ibid.*, XX (1963), 513-526; David S. Lovejoy, *Rhode Island Politics and the American Revolution 1760-1776* (Providence, 1958), 5-31; Charles S. Grant, *Democracy in the Connecticut Frontier Town of Kent* (New York, 1961); Milton M. Klein, "Democracy and Politics in Colonial New York," *New York History*, XL (1959), 221-246; Nicholas Varga, "Election Procedures and Practices in Colonial New York," *Ibid.*, XLI (1960), 249-277; Richard P. McCormick, *The History of Voting in New Jersey: A Study of the Development of Election Machinery, 1664-1911* (New Brunswick, 1953); Theodore Thayer, *Pennsylvania Politics and the Growth of Democracy 1740-1776* (Harrisburg, 1953), 6; and Lucille Griffith, *Virginia House of Burgesses, 1750-1774* (Northport, 1963), 53-79.

19(Princeton, 1965), esp. 270-287. The quotation is from p. 163.

20 Especially Namier's *The Structure of Politics at the Accession of George III* (London, 1929) and *England in the Age of the American Revolution* (London, 1930).

21(New York, 1937), 149-157, 207-242, 291-353.

22The extensive patronage of the Maryland proprietor is analyzed in detail by Donnell MacClure Owings, *His Lordship's Patronage: Offices of Profit in Colonial Maryland* (Baltimore, 1953).

23The classic case is that of Daniel Dulany, Sr. For the details of his switch as well as additional confirmation of the general conclusions reached by Barker see Aubrey C. Land, *The Dulanys of Maryland: A Biographical Study of Daniel Dulany, the Elder (1685-1753) and Daniel Dulany, the Younger (1722-1797)* (Baltimore, 1955).

24Barker, *Background* (New Haven, 1940), esp. 24, 182-183, 372-377. Additional insight into the nature of "out of doors politics" in Maryland is provided by Neil Strawser, "Samuel Chase and the Annapolis Paper War," *Maryland Historical Magazine,* LVII (1962), 177-194.

25(Baltimore, 1942), esp. 11-15. See also Crowl's "Anti-Federalism in Maryland, 1787-1788," *William and Mary Quarterly*, 3d ser., IV (1947), 446-469.

26(Chapel Hill, 1949), 3-43, 219-235. Zeichner's account of the religious origins of Connecticut's political divisions has recently been amplified in several important respects by Robert Sklar, "The Great Awakening and Colonial Politics: Connecticut's Revolution in the Minds of Men," *Connecticut Historical Society Bulletin,* XXVIII (1963), 81-95.

27(New Brunswick, 1950), 69-102. The origins of this split and some of its manifestations in the period prior to the American Revolution can be traced in John E. Pomfret, *The Province of West New Jersey 1609-1702: A History of the Origins of an American Colony* (Princeton, 1956), and *The Province of East New Jersey 1609-1702: The Rebellious Proprietary* (Princeton, 1962); Donald L. Kemmerer, *Path to Freedom: The Struggle for Self-Government in Colonial New Jersey 1703-1776* (Princeton, 1940); and McCormick, *New Jersey from Colony to State, 1609-1789* (Princeton, 1964).

28(Providence, 1958), pp. 1-30, 193-194. A briefer and more pointed analysis of Rhode Island's factional dispute is Mack E. Thompson, "The Ward-Hopkins Controversy and the American Revolution in Rhode Island: An Interpretation," *William and Mary Quarterly*, 3d ser., XVI (1959), 363-375. Both Lovejoy and Thompson make the point that prior to 1755 Rhode Island politics was dominated by representatives of the agrarian towns against the opposition of commercial interests in Newport.

29Jere R. Daniell, "Politics in New Hampshire under Governor Benning Wentworth, 1741-1767," *Ibid.*, XXIII (1966), 76-105. This article is based upon portions of the author's larger unpublished doctoral dissertation, New Hampshire Politics and the American Revolution, 1741-1790 (Harvard University, 1964).

30W. W. Abbot, *The Royal Governors of Georgia 1754-1775* (Chapel Hill, 1959). For somewhat different conclusions and an analysis of the snarled political life of Georgia during the War for Independence see Kenneth Coleman, *The American Revolution in Georgia, 1763-1789* (Athens, 1958).

31W. W. Abbot, "The Structure of Politics in Georgia: 1782-1789," *William and Mary Quarterly*, 3d ser., XIV (1957), 47-65.

32John A. Munroe, *Federalist Delaware, 1775-1815* (New Brunswick, 1954).

33These generalizations are drawn largely from M. Eugene Sirmans, *Colonial South Carolina: A Political History, 1663-1763* (Chapel Hill, 1966). See also Sirmans' "Politics in Colonial South Carolina: The Failure of Proprietary Reform, 1682-1694," *William and Mary Quarterly*, 3d ser., XXIII (1966), 33-55, and "The South Carolina Royal Council, 1720-1763," *Ibid.*, XVIII (1961), 373-392.

34Richard Maxwell Brown, *The South Carolina Regulators: The Story of the First American Vigilante Movement* (Cambridge, 1963).

35There is no adequate study of South Carolina politics immediately after 1776 but see the introduction to William E. Hemphill and Wylma Anne Wates, eds., *Extracts from the Journals of the Provincial Congresses of South Carolina, 1775-1776* (Columbia, 1960), i-xxxiv.

36The threads of North Carolina politics have not been completely unravelled, but some of the more important developments are dealt with in Charles G. Sellers, Jr., "Private Profits and British Colonial Policy: The Speculations of Henry McCulloh," *William and Mary Quarterly*, 3d ser., VIII (1951), 535-551; Lawrence F. London, "The Representation Controversy in Colonial North Carolina," *North Carolina Historical Review*, XI (1934), 255-270; and Desmond Clarke, *Arthur Dobbs Esquire 1689-1765: Surveyor-General of Ireland, Prospector and Governor of North Carolina* (Chapel Hill, 1957). Hugh T. Lefler and Paul Wager, eds., *Orange County—1752-1952* (Chapel Hill, 1953), contains the best discussion of the North Carolina regulator movement.

37Together George Lee Haskins, *Law and Authority in Early Massachusetts: A Study in Tradition and Design* (New York, 1960), and Edmund S. Morgan, *The Puritan Dilemma: The Story of John Winthrop* (Boston, 1958), provide a satisfactory account of the political life of Massachusetts Bay before the Restoration. The social and political divergencies from the ideas of the dominant group are emphasized by Darrett B. Rutman *Winthrop's Boston: Portrait of a Puritan Town, 1630-1649* (Chapel Hill, 1965), and "The Mirror of Puritan Authority," in *Law and Authority in Colonial America: Selected Essays* (George A. Billias ed., Barre, 1965), 149-167.

38(Chapel Hill, 1960), esp. 21-128.

39(Cambridge, 1955).

40*Puritans and Yankees: The Winthrop Dynasty of New England 1630-1717* (Princeton, 1962), 212-257.

41*Ibid.;* Bailyn, *New England Merchants*, 143-197.

42"Succession Politics in Massachusetts, 1730-1741," *William and Mary Quarterly*, 3d ser., XV (1958), 508-520.

43*The Massachusetts Land Bankers of 1740* (Orono, 1959), 17-53.

44See, e.g., Paul S. Boyer, "Borrowed Rhetoric: The Massachusetts Excise Controversy of 1754," *William and Mary Quarterly*, 3d ser., XXI (1964), 328-351.

45John A. Schutz, *William Shirley: King's Governor of Massachusetts* (Williamsburg, 1961). The quotation is from p. 269.

46Ellen E. Brennan, *Plural Office-Holding in Massachusetts 1760-1780: Its Relation to the "Separation" of Departments of Government* (Chapel Hill, 1945), 3-106; Edmund S. and Helen M. Morgan, *The Stamp Act Crisis: Prologue to Revolution* (Chapel Hill, 1953), 7-20, 207-219; John Cary, *Joseph Warren: Physician, Politician, Patriot* (Urbana, 1961); Francis G. Walett, "The Massachusetts Council, 1766-1774," *William and Mary Quarterly*, 3d ser., VI (1949), 605-627.

47The basic study of western attitudes is Robert J. Taylor, *Western Massachusetts in the Revolution* (Providence, 1954).

48*Ibid.;* Lee Nathaniel Newcomer, *The Embattled Farmers: A Massachusetts Countryside in the American Revolution* (New York, 1953), 79-87; Benjamin W. Labaree, *Patriots and Partisans: The Merchants of Newburyport, 1764-1815* (Cambridge, 1962), 1-15; and David Syrett, "Town-Meeting Politics in Massachusetts, 1776-1786," *William and Mary Quarterly*, 3d ser., XXI (1964), 352-366.

49*The Governor and the Rebel: A History of Bacon's Rebellion in Virginia* (Chapel Hill, 1957).

50Bailyn, "Politics and Social Structure in Virginia," in *Seventeenth-Century America: Essays on Colonial History* (James Morton Smith ed., Chapel Hill, 1959), 90-115. On the self-consciousness of the Virginia gentry see Louis B. Wright, *The First Gentlemen of Virginia: Intellectual Qualities of the Early Colonial Ruling Class* (San Marino, 1940).

51See Jack P. Greene, *The Quest for Power: The Lower Houses of Assembly in the Southern Royal Colonies 1689-1776* (Chapel Hill, 1963), 22-31.

52*Gentleman Freeholders: Political Practices in Washington's Virginia* (Chapel Hill, 1952). See also Griffith, *Virginia House of Burgesses;* Jack P. Greene, "Foundations of Political Power in the Virginia House of Burgesses, 1720-1776," *William and Mary Quarterly,* 3d ser., XVI (1959), 485-506; and Carl Bridenbaugh, *Seat of Empire: The Political Role of Eighteenth-Century Williamsburg* (Williamsburg, 1950), 1-43.

53Thad W. Tate, "The Coming of the Revolution in Virginia: Britain's Challenge to Virginia's Ruling Class, 1763-1776," *William and Mary Quarterly,* 3d ser., XIX (1962), 323-343; David John Mays, *Edmund Pendleton 1721-1803: A Biography* (Cambridge, 1952).

54The exact nature and precise importance of this split is unclear, but see Jackson Turner Main, "Sections and Politics in Virginia, 1781-1787," *William and Mary Quarterly,* 3d ser., XII (1955), 96-112.

55Roy N. Lokken, *David Lloyd, Colonial Lawmaker* (Seattle, 1959), and Frederick B. Tolles, *James Logan and the Culture of Provincial America* (Boston, 1957), discuss the role and behavior of the central protagonists.

56Frederick B. Tolles, *Meeting House & Counting House: The Quaker Merchants of Colonial Philadelphia* (Chapel Hill, 1948), 11-28; Thayer, *Pennsylvania Politics.* On the composition of the proprietary group see G. B. Warden, "The Proprietary Group in Pennsylvania, 1754-1764," *William and Mary Quarterly,* 3d ser., XXI (1964), 367-389.

57Ketcham, "Conscience, War, and Politics in Pennsylvania, 1755-1757," *William and Mary Quarterly,* 3d ser., XX (1963), 416-439; John J. Zimmerman, "Benjamin Franklin and the Quaker Party, 1755-1756," *Ibid.,* XVII (1960), 291-313.

58See Sister Joan de Lourdes Leonard, "Elections in Colonial Pennsylvania," *Ibid.,* XI (1954), 385-401; J. Philip Gleason, "A Scurrilous Colonial Election and Franklin's Reputation," *Ibid.,* XVIII (1961), 68-84; and David L. Jacobson, "John Dickinson's Fight against Royal Government, 1764," *Ibid.,* XIX (1962), 64-85.

59*Benjamin Franklin and Pennsylvania Politics* (Stanford, 1964). The quotation is from p. 201.

60*In the Midst of a Revolution* (Philadelphia, 1963). The quotation is from p. 198.

61The analysis of these struggles in Charles Page Smith, *James Wilson: Founding Father 1742-1798* (Chapel Hill, 1956), would seem to support this view.

62*Robert Livingston 1654-1728 and the Politics of Colonial New York* (Chapel Hill, 1961) and "Robert Livingston: A New View of New York Politics," *New York History,* XL (1959), 358-367.

63The best short descriptions of these shifting factions as well as the most thoughtful analyses of the nature of New York politics are two articles by Milton M. Klein, "Democracy and Politics," *loc. cit.,* and "Politics and Personalities in Colonial New York," *New York History,* XLVII (1966), 3-16. Stanley Nider Katz also discusses the factionalism of the early 1730s in his edition of James Alexander, *A Brief Narrative of the Case and Trial of John Peter Zenger, Printer of The New York Weekly Journal* (Cambridge, 1963), especially 2-7.

64Klein, "Politics and Personalities," *loc. cit.,* 9-10; William Livingston and others, *The Independent Reflector or Weekly Essays on Sundry Important Subjects More particularly adapted to the Province of New-York* (Milton M. Klein, ed., Cambridge, 1963), 20-48; Lawrence H. Leder, "The New York Elections of 1769; An Assault on Privilege," *Mississippi Valley Historical Review,* XLIX (1963), 675-682; Nicholas Varga, "Election Procedures and Practices," *loc. cit.*

65Klein, "Democracy and Politics," *loc. cit.,* 231, 238-240; Roger Champagne, "Family Politics versus Constitutional Principles: The New York Assembly Elections of 1768 and 1769," *William and Mary Quarterly,* 3d ser., XX (1963), 57-79; Don R. Gerlach, *Philip*

Schuyler and the American Revolution in New York 1733-1777 (Lincoln, 1964). The quotation is from Gerlach, xvii.

66Champagne, "Family Politics versus Constitutional Principles," *loc. cit.*, and "New York's Radicals and the Coming of Independence ," *Journal of American History*, LI (1964,) 21-40.

67Bernard Bailyn, "The Beekmans of New York: Trade, Politics, and Families," *William and Mary Quarterly*, 3d ser., XIV (1957), 601-602.

68*Pamphlets of the American Revolution 1750-1776* (Cambridge, 1965), I, 91, 188-189, 191.

69See Lovejoy, *Rhode Island Politics*, 2-3; Hanna, *Benjamin Franklin*, ix; Gerlach, *Philip Schuyler*, xiv-xvii; and Klein, "Democracy and Politics," 238-240. The introduction to his recent edition of the *Pamphlets of the American Revolution* indicates that Bailyn does not now hold this view of the role of ideas in early American politics, though it was implicit in much of his earlier work.

70 *E Pluribus Unum: The Formation of the American Republic 1776-1790* (Boston, 1965) and previously *We the People: The Economic Origins of the Constitution* (Chicago, 1958).

71This comment was made recently by Cecelia M. Kenyon in "'An Economic Interpretation of the Constitution' after Fifty Years," *loc. cit.*, 338.

72Among the most important recent studies in this category are Leonard W. Labaree, *Conservatism in Early American History* (New York, 1948); Max Savelle, *Seeds of Liberty: The Genesis of the American Mind* (New York, 1948); Clinton Rossiter, *Seedtime of the Republic: The Origin of the American Tradition of Political Liberty* (New York, 1953); Morgan and Morgan, *Stamp Act Crisis*; and Greene, *Quest for Power*.

73Pole, "Historians and Early American Democracy," *loc. cit.*, 626-646. The quotations are from pp. 628, 641.

74"Democracy and the American Revolution: A Frame of Reference," *William and Mary Quarterly*, 3d ser., XXI (1964), 165-190. The quotations are from pp. 178, 188. See also Pole, "Historians and Early American Democracy," *loc. cit.*, 629, for the phrase from Bagehot. The importance of these ideas in determining political behavior is indicated by McCormick, *Experiment in Independence*, 102; Labaree, *Partisans and Patriots*, 14-15; and my own investigation of Virginia politics immediately before the Declaration of Independence which may sometime be published in a volume tentatively entitled "Virtue and Liberty: Politics in Revolutionary Virginia, 1760-1790," undertaken in collaboration with Keith B. Berwick.

75Especially Miller, *The New England Mind: The Seventeenth Century* (Cambridge, 1939); Morgan, *Puritan Dilemma*; and Haskins, *Law and Authority in Early Massachusetts*.

76Tolles, *Meeting House & Counting House*, and *James Logan*.

77Fink, *The Classical Republicans: An Essay in the Recovery of a Pattern of Thought in Seventeenth-Century England* (Evanston, 1945); Robbins, *The Eighteenth-Century Commonwealthman: Studies in the Transmission, Development, and Circumstances of English Liberal Thought from the Restoration of Charles II until the War with the Thirteen Colonies* (Cambridge, 1959).

78Pocock, "Machiavelli, Harrington, and English Political Ideologies in the Eighteenth Century," *William and Mary Quarterly*, 3d ser., XXII (1965), 547-583, esp. 563-572. The court-country dichotomy as it was expressed in British politics after 1714 is discussed by Archibald S. Foord, *His Majesty's Opposition 1714-1830* (Oxford, 1964). The essential components of the mid-eighteenth century version of the country ideology as it had developed in the colonies are discussed by Buel, "Democracy and the American

Revolution," *loc. cit.*; Bailyn, ed., *Pamphlets of the American Revolution*, 38-59; and H. Trevor Colbourn, *The Lamp of Experience: Whig History and the Intellectual Origins of the American Revolution* (Chapel Hill, 1965).

[79]There is no adequate modern investigation of this particular political motif. The classic expression of it in eighteenth-century Britain was Henry St. John, Viscount Bolingbroke, *A Dissertation upon Parties* (The Hague, 1734), and *Letters on the Spirit of Patriotism: On the Idea of a Patriot King: and On the State of Parties, at the Accession of King George the First* (London, 1749), both written during the author's "country" period.

[80]In this connection see Gerald Stourzh, "Reason and Power in Benjamin Franklin's Political Thought," *American Political Science Review*, XLVII (1953), 1092-1115, and *Benjamin Franklin and American Foreign Policy* (Chicago, 1954); Paul W. Connor, *Poor Richard's Politicks: Benjamin Franklin and His New American Order* (New York, 1965); Jack P. Greene, ed., *The Diary of Colonel Landon Carter of Sabine Hall, 1752-1778* (Charlottesville, 1965), I, 28-48; Zoltán Haraszti, *John Adams and the Prophets of Progress* (Cambridge, 1952); John R. Howe, Jr., *The Changing Political Thought of John Adams* (Princeton, 1966); Edward Handler, *America and Europe in the Political Thought of John Adams* (Cambridge, 1964); Douglass, *Rebels and Democrats;* Arthur O. Lovejoy, *Reflections of Human Nature* (Baltimore, 1961), 37-65; Cecelia M. Kenyon, "Men of Little Faith: The Anti-Federalists on the Nature of Representative Government," *William and Mary Quarterly*, 3d ser., XII (1955), 3-43; and Adrienne Koch, *Power, Morals, and the Founding Fathers: Essays in the Interpretation of the American Enlightenment* (Ithaca, 1961).

[81]See my *Quest for Power;* my review of F. G. Spurdle, *Early West Indian Government: Showing the Progress of Government in Barbados, Jamaica and the Leeward Islands, 1660-1683* (Palmerston North, N.Z., 1963), *William and Mary Quarterly*, 3d ser., XXII (1965), 146-149; and Murrin, "Myths of Colonial Democracy and Royal Decline," *loc. cit.*, 61-66.

[82]Bailyn, ed., *Pamphlets of the American Revolution*, 1-202, esp. 8, 20, 60; Wood, "Rhetoric and Reality in the American Revolution," *William and Mary Quarterly*, 3d ser., XXIII (1966), 31.

[83]This is not to suggest that those variants are not of enormous importance but only that their significance will appear more clearly when they are seen in relationship to the more generalized features of colonial political development.

The Imperial Approach to Early American History

BY LAWRENCE HENRY GIPSON

Few historians of early American history have so influenced the study of their discipline as Lawrence Henry Gipson. Educated at the universities of Idaho, Oxford, Chicago, and Yale, he taught at the College of Idaho, Wabash College, Lehigh University, and Oxford (at the latter as Harmsworth Professor of American History) until his retirement in 1952. During his entire academic career Professor Gipson labored quietly at his research, sometimes at the Huntington Library as he did first in 1946. The results are his multi-volume HISTORY OF THE BRITISH EMPIRE BEFORE THE AMERICAN REVOLUTION, *a monumental work of scholarship that more than any other demonstrates the validity of the imperial approach to the study of colonial America. In the essay that he has contributed to this volume he traces the history of the imperial viewpoint from the days of the Revolution, and argues convincingly that early American history must be viewed from London as well as Boston or Williamsburg.*

THE IMPERIAL APPROACH of American historians to the study of English colonial expansion in the New World is in clear contrast to the more characteristic national approach of most American writers concerned with the same period of history. The latter approach assumes the existence of the United States of America and then probes into the past in order to uncover the beginnings and the development of a group of thirteen English colonies destined to become the nucleus of a new nation. The imperial approach, by comparison, views English colonization of the New World simply as part of the history of the rise and decline of the British Empire. In this approach London, the capital of the Empire, is always the nerve center. Each type of approach has its merits and its disadvantages.

As the national approach has, for obvious reasons, been the one most generally employed by American historians it would be well to illustrate it by what is generally agreed to be the extreme example: George Bancroft's *A History of the United States, from the Discovery of the American Continent*. This impressive work came from the press in ten volumes between 1834 and 1874. The first three were comprehended under the subhead "Colonial History" or, as Bancroft later summarized them, "the History of the Colonization of the United States." In the preface to Volume I Bancroft wrote:

I have formed the design of writing a History of the United States from the Discovery of the American Continent to the present time. . . . I am impressed more strongly than ever with a sense of the grandeur and vastness of the subject. . . . Such an investigation on any country would be laborious; I need not say how much the labor is increased by the extent of our republic. . . . I have dwelt at considerable length on this first period [down to 1660], because it contains the germ of our institutions. The maturity of the nation is but a continuation of its youth. The spirit of the colonies demanded freedom from the beginning.

Consistent with this approach, Chapter 2 of the volume is entitled "Spaniards in the United States" and Chapter 3, "England Takes Possession of the United States"; likewise Chapter 23 of Volume II, is called "The People Called Quakers in the United States"; Chapter 28, "The Southern States after the Revolution [of 1688/9]"; and Chapter 29, "The Middle States after the Revolution [of 1688/9]." Volume IV has as a subhead "The American Revolution. Epoch First. The Overthrow of the European Colonial System, 1748-1763," Volume V is subtitled "The American Revolution. Epoch Second. How Great Britain Estranged America, 1763-1774," and Volume VI, "The Crisis."

Bancroft wrote in the spirit of an ardent Jacksonian Democrat. His *History* was in harmony with the sentiments that he expressed in 1826, when he gave a Fourth of July address at Northampton, Massachusetts, in which he declared: "The government [of the United States] is a democracy, a determined, uncompromising democracy. . . . The popular voice is all powerful with us; this is our oracle; this, we acknowledge is the voice of God."[1]

The views expressed in this great historical work certainly accorded with those of most people living during the period before the Civil War. The books therefore enjoyed almost unbounded popularity. By the time Volume X had been published in 1874, as part of a complete edition of the series, Volumes I and II had reached their 25th reprinting, including revisions; Volumes III and IV, their 23rd; Volume V, its 20th; and Volume VI, its 18th. The series, taken as a whole, represents a remarkable achievement, based as it was upon the use of a vast body of original sources drawn from depositories both in Great Britain and in the United States. But it is not properly a history of the United States; it is, rather, a history of the development of the thirteen colonies and of their movement to cut the political ties that bound them to Great Britain. Nevertheless, in the words of J. Franklin Jameson, "The book at once took rank as the standard history of the United States."[2] Its once great prestige has, however, gradually diminished. Why did this happen?

A number of reasons can be assigned for the decline in esteem of Bancroft as a historian. First of all, in nineteenth-century Germany (where Bancroft himself had studied) among contemporary historians the figure of Leopold von Ranke loomed high above the horizon as one whose influence was to become world-wide. His voluminous writings set an example of intellectual detachment—whether dealing with the history of France, Spain, England, Italy, or of the Papacy. When reading von Ranke's works one is hardly aware that it is a German who is writing, so fully and sympathetically did he enter into the life of a foreign people. As a historian, Bancroft was his antithesis. Under the urge of an indiscriminating and intense patriotism he was apt, in the more purple passages in his *History,* to resort to flamboyancy and gross exaggeration. It is not easy to read today without some amazement the following flight of fancy (especially in light of the fact that, when it was written, hundreds of thousands of Americans were held in abject slavery by other Americans):

But a new principle, far mightier than the church and state of the Middle Ages, was forcing itself into power. Successions of increasing culture and heroes in the world of thought had conquered for mankind the idea of the freedom of the individual; the creative but long latent energy that resides in the collective reason was next to be revealed. From this the state was to emerge, like the fabled spirit of beauty and love out of the foam of the ever-troubled ocean. It was the office of America to substitute for hereditary privilege the natural equality of man; for the irresponsible authority of a sovereign, a dependent government emanating from the concord of opinion; and as she moved forward in her high career, the

187

multitudes of every clime gazed towards her example with hopes of untold happiness, and all the nations of the earth sighed to be renewed.[3]

A much more serious defect than the irresponsible exaggerations and the chief factor in undermining reliance on the authority of Bancroft's *History*, was its careful avoidance of the use of evidence that did not coincide with the thesis that was being propounded: namely, that the English people who came to colonize the New World sought from the beginning and for the best of reasons political independence from their mother country—with all that is implied, both in lack of protection from foreign enemies and pirates and in lack of trade and other advantages enjoyed only by subjects of the English Crown.

The decline in popularity of the work of the most extremely nationalistic historian has, nevertheless, not meant the repudiation of the national approach to the writing of early American history. Most American historians, especially the textbook writers, since the days of Bancroft, have employed such an approach and will, doubtless, continue to do so. Thus, Edward Channing utilized it in his *A History of the United States* that appeared in six volumes between 1905 and 1925, a history that carried the story of the United States from the beginning of the colonization of the New World by Europeans to the end of the Civil War. Similarly in 1965 there issued from the press Samuel Eliot Morison's delightful and thought-provoking *Oxford History of the American People*, apparently designed to take the place of his *Oxford History of the United States* that had been published in 1927. Both of these books bind into a unity the American colonial past and the American national present.

The imperial approach to the writing of early American history by Americans is not new, but began in the early national period with the works of three Loyalist historians: the Reverend Jonathan Boucher, Thomas Hutchinson, and Peter Oliver.

Jonathan Boucher was one-time pastor of St. Mary's Parish Church in Carolina County, Virginia, and was also responsible for the education of George Washington's stepson, John Parks Custis; he later had charge of the parish church at Annapolis and, still later, of the church in Queen Anne's Parish in Prince George's County, also in Maryland. In 1797, as a Loyalist refugee in England, he brought out his *A View of the Causes and Consequences of the*

American Revolution: in Thirteen Discourses, Preached in North America between the Years 1763 and 1775. In seeking to explain why the Revolution occurred, he looked to New England as the chief center of American disaffection. This was due to the fact "that [the] spirit of Republicanism which . . . overturned the Constitution of Great Britain in 1648 . . . was carried over to . . . America by the first Puritan emigrants," whereby these republican principles were transplanted "into a more genial soil. . . . How they have thriven by transplantation, the revolution of America shews."[4] Further in his book he stated: "I believe the people of the four New England governments may challenge the whole world to produce another people who, without actually rebelling, have, throughout their whole history, been so disaffected to government, so uniformly intolerant towards all who differ from them, so dissatisfied and disorderly, and, in short, so impatient under every proper legal restraint not imposed by themselves."[5]

But Boucher also felt, as one who had lived in both Virginia and Maryland, that there were peculiar causes for the spread of this spirit of disaffection from New England to other colonies: "Among other circumstances favourable to the revolt of America, that of the immense debt owing by the Colonists, to the Merchants of Great Britain, deserves to be reckoned as not the least. . . . The being overwhelmed with debt seems always to have been an essential ingredient in the character of a conspirator: in all ages, and in all countries, insurrections have been excited chiefly by 'men that are in trouble, and men that are in debt.' "[6] How little he sympathized as a highchurchman with any revolt against legal authority is indicated by his full acceptance of the doctrine of non-resistance as "a tenet of our Church," and of his approval of such a statement as, "A rebel is worse than the worst prince, and a rebellion worse than the worst government of the worst prince that hath hitherto been."[7] Yet, such quotations from his book hardly do full justice to it. In his *The Literary History of the American Revolution, 1763-1783*, Moses Coit Tyler makes the following comment that is not without pertinence: "Nowhere else, probably, can be found so comprehensive, so able, and so authentic a presentation of the deeper principles and motives of the American Loyalists, particularly from the standpoint of a highchurch clergyman of great purity and steadiness of character, of great moral courage, of great learning, finally, of great love for the country thus torn and distracted by fratricidal disagreements."[8]

Another active participant in colonial affairs, indeed the most prominent of American Loyalists, was Thomas Hutchinson, author of a history of colonial Massachusetts Bay up to 1774. Hutchinson was a man of great distinction and one who had deeply at heart the welfare of the colony where he had been born and educated, and in the affairs of which he had played a leading role for many years—directing its financial policies, supporting its boundary claims against the Province of New York, acting as Speaker of the House of Representatives, as Lieutenant Governor and Chief Justice, and, finally, as Governor. His historical work, as were his public services, was of a high order. In 1764 there appeared *The History of the Colony of Massachusetts-Bay from the first settlement ... until ... 1691*; this was followed in 1776 by *The History of the Province of Massachusetts-Bay, from ... 1691, until the Year 1750*; the final volume, completed in 1778 while he was an exile in England, was edited and published posthumously in 1828 by his grandson, the Reverend John Hutchinson.[9] What enhances the value of Hutchinson's *History* is the inclusion of abundant footnotes and appendices giving the sources of the informative and carefully framed comments that illuminate the text. Although writing as a loyal subject of George III, Hutchinson consistently demonstrates his pride in Massachusetts Bay. Not even in dealing with the activities of his famous ancestor, Mrs. Anne Hutchinson, does he fail to maintain the judicious tone that prevails in his narrative. He relates that the attention paid to her by leading people in Boston "increased her natural vanity. Countenanced and encouraged by Mr. Vane and Mr. Cotton, she advanced doctrines and opinions which involved the colony in disputes and contentions; and being improved, to civil as well as religious principles, had like to have produced ruin both to church and state."[10]

As to Hutchinson's treatment of the exciting events in the 1760's and 1770's in which he himself was so prominently involved, it can be said that, in the main, he holds to a calm tone. This is even true in his statement having to do with his controversial appointment as Chief Justice upon the death of Chief Justice Sewall on September 11, 1760; in his description of the destruction of his Boston mansion by an intoxicated mob on the night of August 26, 1765; in his narrative of the so-called Boston Massacre of March 5, 1770; and in his account of the Boston Tea Party of December 16, 1773.[11] At the same time one is left in no doubt as to his firm commitment to the concept of the supremacy within the empire of the King in Parliament. Yet he presents with fairness the arguments of those who, by pointing to the royal charter of 1691, exalted the claims to power of the people of Massachusetts Bay and, thereby, to exemption from interference by the government of Great Britain. In fact, one has the feeling upon reading the final volume of the *History,* that it is, among other things, Hutchinson's appeal to future generations to recognize the rectitude of his conduct in public office, at the same time as it is his acknowledgment of the strength of the views of those in opposition to him.

Charles Deane of the committee on publications of the Massachusetts Historical Society noted that "Hutchinson's mind was eminently a judicial one; and candor, moderation, and a desire for truth, appear to have guided his pen."[12] In harmony with this, James K. Hosmer, who wrote the leading biography of Hutchinson, has the following to say: "In the main, he is fair-minded, and in the circumstances surprisingly calm. . . . [and his *History*] is the work of a thoughtful brain, whose comments on politics, finance, religion . . . are full of intelligence and also full of humanity."[13]

If both Boucher and Hutchinson, writing from the imperial point of view, sought to give a dispassionate account of the Revolutionary movement in colonial America, the same cannot be said of Peter Oliver and "The Origin & Progress of the American Rebellion" which he composed, as Hutchinson did the final volume of his *History,* while a Loyalist refugee in England. A man of wealth, the owner of Middleboro Iron Works, a member of the Massachusetts Bay Council, and also Chief Justice of the provincial court, Oliver suffered many indignities, including the confiscation of his property, along with other Loyalists. As a result of these accumulated misfortunes, he was an embittered man and gave way to his feelings in his account of the coming and progress of the American Revolution. So furious were his assaults on leading Americans that his book found no contemporary publisher. Although the writing of it was completed in 1781 and copies of it were made (one of which is in the British Museum and another in the Huntington Library at San Marino, California), it was not until 1961 that it was finally published. Under the careful editorship of two scholars, Douglass Adair and John A. Schutz, it appeared under the title of *Peter Oliver's Origin & Progress of the American Rebellion: A Tory View.*

The volume is in the form of an extended letter to a friend, in which the writer gives this friend the following due warning:

You will be presented with such a Detail of Villainy in all its Forms, that it will require some Fortitude to meet the Shock. You will see Religion dressed up into a Stalkinghorse, to be skulked behind, that Vice might perpetrate its most atrocious Crimes, whilst it bore so fair a Front to mislead & deceive the World around. In short, you will see every Thing, sacred & profane, twisted into all Shapes to serve the Purposes of Rebellion; & Earth & Hell ransacked for Tools to work the Fabrick with.[14]

Oliver's contempt for such a colonial leader as Samuel Adams was beyond measure. To him the outstanding characteristic of Adams was "the Malignity of his Heart" in "employing his Abilities to the vilest Purposes"; he was indeed "so thorough a Machiavilian, that he divested himself of every worthy Principle, & would stick at no Crime to accomplish his Ends." As for poor John Hancock, he "was as closely attached to the hindermost Part of Mr. *Adams* as the Rattles are affixed to the Tail of the Rattle Snake. . . . His understanding was of the Dwarf Size; but his Ambition . . . was upon the Gigantick." Nor were the clergy spared. To Oliver, the Reverend Dr. Samuel Cooper, pastor of the Brattle Square Church in Boston, was a man "not deep in his Profession, but very deep in the black Art. . . . No Man could, with a better Grace, utter the Word of *God* from his Mouth, & at the same Time keep a two edged Dagger concealed in his Hand. His Tongue was Butter & Oil, but under it was the Poison of Asps."[15] Thus Samuel Adams, John Hancock, Samuel Cooper, as well as James Otis, were pictured as despicable conspirators who stopped at nothing to gain their ends.

Why, despite the presence of "conspirators," Massachusetts Bay should have turned to rebellion was beyond belief to Oliver. Here was "a Colony, which had been nursed, in its Infancy, with the most tender Care & Attention; which had been indulged with every Gratification that the most froward Child could wish for; which had even bestowed upon it such Liberality, which its Infancy & Youth could not *think* to ask for; which had been repeatedly saved from impending Destruction, sometimes by an Aid unsought—at other times by Assistance granted to them from their own repeated humble Supplications." Why such a colony should "plunge into an unnatural Rebellion . . . must strike 'an attentive mind' with some Degree of Astonishment; & Such a Mind would anxiously wish for a Veil to throw over the Nakedness of human Nature."[16]

The value of Oliver's book lies in the fact that it presents, as no other account does so fully, the deeply emotional reactions of a leading dispossessed Loyalist, a man of learning, a basically good man who, with deep resentment of the treatment he and others had received at the hands of his fellow Americans, sought to give to the world what he thought was a much truer version of the history of the revolutionary movement in his own colony than had been provided by others.

The sort of imperial approach to early American history presented by the writings of Boucher, Hutchinson, and Oliver, was neither desired nor needed by the American people engaged throughout the nineteenth century in the arduous task of consolidating the nation and adding to its prestige abroad. The trend was for early American history to be "patriotic" in the sense that it must glorify the American version of New World colonization together with the causes that finally led to revolution and the creation of the independent United States of America. Only when the nation had become powerful and confident about its great future, only when intolerance of views that did not harmonize with traditional interpretations of the past had given place to a large measure of tolerance—based upon a growing critical spirit that went hand in hand with a growing intellectual maturity—was there a change. It was only at this point that a welcome was given to books that looked at American colonial history within the larger context of the history of the expansion of England and the growth of the first British Empire.

Thus, not until toward the close of the nineteenth century was any American scholar beyond the Loyalist generation moved to deal with the history of the American colonies forthrightly as aspects of the early history of the British Empire. This departure came in the form of a master's thesis written by George Louis Beer, who had studied under John W. Burgess, Herbert L. Osgood, and E. R. A. Seligman at Columbia College (later University). It carried the title of *The Commercial Policy of England toward the American Colonies* and was published in 1893 as one of the *Studies in History, Economics and Public Laws* sponsored by the faculty of political science of the College. This slender volume was concerned with one of the most highly controversial and difficult themes in English colonial history. Nevertheless, Beer wrote with such discriminating judgment and in such a spirit of detachment that the work has retained the respect of scholars.[17] A much more important and detailed study in the same field came from Beer's pen in 1907, when *British Colonial Policy, 1754-1765* was issued. This exhibited a bias in favor neither of the American colonies nor of Great Britain. Thus in dealing with the issue that arose over the Stamp Act, it stated:

In its broader phase, the fundamental question at issue was the political independence of the American colonies. . . . This movement [for independence] came into violent conflict with British imperialism, whose aim was to increase the administrative efficiency of the Empire. Both the British and the colonial ideals were justifiable from their respective viewpoints, each one being in harmony with one of the two underlying tendencies in modern historical evolution.[18]

It also gave due emphasis to the fact that the movement for American political independence was inevitably bound up with another historical event of no less importance—the downfall of French power in North America. Nor could Beer's statement respecting the taxation of the colonies by Parliament be easily improved. As to the right of Parliament to do so, he wrote:

From the legal standpoint, this view was unassailable. It was somewhat vulnerable from the historical standpoint, as Parliament had hitherto not exercised all its legal powers, notably that of taxation. It [Parliament], however, totally failed to take into account that the colonies were growing to political maturity, and that they resented the idea of subordination implied in the doctrine of parliamentary supremacy.[19]

In reviewing Beer's *Commercial Policy*, Professor Charles H. Hull of Cornell University stressed the point that it differed radically, both in approach and method, from all other works concerned with the same period of history and added that these "differences, with scarcely an exception, are to Mr. Beer's credit and to his reader's profit." Before closing his review, Hull paid final tribute to the volume with the statement that "upon its own direct subject it is not only unrivalled but unapproached. . . ."[20]

The following year came Beer's *The Origins of the British Colonial System, 1578-1660,* and in 1912 *The Old Colonial System, 1660-1754. Part I, The Establishment of the System, 1660-1688.* Both of these works display the same mastery of the sources, the same capacity to give a lucid interpretation of the data they presented, and the same spirit of impartiality. In recognition of the merits of the two volumes, they received in 1913 the Loubat Prize "for the best original work published in the English language on the history, geography, archaeology, ethnology, philology, or numismatics of North America during the preceding five years." Unhappily, Part II, that would have traced the evolution of the system from 1689 to 1754, was unfinished at the time of Beer's death in 1920.

Professor Curtis Nettels, while critical of certain aspects of Beer's work, nevertheless stated the generally accepted view of scholars in 1933 when he affirmed that the "writings of G. L. Beer have probably exerted a greater influence in shaping modern views of early British colonial policy than the works of any other historian."[21] However, the general criticism of Beer's work voiced by other colonial historians was that he placed such emphasis on the economic features of the British colonial system, that he tended to slight other aspects of equal importance.

Beer was undoubtedly deeply influenced by Herbert Levi Osgood under whom he studied at Columbia. As early as 1887 Osgood contributed to the *Political Science Quarterly* an article on "England and the Colonies" which supported the eighteenth-century British interpretation of the powers of Parliament and also took the position that the limitations which American colonials placed on these powers were revolutionary in nature.[22] This was followed by a paper presented at a meeting of the American Historical Association in 1898 in which Osgood questioned the soundness of any history of the American Revolution that did not take into account the various forces that brought the British Empire into existence and led to its growth. He also took the position that in any study of English expansion the "political and constitutional side" of it "should be given the first place, because it is only through law and political institutions that social forces become in the large sense operative."[23] Osgood's various articles bearing upon the broad theme of the beginning of the British Empire paved the way for his monumental *American Colonies in the Seventeenth Century* which appeared in three volumes between 1904 and 1907 and was written from the imperial approach. In his review of Volume III, Professor Charles M. Andrews called the series "the most important interpretation of our colonial history that has thus far been made."[24]

With this accomplished Osgood proceeded with the writing of *The American Colonies in the Eighteenth Century* and succeeded in carrying the story forward to 1760 before he passed away in 1918. Happily, under the editorship of his son-in-law, Dixon Ryan Fox, the work appeared in four volumes in 1924-25. While this history represents the most detailed account in existence of the thirteen colonies covering the years 1691 to 1760, the imperial relations are not stressed as forcibly as one was led to believe they would be—doubtless because the final chapters as planned were never written and also because Osgood undoubtedly expected to carry the story beyond 1763 and to include the American Revolution in a treatment that would have been based on the imperial approach.[25]

Osgood was followed by perhaps the greatest American colonial historian, Charles M. Andrews. The year 1912 saw the publication of his small volume, *The Colonial Period*. Popular in form but rich in content, it was not (unlike most earlier histories of the period) concerned primarily with the development of those colonies destined to form the nucleus of what later became the United States of America. For the creation and development of other English colonies in the New World were equally stressed. In the preface, Andrews had the following to say:

In dealing with [English] colonial history in general, three factors stand out for conspicuous treatment: the mother country, the colonies, and the relations between them. It has been customary in the past, when writing of the colonial period of American history, to minimize the importance of the first and last factors, and to lay stress, at least until the period of the Revolution is reached, upon the [North American English] colonies, their institutions, and life. I believe that the balance should be restored, and that if we are to understand the colonies, not only at the time of their revolt, but also throughout their history from the beginning, we must study the policy and administration at home and follow continuously the efforts which were made, on the side of Great Britain to hold the colonies in a state of dependence and on the side of the colonies to obtain a more or less complete control of their own affairs. Upon this belief I have acted in planning the arrangement of this book. . . . My further purpose has been to deal with the colonies in large measure from the vantage ground of their origin. To write as one standing among them and viewing them at close range is to crowd the picture and to destroy the perspective. We must study the colonies from some point outside of themselves, and to the scholar there is only one point of observation, that of the mother country from which they came and to whom they were legally subject.

His preface also explained why he felt obliged to bring into consideration other colonies than those that revolted:

No distinction existed between them in [American] colonial times and none should be made now by the writer on colonial history. To understand the events taking place in one group we must examine to a greater or less extent corresponding events in the others. Only by viewing the colonies as a whole and comparatively can a treatment be avoided which is merely provincial on one side or topical on the other.

Andrews's statement lays down certain canons for the writing of American colonial history which would be hard to improve upon—canons to which he sought to adhere in everything he wrote on the subject. But to think that because he adopted the British imperial approach he was pro-British in his interpretation of early American history would be a serious mistake. For example, his presidential address before the American Historical Association in 1925, "The American Revolution: An Interpretation,"[26] strongly justified the movement that led to the revolt of the American colonies; indeed, Andrews almost managed to exceed Bancroft in his castigation of the government of Great Britain. Typical was his concluding statement: "The American revolutionists had an ideal of living; it can hardly be said that in 1776 the Englishmen of the ruling classes were governed in their colonial relations by any ideals that were destined to be of service to the future of the human race."

Among Professor Andrews' many contributions in the field of colonial history his most important study was *The Colonial Period of American History*. As originally planned, it was to be a series of seven volumes that would cover the entire period of English colonization in the New World down to 1776. However, he was able to complete but four volumes, the first three of which are concerned entirely with the seventeenth century. Volume IV, carrying the subtitle *England's Commercial and Colonial Policy*, while also stressing developments in the earlier century, does give considerable attention to the maturing English policy in the eighteenth century. These volumes, a veritable storehouse of carefully organized information and scholarly critical comment, provide innumerable fresh insights into the history of English colonization; nevertheless, the omission of most of the history of the eighteenth century meant the neglect of some of the most important aspects of the story. It is as it

197

stands an incomplete series, just as is Osgood's on the eighteenth century.

Since restrictions on space make it impossible to deal with other works of distinction that may be categorized as having the imperial approach to early American history (regardless of whether or not they approve the imperial government's point of view), all that can be done is to list some of the more outstanding in the order of their appearance. They are as follows: Evarts B. Greene, *The Provincial Governor in the English Colonies of North America* (New York, 1898); Clarence E. Carter, *Great Britain and the Illinois Country, 1763-1774* (Washington, 1910); Winifred T. Root, *The Relations of Pennsylvania with the British Government, 1696-1765* (Philadelphia, 1912); Oliver M. Dickerson, *American Colonial Government, 1696-1765: A Study of the British Board of Trade in its Relation to the American Colonies, Political, Industrial, Administrative* (Cleveland, 1912); Clarence W. Alvord, *The Mississippi Valley in British Politics: A Study of the Trade, Land Speculation, and Experiments in Imperialism Culminating in the American Revolution* (2 vols., Cleveland, 1917); Viola F. Barnes, *The Dominion of New England: A Study in British Colonial Policy* (New Haven, 1923); Verner W. Crane, *The Southern Frontier, 1670-1732* (Philadelphia, 1929); Leonard W. Labaree, *Royal Government in America, a Study of the British Colonial System before 1783* (New Haven, 1930); Wesley F. Craven, *The Dissolution of the Virginia Company: the Failure of a Colonial Experiment* (New York, 1932); Lawrence A. Harper, *The English Navigation Laws: A Seventeenth-Century Experiment in Social Engineering* (New York, 1930); Max Savelle, *The Foundations of American Civilization: A History of Colonial America* (New York, 1942, and its revision in 1964, in which Robert Middlekauff participated, retitled simply *A History of Colonial America);* Oliver M. Dickerson, *The Navigation Acts and the American Revolution* (Philadelphia, 1951); Jack M. Sosin, *Whitehall and the Wilderness: The Middle West in British Colonial Policy, 1760-1775* (Lincoln, 1961); and Richard W. Van Alstyne, *Empire and Independence: The International History of the American Revolution* (New York, 1965). As for the series written by the author of this essay, *The British Empire before the American Revolution* (12 vols.+, Caldwell and New York, 1936-65+), the title itself dictates the inevitability of the imperial approach that has been used.

NOTES

[1]M. A. De Wolfe Howe, *The Life and Letters of George Bancroft* (2 vols., New York, 1908), I, 186.

[2]J. Franklin Jameson, *The History of Historical Writing in America* (Boston, 1891), 103.

[3]*History of the United States,* IV (Boston, 1852), 12.

[4]Jonathan Boucher, *A View of the Causes and Consequences of the American Revolution: In Thirteen Discourses, Preached in North America between the Years 1763 and 1775* (London, 1797), preface.

[5]*Ibid.,* 474.

[6]*Ibid.,* xl-xlii.

[7]*Ibid.,* 485-486.

[8]Moses Coit Tyler, *The Literary History of the American Revolution, 1763-1783* (New York, 1897), I, 320-321.

[9]For the latest edition of Hutchinson's works see *The History of the Colony and Province of Massachusetts Bay* (3 vols., Lawrence S. Mayo, ed., Cambridge, 1936); see also *Additions to Thomas Hutchinson's "History of Massachusetts Bay,"* (Catherine B. Mayo, ed., Worcester, 1949) reprinted from American Antiquarian Society *Proceedings,* LIX (1949), 11-74, which contains Hutchinson's own valuable addenda.

[10]*History* (Mayo edn.), I, 49-50.

[11]*Ibid.,* III, 63-64, 90-91, 194-201, 303-315.

[12]For Deane's paper on "Hutchinson's Historical Publication," see the Massachusetts Historical Society *Proceedings,* III (1857), 134-150.

[13]*Life of Thomas Hutchinson, Royal Governor of the Province of Massachusetts Bay* (Boston, 1896), 87-88.

[14]Douglass Adair and John A. Schutz, eds., *Peter Oliver's Origin & Progress of the American Rebellion: A Tory View* (San Marino, 1961), 26.

[15]*Ibid.,* 35-45.

[16]*Ibid.,* 3.

[17]A new edition of this work was published in 1948.

[18]George Louis Beer, *British Colonial Policy, 1754-1765* (New York, 1907), 314-315

[19]*Ibid.,* 311-312.

[20]*American Historical Review,* XIV (1909), 817-819.

[21]*New England Quarterly,* VI (1933), 491.

[22]*Political Science Quarterly,* II (1887), 440-469.

[23]American Historical Association *Annual Report for 1898* (Washington, 1899), 63-76.

[24]*American Historical Review,* XIII (1908), 605-609.

[25]Dixon R. Fox, *Herbert Levi Osgood, An American Scholar* (New York, 1924), 59-65, 102-103.

[26]*American Historical Review,* XXXI (1926), 219-232.

The International Approach to
Early Angloamerican History

1492-1763

BY MAX SAVELLE[1]

If Lawrence Henry Gipson's work has demonstrated the validity of the imperial approach to early American history, that of Max Savelle has gone a step further in showing that scholars must view the colonies as a segment of the vast international world of their day. Agreeing that the relationship of the colonies to other parts of the empire is important, he proves that their relationships to each other and to the nations of Europe also shaped their history as well as contributing to important legal precedents. Professor Savelle has distilled these important conclusions from a lifetime of interest in the early history of the Americas. Educated at Columbia University, he has taught at Stanford University and since 1947 at the University of Washington; he used the resources of the Huntington Library first in 1946 and has been a frequent visitor since that time. In the stimulating essay that is his tribute to John E. Pomfret, he draws upon materials from his forthcoming volume on THE INTERNATIONAL HISTORY OF ANGLO-AMERICA, 1492-1763 *to reveal the fresh understanding of early American history made possible by projecting the colonies into the international scene.*

THE INVOLVEMENT OF AMERICA in the web of international relations among the Atlantic community of states has been important and constant from the very beginning of this continent's history.[2] It began at the moment when Columbus, driven by a storm into the Tagus River on his return to Europe from his first voyage, was haled into the presence of King John of Portugal and accused by the King of having trespassed upon Portugal's exclusive colonial sphere as recognized by the Castilian-Portuguese Treaty of Alcaçovas of 1479. One result of this interview, as is well known, was King Ferdinand II's appeal to Pope Alexander VI for a confirmation of Castilian ownership of the lands Columbus had discovered, an appeal that induced the Pope to issue, in 1493, four bulls recognizing Spain's claim and dividing the "New World" between the two kingdoms by a line drawn from the north pole to the south pole one hundred leagues west of the Azores Islands.

From that moment on, throughout the colonial period, America occupied an increasingly important place in the international history of the western world. It is, indeed, difficult to understand the history of colonial Angloamerica without a constant reference to this context.

In the international history of Angloamerica in the colonial period there are to be seen two parallel but generally interlocking streams of events, developments, and ideas. One of these was the course of European diplomatic exchanges with regard to America; the other was the intercolonial contacts and quasi-diplomatic exchanges that took place among the various sets of European colonies in America itself.

In the course of European international exchanges relative to America many subjects were discussed, such as rival territorial claims, European commerce with colonial empires, questions having to do with the freedom of the seas, and so on, and certain principles of international law and custom were formulated, always in the interest of the citizens of the European countries involved. Along the "great frontier" in America intercolonial, quasi-diplomatic exchanges were concerned with such local matters as boundaries and the national ownership of territories, fisheries, missionaries, Indian trade and alliances, and intercolonial commerce, licit and illicit. These exchanges, especially after the Peace of Utrecht of 1713, exposed the specific local issues that provided the factual groundwork for the demands of the mother countries upon each other in Europe. In general, the claims made by English colonies against non-English colonies, or the reverse, were claims made in the interest of the colonies themselves. Nearly always, the local intercolonial objectives of the colonies became parts of the diplomatic objectives of the mother countries. In only one major area of intercolonial relations, that of commerce, did the international objectives of the colonies run counter to the diplomatic objectives as well as to the laws of the mother countries, and that was because the commercial needs and ambitions of the colonies stood in positions essentially of economic rivalry with those of the mother countries. Thus it was that whereas, in most areas other than that of commerce, the international objectives and policies of the colonies coincided with those of the mother countries, they were not always identical, since the American objectives were formulated to serve American, rather than European interests. Indeed, a colony might differ from the mother country, and often did, in its policy with regard to any particular local or colonial issue. It was out of this circumstance that there appeared in the colonies certain diplomatic inclinations, or policies, that may properly be called American, as distinguished from English or European policies.

I

European diplomacy with regard to America in the sixteenth, seventeenth, and eighteenth centuries was a diplomacy of rival colonial empires.

The first of these imperial rivalries was between Portugal and Spain over their respective domains in Africa, the Far East, and America. It began in conflicting claims to the coast of Africa explored by Prince Henry the Navigator's captains and to the Canary Islands, earlier granted to a Spanish nobleman, Luis de Cerda, by Pope Clement VI. The "new world," as it came to be explored, was divided between Spain and Portugal by a series of papal bulls, beginning in 1455 and running well into the sixteenth century, and by the Hispano-Portuguese treaties of Alcaçovas (1479), which awarded the Canaries to Spain and the African coast to Portugal, of Tordesillas (1494), which drew a line through the Atlantic, from pole to pole three hundred seventy degrees west of the Cape Verde Islands, the lands west of which were assigned to Spain and the lands east of which to Portugal; and of Saragossa (1529), by which a similar line was drawn in the Pacific seventeen degrees east of the Moluccas, a line of longitude that was supposed to pass through the islands of Santo Tomé de las Velas.

In the course of this imperial rivalry, the first to be concerned with non-European lands lying about the Atlantic basin, there were formulated certain principles of international relations and custom, relative to colonies, that were to underly European diplomacy relative to America for centuries.

Out of the disputes over the ownership of territories there emerged the basic and generally accepted proposition that prior discovery of hitherto unknown territory gave prior title of national ownership of that territory. Not only that, the ownership of overseas territory was understood to convey with it national title to the natives of those territories and to the oceans over which the sea routes to the colonies lay. Thus, for example, after the Treaty of Tordesillas Portugal understood—and Spain agreed—that the oceans east of the "Line" over which Portuguese ships must pass in going to the Portuguese colonies in Africa and India belonged exclusively to Portugal, and that oceans west of the Line, over which Spanish ships must pass en route to and from Spanish colonies west of the Line, belonged exclusively to Spain.

Once a territory was effectively occupied by a colonizing power and its ownership of that territory recognized, tacitly or explicitly, by the other imperial powers, the state owning the territory or colony customarily sealed it off from penetration, for trade or any other purpose, by citizens of other empires. It was generally recognized that the trade of the colony was the exclusive, monopolistic property of the mother country, and it was one of the international tenets of mercantilism that the colonies and their economies existed chiefly for the profit of the mother countries. The commerce of colonies was expected to enrich the mother countries; presently the colonial commerce of any European state came to be thought of as the most important determinant of its national wealth and, therefore, of the mother country's position in the scales of the international balance of power in Europe. Colonial commerce, therefore, was of prime national interest in the diplomatic exchanges among European powers, and the stringent closing of the doors of the commerce of their colonies to all foreigners was undertaken in the interest of the mercantile doctrine that such commerce should be a national monopoly.

Similarly, it was generally agreed, in these early stages of the evolution of European diplomacy with regard to the new world, that the religion of the colonies should be the religion of the mother country. In the case of the Iberian powers, although both were Roman Catholic, the principle of national monopoly still held: the religious conversion and development of an acquired colonial area was generally entrusted to religious orders of national character and connections. Thus the imperial rivalries of the maritime powers was religious and cultural as well as political and economic.

The Iberian paper monopoly of the entire new world "discovered and to be discovered," could not be expected long to stand unchallenged. In the realm of diplomacy the challenge came in the repudiation of the monopoly by French, English, and Dutch governments, their diplomatic representatives, and their theorists. Such, for example, was Francis I's sarcastic quip at the preposterous claims of the Iberian powers: "The sun shines for me as well as for others; I should like to see the clause in Adam's will that excludes me from the division of the world."[3]

Similarly, when the Duke of Mendoza, the Spanish ambassador, protested to Queen Elizabeth Francis Drake's violation of Spain's *mare nostrum* in the eastern Pacific, Elizabeth replied bluntly that

For that their [the Spaniards] having touched only here and there upon a coast, and given names to a few rivers or capes, were such insignificant things as could in no ways entitle them to a propriety further than in the parts where they actually settled and continued to inhabit.[4]

In thus stating the doctrine of effective occupation, subsequently to be accepted by all of the colonizing powers, Queen Elizabeth was also informing the Iberian monopolists that England would not recognize, any more than France, their self-awarded monopoly of the new world. It was precisely upon the basis of this doctrine, indeed, that King James I was to justify to Philip III of Spain the occupation of the lands upon which was founded the colony of Virginia.

Out of the conflicts over the new world, and particularly out of the French, English, Dutch and other challenges to the Hispano-Portuguese monopoly, there also appeared the proposition that Europe was one sphere of international institutions, law, and custom and that the new world of the colonies, beyond European waters, was another. This was the so-called "doctrine of the two spheres," under the terms of which, for example, treaties between two European states did not necessarily apply to the colonies or special treaties relative to America might be made between two such powers which did not apply to Europe. More informally, under this doctrine, it was understood that seizures of ships, violent disputes over territory or trade, or other conflicts in the new world "beyond the lines of amity" were not necessarily to be taken as causes for war in Europe.

This doctrine was made explicit, for example, at the time of the Franco-Spanish Treaty of Cateau-Cambrésis (1559), where it was orally agreed that

They [the French] would not go to the lands possessed by your Majesty [Philip II of Spain] and by the King of Portugal, or that one would abide by the terms of past treaties, according to which the Indies are not mentioned, and if they [the French] were found doing anything there that they should not be doing, they would be punished. . . . We [the Spanish negotiators] declared to them [the French] that if they went there in time of peace, one [the Spaniards] would throw them into the sea, with the understanding that this action would not be thought a contravention of the treaties of friendship between us. . . .[5]

The "doctrine of the two spheres" continued for centuries to be one of the basic principles of European diplomacy relative to America. It was explicitly written into the Anglo-Spanish Treaty of Madrid of 1670, the Aglo-French Treaty of Whitehall of 1686, and the Hispano-Portuguese Treaty of Madrid of 1750. But it was also invoked by the colonies themselves in such treaties as that of Sandy Point, St. Christopher (1678), by which the English and French colonists agreed to remain neutral in case of war between their mother countries in Europe. It was this doctrine, and the experiences that substantiated it on both sides of the Atlantic, that provided a host of precedents in the colonial period for the basic principle contained in the famous pronouncement of President James Monroe in 1823.

It was not, however, until the other maritime states of western Europe achieved colonial empires of their own that they became deadly rivals both of the Iberian empires and each other. This situation became a condition of fact in the seventeenth century, in the course of which England, France, Holland, Denmark, and Sweden established colonies in territories formerly claimed by Spain or Portugal. Much of European diplomacy with regard to America in that century, therefore, was concerned with the settlement of these new colonies and their relations with the colonies of other countries. Such, for example, was the diplomatic duel between England and Spain over the settlement of Virginia, or that between England and France on the one side and Spain on the other over the occupation of the islands in the West Indies, or that between Holland and Sweden over their respective colonies around Delaware Bay.

Actually, it was only under duress, and very slowly, that Spain and Portugal were led even to admit that other countries had a right to send ships to the new world. The first breach in the monopoly was made in 1609, in the Twelve Years Truce between Spain and Holland, in which, in carefully veiled language in which the Indies were not mentioned, Spain finally admitted the right of the Dutch to sail, for the purposes of trade, to the "lands of all other princes, potentates, and peoples who are willing to permit them to do so," which really meant the countries in the East and West Indies not actually under the domination of Spain.

The breach was widened in the Dutch-Spanish Treaty of Münster (1648), by which Spain agreed specifically that

The Navigation and trade in the East and West Indies shall be maintained as under present arrangements [that is, the charters of the Dutch East India Company and the Dutch West India Company] or under contracts to be made later, . . . and the King [of Spain] and the Estates-General, respectively, shall remain in the possession and enjoyment of the . . . commerce and the countries in the East and West Indies, as also in Brazil and on the coasts of Asia, Africa, and America respectively that the said King and Estates-General [now] have and possess.[6]

This surrender by Spain marked the beginning of the final end of the Hispano-Portuguese claim to a monopoly of the new world. The end did not come all at once, however, for it was not until the Anglo-Spanish "American" treaty of Madrid of 1670 that Spain made the same concession to England. Even so, Spain was still not ready to admit the right of England, France, or Holland to seize unoccupied lands in America that were claimed by Spain, and continued to protest the occupation of islands in the West Indies, as well as of Georgia, well into the eighteenth century.

All of the non-Iberian challengers of the Hispano-Portuguese colonial monopoly were heavily involved in overseas commerce, and all, following the precedent set by the Iberians, closed their colonies, with varying degrees of tightness and rigidity, to commercial contact with foreigners. Such a mechanism of exclusion or semi-exclusion, for example, was the English system of laws of navigation and trade. Spain, France, Holland, Sweden, and Denmark all had similar systems of national regulation and control, although they varied in specific application and in the rigidity with which they were enforced.

It thus fell out that a significant portion of the diplomatic correspondence of western European states relative to their American colonies in the seventeenth century was concerned with commercial relations with or between colonies. Such a correspondence was that between England and the Netherlands in the middle of the seventeenth century, in which the Dutch sought to procure some sort of relaxation of the English navigation laws that might enable them to continue their lucrative trade with the English colonies in North America.

Many European treaties were made, in the seventeenth century, providing for and regulating commerce between the subjects of the signatory nations. Most of these commercial treaties were understood not to apply to America. They did, however, as in the case of the Anglo-Dutch marine treaty of 1674, define "contraband" and "non-contraband" goods, among which generally appeared such American products as tobacco, sugar, and dye-woods. They also contained the principle that "free ships make free goods," which was calculated to establish in international law the right of a neutral nation to trade with belligerents in time of war.

It was out of the activities of colonial commerce, also, that there emerged the classic expression of the doctrine of the freedom of the seas, formulated by Hugo Grotius in 1609. This principle, even before Grotius, was one of the chief bases of the English claim to the right of going to America in the first place, and, later, to the exemption of English and colonial ships upon the high seas from search and seizure by Spanish *guarda-costas* in the bitter years of controversy that preceded the War of Jenkins' Ear.

Although the interest of all the European states with colonies in America was focused chiefly upon the contributions to the national wealth that the colonies could make, whether derived from commerce, from the production of raw material not produced in the mother country, or from the mining of gold and silver, European diplomatic interest in America was not solely economic or purely mercantilistic. For there were strong elements of imperialism for its own sake, of political or dynastic interest, of nationalism, and of religion present in the thinking of most European statesmen relative to America, throughout the colonial period.

Thus, it was by reason of a combination of motives that the European colonial empires became world-wide rivals, and European diplomacy with regard to them was a diplomacy of nationalistic and imperialistic rivalries. In the course of such rivalries England came almost to eliminate the Dutch from the colonial world in America and to dominate the American colonial commerce of Portugal. The Dutch had already absorbed the Swedish holdings on the Delaware when England seized New Netherland; the Danish colonies in America (the Virgin Islands) were claimed by both Spain and England, but they were never very significant in the total panorama of European imperial rivalries in America. As the eighteenth century dawned, only the French and British American empires were active and aggressively expansive. The Spanish Empire, while not exactly moribund, was somewhat less than a rival of the other two. Indeed, France and England were both seeking to expand in America at Spain's expense, or, at the very least, to reap the greatest possible profit from Spanish colonial commerce.

But no colonial empire was to be allowed to become so large as, by contributing an overwhelming national wealth to any single state, to give that state an inordinately preponderant weight in the balance of power in Europe. As François de Salignac de la Mothe Fénélon, Archbishop of Cambrai, wrote, about the end of the seventeenth century, "Anything that upsets the balance [of power among the nations], and which gives any nation a decisive power to establish a universal monarchy, cannot be just, even though it be founded on the written laws of a particular country." The careful maintenance of this sort of equality and balance among the nations, he wrote, assured the common security.[7]

The greatest and most tempting American plum to appear in the second half of the seventeenth century had been the American segment of the Spanish inheritance, which began to dangle before the eyes of European imperialists from the moment of the accession of the childless and ailing Carlos II to the throne of Spain. The American possessions of Spain had been promised to one after another of a number of aspiring monarchs between 1668 and 1698, but Carlos had reversed the field by making a will, prior to his death in 1700, which left all his kingdoms and territories, *in toto* and including Spanish America, to Philip of Anjou, the grandson of Louis XIV. Since Philip was potentially an heir to the throne of France, in the fear that he might one day rule over both France and Spain and all their dominions and, thereby, upset the balance of power both in Europe and America, the other aspirants to parts of the Spanish inheritance organized themselves into the Grand Alliance of 1701 to prevent Philip from ascending the throne of Spain.

The maintenance of the balance of power, then, both in Europe and in America, was the chief reason for the so-called War of the Spanish Succession. As the allies stated it in the treaty of the Grand Alliance, since

the Kingdoms of France and Spain are so closely united [by the naming of Philip, Duke of Anjou, as Carlos II's heir] that . . . the French and Spaniards being thus joined will in a short time become so formidable to all that they may easily arrogate to themselves empires all over Europe, . . . and since France and Spain are taking advantage of this state of affairs to unite more and more closely for suppressing the liberty of Europe and destroying trade, . . .

the signatories have been forced to take military action and to form a close alliance to prevent any such upset of the balance of power, whether in Europe or in the new world.

The war that followed, the War of the Spanish Succession, was, on final balance, a victory for the allies. By the Peace of Utrecht (1713) Philip was admitted to the Spanish throne, but he was forced to forswear any future claim he might have to the throne of France. As for America, Philip was required to promise in the Anglo-Spanish treaty of peace never to alienate any part of the Spanish American empire, to France or any other nation. England, on its side, undertook to guarantee the territorial integrity of Spain's American colonies.

At the same time, in the Anglo-French treaty of Utrecht Louis XIV was required to make a similar disclaimer, to the effect that he renounced any

intention to try to obtain or even in the future to accept for the benefit of his subjects that anything be changed or that innovations be made, either in Spain or in Spanish America, whether in matters of commerce or in matters of navigation, from the usages practiced in those countries under the reign of the late King of Spain Charles Second. . . .[8]

Thus England, in the name of the balance of European power, forced upon Spain and France its own eighteenth-century analogue of the Monroe Doctrine for the preservation of the territorial *status quo* in Spanish-America.

More specifically, by the Anglo-French Treaty of Utrecht England was ceded vast territories in America by France—Hudson Bay, Newfoundland, Acadia, and St. Christopher, along with a vague recognition of Britain's suzerainty over the Iroquois Indians, while Spain granted to the English South Sea Company the *Asiento,* or contract for supplying slaves to the Spanish colonies, along with certain very promising commercial privileges in Spanish America. Thus, while the Peace of Utrecht, by preventing the union of the crowns of France and Spain, ostensibly preserved the balance of power in Europe, its provisions, with regard to America rather sharply tilted the balance in England's favor in the western hemisphere. The theory of the European balance, however, along with its corollary, the idea that the balance of power in Europe depended upon the balance of colonial and commercial power in America, continued to be one of the major principles in the conduct of eighteenth-century European diplomacy dealing with colonial matters. As the Duke of Newcastle put it, speaking to the House of Lords on May 2, 1738, if no nation had a monopoly of the Spanish colonies or their trade, all European states benefit from it equally,

Whereas, should too large a share of them [the Spanish colonies] come into the hands of any other nation in Europe... they might be employed to purposes inconsistent with the peace of Europe, and which might one day prove fatal to the balance of power, that ought to subsist amongst her several princes.

A combination of other states would inevitably be formed against the strong one.[9]

In the three decades following the Peace of Utrecht the "Concert of Europe" gave attention to many of the conflicts among the European nations over their possessions in the colonial world.

Actually, Europe did not achieve a full pacification until some seven years after Utrecht, because Spain and Austria were still in armed disagreement over their respective claims in Italy. But France and England drew together in 1716 in an alliance for the maintenance of the balance of power, and this alliance presently grew into the Quadruple Alliance by the accession of the Netherlands and Austria. The Alliance invited Spain to make peace, but Spain refused. On the contrary, it attempted to seize by force certain territories it claimed in Italy, and the Alliance resorted to war in 1718 and 1719 to force Spain to accept its peace terms. Spain finally acceded to the Alliance in 1720.

By the terms of the general treaty, the details of peace were left to be settled at a Congress to be held at Cambrai, in France. The treaty did, however, embody a general agreement to the mutual suppression of the activities of corsairs against the commerce of the signatories; the signatories also agreed to protect each other's territories. The colonies were not specifically mentioned, but it would appear from the wording of the treaty and its annexes that these provisions were expected to apply to the commerce and the territories in America and in other parts of the world.

With the accession of Spain to the Quadruple Alliance and its acceptance of the terms of peace, France, England, and Spain drew together, and there ensued a series of complicated negotiations in 1721 relative to the colonies of the three powers in America. By the Franco-Spanish treaty, after much dickering with regard to American possessions, Pensacola, seized by France during the short war, was returned to Spain. Similarly, after much haggling over England's proposal to give Gibraltar back to Spain in return for some American territory, the Anglo-Spanish treaty of friendship provided only for a renewal of the *Asiento,* although the British guarantee of the territorial integrity of the Spanish colonies in America contained in the Peace of Utrecht was repeated. Other disputes, either between Spain and France or between Spain and England, were referred to the Congress of Cambrai.

The Congress of Cambrai was eventually held in 1724, and representatives of France, Spain, and England went prepared to debate their American disputes. But the Congress bogged down in matters of protocol, and the attention of England and the Netherlands was diverted to the business of getting the Emperor of Austria to abolish the Ostend Company, a company founded in the Austrian Netherlands to procure for Austria a share of the rich profits of the colonial trade. Because of certain vicissitudes of European international politics, the Congress of Cambrai presently dissolved in confusion, and Spain made an alliance with Austria for mutual defense of the commerce and territories of the two signatories, "whether on this or the other side of the Line," with special privileges and encouragements provided for the Ostend Company.

The Austro-Spanish Alliance of 1725 presented the threat of a new general European war, and led to the formation of a new alliance, called the Alliance of Hanover. Hostility, never entirely ended, flared up between England and Spain in the Caribbean area, and Europe stood once more on the brink of war. Thanks, however, to the efforts of Cardinal Fleury, now the ruling minister in France, the members of the "Concert of Europe" were once more brought to the conference table, this time at Soissons, near Paris. Again, after endless wrangling over European and American questions, this Congress, also, arrived at a stalemate, chiefly because of the obstinacy of Spain. But the stalemate was broken by the collapse of the Austro-Spanish alliance of 1725, and Spain finally acceded to the terms proposed by the Congress in the Treaty of Seville, signed by France, England, and Spain on November 9, 1729.

By the terms of this treaty, Spain and England promised to make mutual restitution for damages done each other in America; other claims and counter-claims were to be adjudicated by a joint commission; the *Asiento* granted to England in 1713 was specifically reviewed. But Spain had acceded to the Treaty of Seville chiefly as a concession to France and England in return for their support of Spain's effort to seat Don Carlos, eldest son of Queen Elizabeth Farnese, upon the ducal thrones of Parma, Placentia, and Tuscany. The settlement of colonial disputes in America was thus linked to the dynastic disputes of Spain and Austria in Italy.

When England and France procrastinated in effectuating the terms of the Treaty of Seville relative to Italy, Spain threatened to denounce that treaty. But England saved the day by making a treaty of friendship with Austria by which Austria agreed to a final dissolution of the Ostend Company and an acquiescence in the occupation of the ducal thrones by Don Carlos, in return for England's acceptance of the Emperor's Pragmatic Sanction assuring the Crown of Austria to his daughter, Maria Theresa, after Charles VI's death. Once this was achieved, Don Carlos proceeded to Italy and the Anglo-Spanish commission for the adjudication of American disputes could proceed—which it did, without success.

With the outbreak of the War of the Polish Succession, France, isolated by the Anglo-Austrian Treaty of 1731, fearing England might side with Austria, and needing the aid of Spain, turned to that country for aid, and signed with it the so-called Bourbon Family Compact. This treaty was ostensibly an alliance between France and Spain against Austria; but here, again, the American interests of the two signatories were tied to the dynastic ambitions of the European powers. For the compact was aimed, so far as Spain was concerned, chieflly at England, and it provided that France would assist Spain, both in Europe and in America, should England attack Spain. Should Spain, because of English abuse of its commercial privileges in Spanish America, see fit to suspend those privileges, and should England therefore begin hostilities against Spain or its colonies, France would make common cause with Spain against England. At the same time, France was granted most-favored-nation treatment in the commerce of Spanish America conducted through Cadiz, and Spain agreed to ameliorate French complaints, whether pertaining to ships seized, commerce at Cadiz, or territorial conflicts in America.

England did not join in the War of the Polish Succession. But France and Spain remained allies, with France generally supporting Spain's complaints relative to America against England and assuming a role of benevolent neutrality in the Anglo-Spanish War of Jenkins' Ear that broke out in 1739.

Meanwhile, after the Peace of Utrecht, the French and British empires had emerged as the two great contestants for the domination of North America. They faced each other along the entire continent, from Canada to the Gulf of Mexico and across the Caribbean to the coast of South America. Despite the Anglo-French entente in Europe that lasted, roughly, from 1716 to 1731, in all the areas in America where French colonies confronted English colonies—Acadia, the Lakes area, the Ohio Valley, the lower Mississippi Valley, and the West Indies—conditions of conflict at times approximating actual warfare existed throughout the third and fourth decades of the eighteenth century. Neither the Anglo-French joint commission of 1719 nor the joint commission of 1750, both created for the purpose, was able to settle these disputes; that settlement had to await the final adjudication of war in the Peace of Paris of 1763. It was this peace that, once and for all, ended the Anglo-French diplomatic contest for domination of America by the almost total elimination of France from possession of any significant parts of the hemisphere. It was this peace, also, that marked the end of the European phase of the international history of Angloamerica during the colonial period. From this date onward, the international history of Angloamerica centers about the history of the independent United States of America.

If the imperial rivalry of France and England was a rivalry for the domination of territory, the commercial aspects of the relations of the two empires in America amounted almost to a conflict between the two mother countries on one side and the English and French colonies on the other.

It is true that, from the point of view of the mother countries, the imperial policies of each of the metropoli were identified with the expansion of the interests of the national commerce. Indeed, it is difficult to distinguish between the direct profit motives of merchants, such as those who composed the English Hudson's Bay Company and the South Sea Company, and the high policy of government. Both these commercial companies participated directly in the diplomatic negotiations of their government relative to the areas of America in which they were interested. Their interest, of course, was in profits, and hardly anything more. But the statesmen who planned and conducted national diplomatic policies were mercantilists who reasoned that the expansion of the national commerce in America would redound to the benefit of the whole nation. Thus the English diplomats fought at Utrecht for the whole of Hudson Bay, with its fur trade, and at Madrid for the *Asiento,* with the rich anticipated profits to be derived from the trades that would be conducted under it. Thereafter, throughout the eighteenth century, English international policy with regard to America was focused upon the promotion of the expansion of imperial commerce. France, on the other hand, excluded from the *Asiento* by the Peace of Utrecht, directed its diplomacy with Spain relative to American commerce toward controlling a major share of the commerce of the Spanish empire that flowed through Cadiz, while it constantly reminded the Spanish rulers of the extent and the unscrupulousness of the English contraband trade with the Spanish colonies, conducted by Englishmen and Angloamericans, both under cover of the *Asiento* and apart from it.

But English international colonial policy directed at expanding the commerce of the Empire involved the effective enforcement of the English laws of trade and navigation, just as France's international policy with regard to its own colonies was thought to involve the rigid enforcement of prohibitions upon the foreign trade of the French colonies. When it came to enforcing their systems of commercial control in the colonies, however, both France and England had to face the open violation of their systems by their own colonists. If France and England failed to achieve the great colonial commercial monopolies they sought, that was less because of their rivalry with each other than because of the nullification of their restrictive laws by the colonists in America.

It is to be noted that all of the diplomatic policies and practices of the European colonizing powers having to do with colonies derived from the interest of the mother countries, and had little or no regard for the interests of the colonists or of the natives in the colonies. The rights of the aborigines, however, were not without their defenders, for there appeared in Spain an extraordinary group of legal theorists—Francisco de Vittoria, Francisco Suarez, Luis de Molina, Domingo da Soto and others—who raised embarrassing question of international law relative to title to new countries by conquest, the rights of the aborigines, and limitations upon forced religious conversion. The theories of these great jurists, although of great significance in the history of international law, had little or no practical effect upon the conduct of international relations.

In other areas, however, the formulation of a body of international law and custom was a direct outgrowth of the experiences of the European states in their rivalries and conflicts with each other in the colonial world. Out of the Hispano-Portuguese monopoly, for example, came the principle of the "closed door" in colonial empires. Out of the French, English, and Dutch challenges to that monopoly came the principle of the freedom of the seas and the doctrine of effective occupation. Out of the disputes over participation in colonial commerce came, in part, at least, the doctrines of the rights of neutrals, "free ships make free goods," definitions of "contraband" and "non-contraband," the British "Rule of the War of 1756" and "doctrine of continuous voyage." Out of the many efforts to solve colonial disputes by joint commission or by arbitration there came a general acceptance of the idea that colonial disputes might be settled by peaceful methods, although there is no record of any international dispute with regard to America that was actually resolved in that way.

II

In contrast to the history of European diplomacy relative to America, the history of the international relations of Angloamerica itself was a history of the direct contacts between the Angloamerican colonies and the French, Dutch, Swedish, Portuguese, Spanish, and Danish colonies in the hemisphere and the correspondence, the agreements and disagreements, and the intercolonial treaties that were produced by them.

These international contacts among the European colonies during the seventeenth century arose out of local situations, and the agreements and correspondences that grew out of them were made or conducted by Americans on the spot, often entirely without or with a minimum of instruction from Europe. They sprang from the needs of the Americans themselves and were calculated to promote American interests. Not only that, in the course of the history of the contacts of the Angloamerican colonies with their neighbors there were formulated certain generalized principles or policies that represented the long-term interests of the Americans, although those principles of colonial self-interest did not always coincide exactly with the principles governing the international relations of the mother country. Thus, in the Treaty of Boston between Massachusetts and Acadia (1644) and in the negotiations surrounding it there were clearly enunciated the principles of freedom of trade and of the freedom of the seas; in the Treaty of Hartford between the New England Confederation and New Netherland (1650) is to be seen the importance of territorial expansion of the colonies; into the Virginia-New Netherland Treaty of 1660 there was written a principle of freedom of commerce that ran directly counter to the British Navigation Act of the same year and the English position in the Anglo-Dutch negotiations going on in Europe at the same time.

In the eighteenth century, and especially after the Peace of Utrecht, there were fewer directly negotiated agreements between colonies. But there was a vast amount of correspondence between English governors and French, Spanish, Dutch, and Danish governors, a correspondence that constituted a corpus of international negotiation, as it were, on the frontiers of empires.[10] The colonial governor became, in reality, a diplomatic agent of his mother country, operating semi-independently in the field. In the eighteenth century the governor was more closely bound by his instructions than had been the case earlier, but, more often than not, his instructions relative to his correspondence with the governors of neighboring foreign colonies were based upon reports of the local situations that he, himself, had made to his home government and recommendations that he had suggested as to the international policies to be followed, locally or in Europe. The colonial governor was thus no mere agent in the field executing the wishes of his home government, based purely upon the interests of his mother country; he was, in fact, and in a number of ways, the instrument of American inter-colonial contacts and a formulator of international policies to be followed with regard to them. The situations he reported were local, and often had no direct connection with diplomatic negotiations in Europe. The self-interests he served in the recommendations he made, while usually integrated, in his mind, with those of his empire as a whole, were local, American self-interests, and the mother country was expected by the Americans to use its European diplomatic machinery to promote their interests—as it usually, but not always, did. The American colonial frontiers, then, whether the frontiers of commerce, of fishing, of territorial expansion, or of relations of the colonies with the Indians, were, in this sense, the matrix in which the origin and the gestation both of European diplomatic policies with regard to America and of later international policies of the United States took place.

The governor-to-governor relations between the governors of the Angloamerican colonies and those of the neighboring foreign colonies were concerned with many issues. Rival imperial claims to territory and the boundaries between empires loomed large in this corpus of colony-to-colony correspondence, and the territorial rivalry on the continent of North America had its Caribbean counterpart in rival claims to the ownership of hitherto unoccupied islands. But much of this intercolonial correspondence, especially in the West Indies, also had to do with commerce, licit and illicit; much was concerned with relations with the Indians, piracy, the seizure of ships thought to be violating territorial waters, freedom of the seas, and so on. It was often concerned with military matters, such as fortifications, Indian alliances, and the exchange of prisoners. But it was often concerned, also, with the legal or religious rights of national or cultural minorities in ceded territories, the sending of missionaries to the Indians, and the transfer of populations.

The intercolonial disputes over territory in America began immediately after settlement. Governor Thomas Dale sent Captain Argall to destroy the French settlements in Acadia in 1613, in time of peace, because, as he claimed, the French on Mt. Desert Island and at Port Royal were trespassing in English territory. The area was seized again by the English in 1628, in the course of the Huguenot War, but it was returned to France by the Treaty of St. Germain-en-Laye in 1632. From that time on the ownership and extent of Acadia and the lands lying along the Bay of Fundy constituted an area of constant and bitter dispute between the English governors of the New England colonies and the French governors of Canada until the final cession of Canada itself to England by the Treaty of Paris in 1763. Similarly, the Dutch governors of New Netherland challenged the English title to Connecticut on the east and the Swedish title to Delaware on the south. After the English seized New York the English governors of that colony disputed for a century with the governors of French Canada the boundaries between New York and Canada. Out of those disputes there came the French claim to the watershed as a boundary, as against the English claim to the highly flexible boundaries marked only by the limits of lands owned by the Iroquois Indians, whom the English claimed as subjects of the British King under Article XV of the Anglo-French Treaty of Utrecht. As the population of the English seaboard colonies began to trickle over the Alleghenies into the valley of the Ohio, that valley became a base of intercolonial contention, culminating in the mission of George Washington from the colony of Virginia to the French commandant at Fort Le Boeuf in 1753. Farther south, the governors of Carolina and, later, Georgia, corresponded with the Spanish governors of Florida and Havana over the boundaries between English colonies and Florida and with the French governors of Louisiana and "Mississippi" over the Anglo-French boundary in that region. In the West Indies, governor corresponded and disputed with governor, especially after the Peace of Utrecht (1713), over the ownership of the Virgin Islands, St. Lucia, Dominica, St. Vincent's, Tobago, and others.

The territorial claims of the governors on both sides were invariably expansionist, while the protagonists on each side professed to believe that the other was consciously and diabolically determined to drive their people out of the hemisphere. This imperialistic rivalry reached a climax about the middle of the eighteenth century, when the English, beginning to flow over the Alleghenies, aroused in the French the dread of English domination. The most eloquent of the French Cassandras was the Marquis de la Galissonière, one-time governor of Canada. "Motives of honor, glory, and religion," he wrote in 1750, "forbid the abandonment of an established colony. . . ." Canada had always been a burden to France, and must be expected to continue such for a long time into the future, but it constituted "the strongest barrier that can be opposed to the ambition of the English." Canada alone was in a position to wage war against the English possessions, "possessions which are as dear to them as they are precious in fact, whose power is daily increasing, and which, if means be not found to prevent it, will soon absorb not only all the colonies located in the neighboring islands of the Tropic, but even all those of the continent of America."[11]

But the English felt almost exactly the same way about the French. The Albany Congress expressed its conviction in 1754,

That it is the Evident Design of the French to Surround the British Colonies, to fortifie themselves on the Back thereof, to take and keep Possession, of the heads of all the Important Rivers, to draw over the Indians to their Interest, and with the help of such Indians added to such Forces as are already arrived and may hereafter be sent from Europe to be in a Capacity of making a General Attack on the Several Governments, and if at the same time a Strong Naval Force be sent from France, there is the utmost danger that the whole Continent will be subjected to that Crown and that the Danger of such a Naval Force is not merely Imaginery....[12]

The Angloamericans were not only conscious of the continent-wide nature of the life-and-death territorial struggle of the two empires for the control of the continent of North America; their most aggressive leaders were out-and-out imperialists, determined to drive the French out of America; they urged the mother country to undertake the task; and they took pride in being associated with the mother-country in that enterprise. And always, it was the colonial governor who was, as it were, the aggressive activist leading the forces of the empire westward.

From the very beginning of their existence the American colonies of the European powers traded with each other. This commerce, wherever found, ran counter to the mercantilistic policies growing out of the doctrine of the monopolistic, "closed door" commercial and colonial policies of the mother countries, as illustrated by the English navigation laws or the rigid Spanish or French prohibitions of foreign trade in Spanish and French colonies. These "closed door" policies were mutually accepted by the European states, and were written into such treaties as the Anglo-Spanish Treaty of Madrid of 1670 and the Anglo-French Treaty of Whitehall of 1686. Even the Dutch were compelled by the British, in a series of treaties beginning with the Anglo-Dutch Treaty of Westminster of 1654, to recognize the "closed door" in the English colonies represented by the British Navigation Acts.

Despite the near unanimity of the European powers in their formal agreements, the "free" or "illicit" trade of English, French, Dutch, and Spanish colonies with each other flourished, especially after the Peace of Utrecht. For the Spanish and French colonies the trade with foreigners was clearly and entirely prohibited by law. For the English colonies, trade with French, Spanish, Dutch, or Danish colonies was not illicit except insofar as it might directly or indirectly violate the Staple Act of 1663, or the Treaty of Whitehall (1686), which never was implemented by English municipal law. The English government made various attempts to stop it, nevertheless.[13]

This trade with foreign colonies, while shared by merchants in the mother country, as in the case of the South Sea Company, was of prime importance to the continental colonies and, on the face of it, ran counter to the mercantilistic interests of the mother country. However, as many a colonial governor was to point out to the British ministry and the Board of Trade, this trade was also of great value, not only to the British colonies, but to the mother country itself, since with the profits of foreign trade the continental colonies could import a vast quantity of goods from England that they would not have been able to afford, otherwise, to buy.

For the British colonies in the West Indies, however, the sugar and molasses trade of the northern colonies with the Dutch, Danish, French, and Spanish colonies in the Caribbean area actually brought the foreign colonies into a direct competition with the British West Indies for the trade of the English colonies on the continent, even though many merchants in the British Islands were partners in it. It was against this competition that the British West Indies protested and agitated until they brought about the passage of the Molasses Act of 1733, which was just as futile as a mechanism for restraining the foreign trade as all other efforts had been.

Because of this divergence of economic interest between the continental colonies and the British West Indies, on the one side, and between the continental colonies and the mother country, on the other, the governors of the continental colonies were often torn between the Charybdis of obedience to their instructions to suppress the trade and Scylla of their realization, immersed, as they were, in the commercial interests of the colonies they governed, that to stop the foreign trade must have disastrous effects upon the economic life of those colonies.

In their correspondence with the governors of the French colonies in the Caribbean area, therefore, the British West Indian governors were generally disposed to collaborate with their French colleagues for the suppression of the trade, even though the French governors often actually winked at it because they, too, as their English colleagues on the continent, realized that this commerce was essential to the economic welfare of the colonies they governed. The Spanish governors were much more sincerely disposed to enforce their laws prohibiting foreign trade than their French colleagues, and they issued commissions to the Spanish *guarda costas* for the enforcement of those laws. Where the French governor might quietly share in the profits of the trade with the English northern colonies, despite the activities of his own *garde-côtes,* the Spanish governor was likely to share in the profits of the *guarda costas*.

It thus came about that whereas the correspondence of the British West Indian governors with the French governors was aimed at suppressing the northern trade, their correspondence with the Spanish governors was weighted with complaints against the activities of the *guarda costas* in suppressing trade with the Spanish colonies, since the *guarda costas* seized many North American, English, and British West Indian ships, innocent as well as guilty, far out on the high seas as well as in waters that the English would recognize as territorial.

On the other hand, the Dutch and Danish colonies were heavily committed to trade with all their neighbors, English, French, and Spanish, and in great measure they lived by it, especially the trade with the English continental colonies. They also profited by their role as middle-men in trade among all of them and between them, on the one side, and continental Europe, on the other. The little governor-to-governor correspondence between the English governors and their Dutch and Danish colleagues relative to trade, therefore, was likely to be confined chiefly to matters pertaining to the control of piracy, with little or no correspondence relative to trade itself.

But there was a lively and acrimonious correspondence between the British governors and French and Spanish governors, especially the latter, over the seizure of British (English and North American) ships by French and Spanish cutters and retaliation by the British. Since the British were the most numerous "interlopers" in Spanish colonial trade, more British ships were seized, probably, than of any other nation. Needless to say, the seizures and reprisals became the subject-matter of a vast correspondence of claim and counter-claim in the diplomatic relations of Spain and England in Europe.

If the governors of the British West Indies shared the opposition of most of their constituents to the North American trade with for-eign colonies, the governors of the North American colonies shared, as extensively as they could, in view of their position, the sentiment of their constituents in favor of it. Thus, for example, Jeremiah Dummer, brother of Lt. Governor William Dummer of Massachu-setts and agent for Massachusetts and Connecticut in England, wrote, in his famous *Defence of the New-England Charters* (1721) a defence, also, of the intercolonial trade:

Why then should not Great-Britain form the same Judgment, and pro-ceed by the like Measures [in encouraging foreign trade] in regard to her American Dominions, from whence she receives the greatest Advantages? It were no difficult Task to prove that London has risen out of the Plan-tations, and not out of England. Tis to them we [England] owe our vast Fleets of Merchant Ships, and consequently the Increase of our Seamen, and Improvement of our Navigation. 'Tis their Tobacco, Sugar, Fish, Oil, Logwood and other Commodities, which have enabled us to sup-port our [English] Trade in Europe, which would otherwise be against us, and to make the Figure we do at present, and have done for near a Century past, in all Parts of the Commercial World. . . .
As this is evident, so is it that whatever injures the Trade of the Planta-tions, must in Proportion affect Great-Britain, the Source and Center of their Commerce; from whence they have their Manufactures, whither they make their Returns, and where all their Superlucration is lodg'd. The Blow then may strike the Colonies first, but it comes Home at last, and falls heaviest on our selves.[14]

The great climax in the history of intercolonial commerce came during the Seven Years' War, during which the northern colonies furnished vast supplies of provisions to the French colonies, both directly and indirectly by way of neutral Dutch, Danish, and Span-ish ports in the West Indies. So great was the injury thought to be done by this trade to the British cause in the war that Parliament passed the so-called Flour Act of 1757, which placed provisions on the list of enumerated articles, and William Pitt issued his famous circular letter of August 23, 1760, to the colonial governors requir-ing them to suppress the trade with the enemy, in all its forms and by every means. A number of colonial legislatures passed laws intended to stop the direct "flag-of-truce" trade, or the indirect trade with the enemy by way of neutral Spanish, Dutch, or Danish ports. Despite all the efforts to suppress it, however, this international commerce continued.

The fact of the matter was that the international trade of the continental colonies with the foreign colonies in America lay so close to the natural economic growth of the English colonies, and was so nearly essential to their economic existence, that it was next to impossible to suppress it. To have suppressed it, whether in peace or in war, as several of the colonial governors recognized, would have been a disastrous blow to the colonial economy. Besides which, as these governors pointed out, such a suppression would have been a serious blow at the economic prosperity of England itself, since it was with the profits from this foreign trade that the colonies paid the unfavorable balance of their trade with the mother country. As Cadwallader Colden, Lt. Governor of New York, for example, wrote William Pitt in 1760,

The Northern Colonies cannot pay for their consumption of the British manufactures by their own produce, exported only to the British Colonies. . . . The result of the whole trade of North America, taking it in every shape, as [is] barely sufficient to pay the ballance due to Great Britain. The consumption of British manufactures in the Northern colonies increases in proportion to their ability to purchase them, and nothing can make the Northern colonies interfere with the British manufactures, but their poverty or inability to purchase. . . .

I have informed you Sir of these things, in hopes that my doing of it may be of use, not as an excuse for any remissness on my part. However as to presemtious or penal laws, I must beg leave to observe, that it is difficult to prosecute with success against the bent of the people, while they are under the prejudice to think that the Sugar Islands have gained a preference inconsistent with the true interest of their Mother Country, and whence prosecution fails of success it is of prejudice to the service it was designed to promote.[15]

Thus, from the role of negotiator for his colony with the governor of a foreign colony the English governor turned, as it were, to that of negotiator for his colony with his own home government in the interest of promoting his colony's trade with that same foreign colony. In demanding a greater, if not a complete freedom of foreign trade, these governors, as agents of their colonies, were express-

ing an international outlook that was to become one of the corner-
stones of the international policies of the later United States.

If the Angloamericans were ardent imperialists, rejoicing in a
close collaboration with the mother country in the territorial expansion of the Empire in America, they were the reverse of that,
they were isolationists, in everything that might draw them into
purely European conflicts. And if the English guarantee of the territorial integrity of the Spanish dominions in America contained in
the Anglo-Spanish Treaty of Utrecht of 1713 was an European analogue of the Monroe Doctrine calculated to block French colonial
and commercial expansion at Spain's and England's expense, that
doctrine was also anticipated in the strong feeling among Americans of the reality of the "two spheres" and of the desirability of
American isolation from European affairs—a mood that found
expression in the writings of many Americans.

This sense of the desirability of isolation and abstention from
European involvements was expressed by the Massachusetts General Court as early as 1651, when it reminded Oliver Cromwell that
it was to escape the conditions of Europe that the original settlers
of Massachusetts had emigrated in the first place. They had found
peace in America, they said: "We know not any country more
peaceable and free from Warre [than Massachusetts]."[16] And Francis Daniel Pastorius, in Pennsylvania, expressed the same mood
when he wrote back to his friends in Germany that "after I had
sufficiently seen the European provinces and countries, and the
threatening movements of war. . . . I was impelled through a special guidance of the Almighty, to go to Pennsylvania."[17]

But the American feeling of isolation was not limited to sentiment. Governor Peter Stuyvesant, for example, when the first
Anglo-Dutch war broke out in 1652, proposed to the New England
Confederation that the English and Dutch colonies maintain a policy of neutrality in the war then beginning between their "Nations
in Europe." Connecticut welcomed the prospect of war in the hope
of territorial gain, but the Massachusetts General Court voted for
neutrality, because, as it said, "it was most agreeable to the gospel
of peace which we profess, and the safest for these colonies at this
season, to forbeare the use of the sword."[18]

The same mood of isolation from European wars was also written
into the Treaty of Sandy Point, made between the French and English colonists in the island of St. Christopher in 1678, a treaty which

provided that the two groups would remain neutral in any war that might break out between France and England in Europe. Similarly, the French merchants of Montreal, when Queen Anne's War was approaching in 1701, proposed that New York and Canada remain neutral for the sake of their trade, the trade with the Indians, and the stability of the frontiers, and the New York merchants and Assembly agreed. New York thus remained neutral until 1709, when the British government inaugurated plans for a massive land and sea attack upon Canada, and neutrality could no longer be maintained by either the French or the English colony.

In general, then, the Angloamericans had formulated, by the middle of the eighteenth century, a strong aversion to inclusion in purely European conflicts. On the other hand, they were almost eager for conflict in America whenever such a conflict might promote either their territorial expansion, their control of the Indians, or their international commerce. Essentially, the policy of most Americans was still one that might be called the mood of the two spheres: isolation from Europe, to be sure, but conflict in America.

By the middle of the eighteenth century, literate Angloamericans were highly conscious of the international affairs of the world and their place in them. They were also conscious of the cultural differences that set them off from their non-English neighbors, especially the Spanish and the French. This consciousness of cultural differences was closely linked with the Angloamericans' thinking about the imperialistic competition for the continent, and was used to justify their demand that the French be driven out.

The most hysterical voice of this Angloamerican cultural nationalism and imperialism was probably that of the Reverend Jonathan Mayhew, of Boston. In his election sermon delivered before the governor and legislature on May 29, 1754, Mayhew preached a crusade of Angloamerican cultural nationalism and imperialism:

And what horrid scene is this, which restless, roving fancy, or something of a higher nature, presents to me; and so chills my blood? Do I behold these territories of freedom, become the prey of arbitrary power? . . . Do I see Christianity banished for popery! the bible, for the mass-book! the oracles of truth, for fabulous legends! Do I see the sacred Edifices erected here to the honour of the true God, and his Son, on the ruins of pagan superstition and idolatry; erected here, where Satan's seat was; do I see these sacred Edifices laid in ruins themselves! and others rising in their places consecrated to the honour of saints and angels! Instead of a train of Christ's faithful, laborious ministers do I behold an heard of lazy Monks, and Jesuits, and Exorcists, and Inquisitors, and cowled, and un-cowled Imposters! Do I see a Protestant, there, stealing a look at his bible, and being taken in the fact, punished like a felon! What indignity is yonder offered to the matrons, and here, to the Virgins! . . . Do I see all liberty, property, religion, happiness, changed, or rather transubstanti-ated, into slavery, poverty, superstition, wretchedness! . . . O dishonest! profane! execrable sight! O piercing sound! that *entereth into the ears of the Lord of Sabbath!* Where! in what region! in what world am I! Is this imagination? . . . Or is it something more divine? I will not, I cannot believe 'tis prophetic vision; or, that God has so far abandoned us![19]

And Mayhew urged his people to war:

Shall the sword rust? . . . Shall our military garments be moth-eaten for want of use, when such things are doing! It is impossible, Gentlemen, you should be any ways backward, or parsimonius, in such a cause as this; a cause wherein the glory of God, the honour of your King, and the good of your country, are so deeply concerned; I might perhaps add, a cause, whereon the liberties of Europe depend. For of so great conse-quence is the empire of North America, . . . that it must turn the scale of power greatly in favour of the only Monarch, from whom those liberties are in danger; and against that Prince, who is the grand support and bul-wark of them. . . . It is even uncertain, Gentlemen, how long you will have an House to sit in, unless a speedy and vigorous opposition is made to the present encroachments, and to the further designs, of our enemies![20]

These are Angloamerican voices which, among many, expressed a cultural and nationalistic self-consciousness which provided a deeper and broader emotional and ideological base for the hatreds and jealousies engendered by imperialistic rivalry. The "cold war" against the French was now a moral crusade; such preaching as this furnished the needed moral rationalization for driving the French out of the colonies they occupied on the continent.

III

The international history of Angloamerica in the colonial period is a double history. On the one side, the "thin red-line" of the inter-national history of America runs unbrokenly and inseparably through the diplomatic history of the community of states of west-ern Europe. In this sense, the history of colonial America is an integral part of European history. It is to be noted, however, that the American concerns of the European powers occupied only a part of the total context of their international relations. Their diplomatic policies relative to their European self-interest and objectives generally overshadowed their interests in America, although it may be said that for some states, such as England in the War of the Spanish Succession and in some wars, such as the Seven Years' War, the American interests of the maritime powers outweighed in importance their European interests. In all cases except the Seven Years' War, their diplomatic relations with each other were calculated to promote the interests of their citizens in Europe, first, and those of their colonists only incidentally. This meant that in many cases, as in that of the return of Louisbourg to France by England in 1748, and in many ways, as, most notably, in the mercantilistic restrictions upon colonial trade, the interests of the colonies were clearly and consciously sacrificed to those of the mother country. Because of their subservient position in the overall imperial perspective of British diplomatic history, the international history of the colonies was in significant measure moulded by the policies of the mother country. At the same time, the existence of the colonies and the deep involvement in them of many Englishmen, as well as of the British government itself, the colonies and their activities also had an increasingly significant influence upon the mother country itself.

On the other side of the ocean the international experiences of the European colonies centered in America itself. Whatever part they consciously played in international affairs was calculated to promote their own self-interests, first, and those of the mother country only secondarily.

But the international evolution of the colonies did not follow exactly the international ideologies and policies of their European metropoli. For the colonies soon discovered that they had international objectives of their own that often did not coincide with those of the mother countries. Thus, in America there emerged a body of international custom, such as the *de facto* practice of freedom of commerce, or the governor-to-governor diplomacy along the "great frontier," which often departed rather sharply from the desires and intentions of the home governments in their international dealings with each other. Furthermore, in the colonies there emerged a body of international concepts, or impulses, that diverged from the policies, customs and moods, of their metropoli. Such, for example, was the impulse toward freedom of international trade among the colonies; such was the American mood of isolation from Europe; such, indeed, was the rabid Angloamerican cultural imperialism that seems to have exceeded in fervor any comparable emotion in England or any other European country. Where the "enlightened self-interest" of the Angloamericans coincided with the policies of England, as in the matter of territorial expansion, the colonies enthusiastically allied themselves with the mother country. But, even here, the motivation was not the same. English motivation for defeating the French empire around the world was one thing; American ambitions to drive the French out of the West Indies and North America were something else. In any case, the general attitudes and the specific aims of Angloamerica in the world of international relations originated in and fed upon American experiences. They were not basically English or European, nor calculated primarily to serve English or European self-interests; they were American, and they evolved to serve the "enlightened self-interest" of the Americans in the new world. Representing what might be called the "natural" objectives of the Americans in international affairs, they clearly anticipated the basic diplomatic principles of the United States after independence.

¹It is a pleasure to acknowledge my great indebtedness to Miss Margaret Anne Fisher, who contributed much to the research and the thought upon which this essay is based.

²It is an arresting fact that since the publication of Frances Gardiner Davenport's magnificently edited *European Treaties Bearing upon the History of the United States and Its Dependencies* (3 vols., Washington. The Carnegie Institution of Washington, 1917-1934), the second and third volumes of which were brought to publication posthumously by J. Franklin Jameson, no significant study of the international history of the English colonies in America has been undertaken or published.

³Quoted in Charles de la Roncière, *Histoire de la Marine Française* (6 vols., Paris: 1899-1934), III, 300.

⁴*Camden's Annals*, year 1580, quoted in J. Holland Rose, *et al.*, eds., *The Cambridge History of the British Empire* (8 vols., New York, 1929-1959), I, 185.

⁵Quoted in Frances G. Davenport, ed., *European Treaties*, I, 220-221, fn. 9.

⁶*Ibid.*, I, 363.

⁷François de Salignac de la Mothe Fénélon, Archbishop of Cambrai, *Oeuvres Choisis de Fénélon* (4 vols., Paris, 1872), IV, 361.

⁸Davenport, ed., *European Treaties*, III, 210-211.

⁹William Cobbett, ed., *Parliamentary History of England from the Norman Conquest in 1066, to the Year 1803* (36 vols., London, 1806-1820), X, 772.

¹⁰This correspondence reposes chiefly in the colonial archives of England, France, Holland, and Spain. The greatest single collection of printed examples of it, often in the form of "calendars" or digests, is in the *Calendar of State Papers, Colonial Series,* published by the British Public Record Office.

¹¹The Marquis de la Galissonière, "Memoir on the French Colonies in North America," December, 1750, in E. B. O'Callaghan and Berthold Fernow, eds., *Documents Relative to the Colonial History of the State of New York* (15 vols., Albany, 1857-1887), X, 220-232.

¹²Albany Congress: "Representation of the Present State of the Colonies," July 9, 1754, *The Papers of Benjamin Franklin*, ed. by Leonard Labaree, *et al.* (8 vols to date. New Haven, 1959-   ), V, 366-374.

¹³In 1728 the Board of Trade asked the Attorney-General and the Solicitor-General of England for an opinion as to the legality of Angloamerican trade with the foreign colonies in the West Indies. It explained that the colonial governors were customarily instructed to prevent Angloamerican trade with foreign colonies in accord with Articles Nos. 5 and 6 of the Treaty of Whitehall of 1686, but that there was some doubt as to whether such instructions were proper. The Attorney-General and the Solicitor-General, in their opinion, ruled that the Treaty of Whitehall, being a Treaty between the kings of France and England, simply gave either king the right to seize the ships of subjects of the other if caught trading in his dominions. It was not intended by the treaty, they said, to lay down a law prohibiting Englishmen from trading with the French colonies if they wished to run the risk involved in doing so, nor was it intended to authorize the king of either signatory to seize and condemn the ships of his own subjects in such a case. The trade, therefore, they ruled, was entirely legal for Englishmen, since there was no English law prohibiting it. This ruling was of importance among the considerations underlying the steps that led eventually, in 1733, to the passage of the so-called Molasses Act of that year (Secretary Popple to Mr. Attorney and Mr. Solicitor General, May 16, 1728, Great Britain, Public Record Office, *Calendar of State Papers, Colonial: America and West Indies, 1728-1729,* No. 195, pp. 92-93; Mr. Attorney and Mr.

Solicitor-General of the Council of Trade and Plantations, June 3, 1728, *ibid.*, 1728-1729, No. 230, pp. 107-108). See, also Ira W. Taylor, "Massachusetts Trade With the French West Indies 1686-1733," unpublished Master of Arts Thesis (1959), University of Washington Library.

[14]Jeremiah Dummer, *A Defence of the New-England Charters* (London, 1721), pp. 38-40.

[15]Cadwallader Colden to William Pitt, December 27, 1760. New York Public Library, Manuscripts Division: "Colden Papers." Printed, *Colden Letter Books*, I, (*N.Y.H.S., Colls.*, 1876), 52.

[16]Hutchinson, *History of Massachusetts*, I, Appendix IX, 450-452.

[17]Quoted in J. Fred Rippy and Angie Debo, *The Historical Background of the American Policy of Isolation (Smith College Studies in History*, IX, Nos. 3 and 4, April-July, 1924), 71.

[18]Hutchinson, *History of Massachusetts*, I, Appendix X, 452-453.

[19]Jonathan Mayhew, *A Sermon Preach'd in the Audience of His Excellency William Shirley, Esq., . . . May 29th, 1754* (Boston, 1754), 32-47.

[20]*Ibid.*

"The Historian's Day"—From Archives to History*

BY LESTER J. CAPPON

The learning explosion that has revolutionized the writing of early American history since the 1940's is traceable not only to able scholars but to the selfless labors of countless individuals— editors, museum directors, bibliographers, librarians, archivists —who have provided the tools essential to their labors. That is the thesis of the essay that Dr. Lester J. Cappon has prepared for this volume. Calling on his own vast learning and his experience in virtually all of these capacities, he has not only expertly sum- marized the extensive developments in these areas, but has shown their impact on scholarship and revealed their weak points needing correction. Dr. Cappon first became associated with John E. Pomfret in 1945 when, after earning a Harvard doctorate and teaching at the University of Virginia, he joined the staff of the Institute of Early American History and Culture. There he has remained since that time, as director after 1955, to provide aid and enlightenment to a generation of historians.

D URING THE TWENTY YEARS since World War II the field of early American history has undergone a transformation from apathy to enthusiasm among professional scholars as writers and critics and a segment of the public as readers and in- quirers. This renaissance, in large part an expression of renewed interest by Americans in their origins as a people, their national government born of revolution, and their democracy, has been fed by scholars. It is the scholarship in books and magazine articles, in indoor and outdoor museums of repute, in seminars and confer- ences translated into written record, that has multiplied our knowl- edge and increased the citizen's understanding through popular and semi-popular media. In view of the far-reaching nature of this

*The phrase is J. H. Hexter's.

renaissance, in breadth and depth, it is pertinent to examine the method and substance, the means and ends, that are producing the written history of the colonial and revolutionary period. It is timely to emphasize the basic contribution of scholars in making the sources of history more accessible and usable and to point out along the way some shortcomings in this pursuit of learning.

The decline of interest in early American history, evident between the two world wars, has been attributed to absorption in contemporary problems that seemed unrelated to a remote past, to the relevance of the expanding social sciences concerned with current issues, and to the accompanying popularity of "recent history" as adequate background. At the turn of the century the study of American history still concentrated largely on the colonial and revolutionary periods, but up to World War I graduate schools were small. During the expansion of the 1920's students responded to new opportunities in nineteenth- and twentieth-century history, although scholars working in the early period, like Charles M. Andrews, Edward Channing, Thomas J. Wertenbaker, and Evarts B. Greene, had achieved distinguished reputations. Social history was in vogue (the "new history" which Edward Eggleston had propounded in 1900—"the history of culture, the real history of men and women"[1]— and James Harvey Robinson a decade later[2]), but the common man was not the concern of the "imperial school" which dominated colonial history, and students interested in social history were inclined, with few exceptions, to turn to the nineteenth century or the twentieth.

World War II precipitated the American people from would-be isolationism into world affairs, but paradoxically contemporary world problems led Americans to re-examine their own beginnings. Challenges at home and abroad to American democracy, to American ideals and shibboleths, to principles of government and natural rights, which cannot be explained or comprehended apart from their historical development, brought a resurgence of interest in early American history. Whatever the effects of communism in tempting Americans to sacrifice their civil liberties on the one hand, and in threatening their position in world affairs on the other, the serious citizen derives some sustaining power from a knowledge of origins and historical sequence, from a critical appraisal of conservatives and revolutionaries in the era of the young republic. The phenomenal number of subscribers to *American Heritage* magazine since 1954 echoes the popular interest in local and national history that Benson J. Lossing's *Field Book of the American Revolution* enjoyed in the 1850's.

Within surprisingly few years the study of early American history was no longer a neglected subject. New articles and books explored new questions and reconsidered old ones, more colleges and universities added courses in early American history, more people discovered the fascination of visiting historic sites. The contribution of the museum to research and public education is amply demonstrated by the mounting interest in "three-dimensional history" portrayed through historic preservation and restoration. Many a site or building, long recognized as historic, now became an attraction as the "first" or "the earliest known" of its kind, dating from seventeenth- or eighteenth-century America. Thus the teaching and absorption of early American history took on a variety of expression. This is illustrated most aptly and forcefully in Williamsburg, Virginia, by Colonial Williamsburg's multiple educational program for adults and children, by the augmented graduate and undergraduate curriculum in history at the College of William and Mary, and by these institutions' joint sponsorship of the Institute of Early American History and Culture.

As scholarly periodical publications provide the widest opportunities for the author to test his ideas and add his bit to the accumulation of knowledge, so this medium may serve as a convenient point of entry for surveying and evaluating the dissemination of early American history since the war. The well-known national, regional, and state historical magazines of long standing continue to devote space to this field, but more significant is the fact that scholars in early American history now have "their own" magazine, to be discussed below.

It is also noteworthy, however, that the current era of specialization has produced a considerable number of historical periodicals in which the American historian of any period may obtain a hearing. Some of them reflect new trends in research, new concepts in history and related disciplines, sometimes encumbered with terminology horrendous to contemplate. The *Journal of the History of Medicine,* founded in 1946, and *Technology and Culture* (1959) testify to the rapid increase of interest in the history of science and technology, and science in relation to society, since the war. *Ethno-History* (1954) suggests in its title the interdisciplinary approach increasingly prevalent among the social sciences, as does the new *Journal of the History of the Behavioral Sciences* (1965) for its field. A modification of this point of view may be sensed in the *Journal of the History of Philosophy* (1961). All these magazines have special interests to serve—that is their *raison d'être,* but history is their common denominator.

The *Journal of the History of Ideas* (1940), antedating all the others, was a response to what purports to be a separate field of study. In the college catalogues the subject first appeared as a compound, social and intellectual history, which suggests its broad coverage. After World War II an even broader concept emerged. The newest of the new history was "civilization," equated with cultural history. The concept of "American Civilization" (Eggleston would have recognized it as next-of-kin) spawned the American Studies Association, which took over the *American Quarterly* (1949) in 1951. Here, under one roof, are to be accommodated the social and behavioral scientists, the humanists, and the historians who must be on guard against loss of identity and method in the controversy between past and present. How well can *American Quarterly* serve history, early American history in particular?

In the first exposition of *American Studies,* Tremaine McDowell, pioneer and prophet of the new discipline, declared that they "move toward the reconciliation of the tenses, the reconciliation of the academic disciplines, and a third long-range goal, namely, a reconciliation of region, nation, and world."[3] Every student of American culture, he wrote on another occasion, must ask and answer for himself this question, among others: "Do I recognize that in American studies the present is as relevant as the past?"[4] The stated aim of *American Quarterly* is "to aid in giving a sense of direction to studies in the culture of the United States, past and present."[5] But what direction, historians ask with misgivings. They have long since abandoned belief in the attainment of "scientific objectivity"; and if they are conscious of current influences as men of the present, they must still give priority to historical contexts derived from the sources before connecting the "relevant past" with the present.[6] The study of present problems is not history, and the self-conscious historian who judges all research in terms of "presentism" does disservice to his profession. Adoption of current catch-words links the historian with the faddist—myth-makers and image-identification, neo-conservatives and devotees of the "cult of consensus"—so that every current historical writer of any reputation is classified and tagged, for the present.[7] This is high-sounding pedantry, a travesty on history and the concept of American civilization.

"Civilization," like the word "documentation," means all things to all men. What theory, what piece of research, what contribution to knowledge, could not fall within this all-embracing term? It would seem that *American Quarterly* could only become an *omnium gatherum*, a latter-day journal of both universal and specialized knowledge in which the status of historiography without metes or bounds is precarious, riding the wave of the present.

While early American history was in the doldrums, the Third Series of the *William and Mary Quarterly* came into being in January, 1944, as "a magazine of early American history, institutions, and culture." The subtitle indicated a broadening of scope from that of Virginia history in the Second Series of the *Quarterly* under the able editorship of Earl Gregg Swem, librarian of the College of William and Mary and distinguished bibliographer.[8] To launch the Third Series during war-time was an act of faith on the part of the College (*i.e.*, of its president, John E. Pomfret), who hoped to retain most of the old subscribers but fully expected to alienate the genealogists among them. "At present," Pomfret pointed out in the first number, "there is no single historical journal dealing with this broad field" of early American history. Yet it "becomes evident that this broadening of horizons hardly involves the exclusion of Virginia history."[9] The embryonic Institute of Early American History and Culture, which did not go into full operation until the fall of 1945, would succeed the College as publisher of the *Quarterly*.

To a far greater degree than the sponsors and historical advisors of the Institute could anticipate, the *William and Mary Quarterly* became within a decade the chief vehicle for current essays and book reviews in its field. Under successive editors of high caliber[10] the magazine improved the quality of historical publication by careful selection. Gresham's Law could not apply when the editor had achieved the enviable position of choosing only from the better essays on hand, even though he might still wish that the lead article could always be distinguished. If scholars in early American history turn first to the *Quarterly* for publication of their manuscripts, we may aver that they like to be found in good company; but scholarship of superior quality is not a matter of "snob appeal" but rather of rigorous criticism to which the editor subjects the work of the distinguished historian no less than that of the promising graduate student. The educational exchange between editor and author is at the heart of the matter, affecting for the better, in turn, what follows between author and reader.

As early American history has become a lively field of research and criticism, so the concentration of articles and reviews in the *William and Mary Quarterly* provides an authentic basis for judging trends and substance, thesis and hypothesis, even synthesis. From the perspective of contemporary history the magazine may appear to be traditional, highly factual, and "inner-directed." Dedicated to the old virtue that labor in the primary sources is indispensable for the writing of authentic history, the *Quarterly* has also presented the flowering of new research and the spinning of new theses from both well-known and freshly discovered sources. It has aired the controversies of historians, involving method as well as interpretation, semantics as well as historical criticism. It has published essays containing some relevance for the present but letting the reader, by and large, arrive at his own deductions. It announced no stated objectives at its inception and soon dropped the redundant "culture" from its sub-title. Yet its contents include numerous articles on "cultural history," not always identified as such, and it has devoted space to such diverse concepts as "Atlantic civilization," the "noble savage," and the "Whig myth." It unravelled the "Mystery of the Horn Papers" and traversed new ground broken by Wyatt and Willcox's "Psychological Exploration in History," with Sir Henry Clinton on the couch.[11]

The proliferation of historical publication since the war offers a means of measuring this period of unprecedented growth in quantity, and statistics could be extracted from the files of *Publisher's Weekly*. It is sufficient, however, to note a few facts and conditions. Historical and biographical works by scholars who have established reputations beyond professional circles are sought, indeed contracted for in advance, by commercial publishers. So keen is the competition for textbooks, source books, and brief monographs in series that publishers will pay advance royalty in sealing the contract with many a lesser light, the quality of whose product is gambled on, not guaranteed. Most scholars, however, depend on the university press to publish and to subsidize their works. During the years immediately after World War II the young author who had to provide the subsidy for his first book found this outlay a serious burden. To help solve this problem, the Institute of Early American History and Culture was publishing its books without financial obligation of the authors. Most of these were first titles of young scholars. Although it has continued to assume the obligation, this procedure, almost unique when the Institute's book program was initiated, is now the rule rather than the exception among university presses.

The Institute's book publication program—monographs, primary sources, "documentary problems," bibliographies—derives from manuscripts submitted by scholars throughout the United States.[12] This is not the occasion for surveying these publications, comprising more than 50 titles, or commenting on the several categories, but rather to point out that they are university press books, published by the University of North Carolina Press, competing with the output of other university presses and occasionally with the commercial houses. However, the Institute has offered special editorial services in its field that may account in part for the improvement in quality of scholarly production, although that is a matter of individual opinion.

In the service rendered to scholars and scholarship, which is the primary purpose of the university press, there is a hidden cost varying widely in amount and too critical to be overlooked. This is the cost of historical editing. Has the author made a contribution to knowledge deserving publication? Does his theme or interpretation offer a fresh concept to stimulate further research? Will he command the attention of his readers or lose them in a wilderness of words and inept figures of speech? Perhaps more than most university presses, the Institute has subjected every manuscript worth serious consideration to this kind of editing as an educational service that has helped raise the level of historical publication. Many manuscripts have been rejected after such service was rendered; nevertheless, some authors have secured publication elsewhere. Although it is not unduly difficult for a respectable monograph to find a publisher, the young scholar may have to learn by the hard way that his dissertation is not yet a publishable manuscript, that it may yield only a substantial magazine article, not constitute a book. Clearly, the primary consideration should be the quality of the work for book publication, not how cheaply it can be put into a disguise of book publication.[13]

In the process of historical writing the first product is the monograph (in crude form, the dissertation), with its findings and conclusion, indispensable to broader works with more expansive range of interpretation and generalization. But the findings are among primary sources, for which the demand has increased as research in early American history and other fields has multiplied. Thus it is pertinent to ask whether these cultural resources, manuscript and printed, are more voluminous than they were a generation ago, and more useable? To what extent have accessibility and new tools for research stimulated the historian's productivity?

These post-war years, unlike the 1920's, have witnessed not the establishment of new special libraries for historical research, the crowning deed of the private collector, but rather the enrichment of existing institutions by benefactors. The initiative of curators has worked to the same end through "rational" collecting by a rule of thumb if not a systematic program for building onto foundations already laid. Of manuscript collections newly discovered there seems to be no end, although yields of the seventeenth century have become exceedingly lean. Since the scholar finds it difficult to keep abreast of current acquisitions, some curators of manuscripts have felt a responsibility to make their holdings known through published guides. The Historical Records Survey initiated a number of projects to this end in the late 1930's and the William L. Clements Library set an enviable example in its *Guide* of 1942.[14] Others have followed with a uniformity of format and content that is advantageous to the scholar; and though relatively few institutions have provided this boon, there is much to be said for an approach to these resources by repository because the collections of most libraries have a geographical orientation which is often well geared to the scholar's research.

In the field of governmental records the National Archives has set the pace for a generation. From its founding in 1934 an enlightened administration by historians has accomplished far more for their professional colleagues than the latter have ever appreciated. With the publication of its first *Guide to the Records* (1948)[15] the National Archives has made its resources increasingly better known and readily accessible through a series of *Preliminary Inventories*. For early American history these include the valuable corpus of "Pre-Federal" records, enriched by transfer of the Papers of the Continental Congress from the Library of Congress. But scholars often overlook the fact that federal agencies have also created "local" records from the beginning of the Government, in courts and custom houses, for example. Many of these have escaped destruction, to be preserved not in the National Archives but in the Federal Record Centers.[16]

For an approach to colonial and early state records the historian must consult Ernst Posner's comprehensive *American State Archives* (1964), if only to read his first chapter on "The Genesis and Evolution of American State Archives." For more detailed, though limited, information on the records of particular states he must still turn in most instances to the preliminary survey reports prepared sixty years ago under the auspices of the Public Archives Commission.[17] For the documents themselves, by series, Jenkins' *Guide to the Microfilm Collection of Early State Records*[18] provides virtually complete coverage in positive prints through the Library of Congress.

The printing of selected colonial documents under state auspices has been going on intermittently for well over a century and in a few instances, like the *Archives of Maryland* (1883-), on a long-time basis. Recent large-scale editorial projects have concentrated on persons rather than on agencies or departments of state government. The exception is the *Colonial Records of South Carolina* (1951-), impeccably edited by Harold Easterby in eleven volumes, but suspended after his untimely death. By and large, state archival agencies have been remiss about publishing guides to their records, and the historian must remember that most printed series are incomplete.

Local records—of towns and counties, churches and social organizations—have held a stronger attraction for historians in recent years than hitherto because the study of government and society in microcosm, seen through specific actions of identifiable individuals, provides a relatively sound basis on which to make generalizations of broader significance concerning the state or region. Furthermore, some state and antecedent colonial records contain information of a local nature about individuals or, for statistical purposes, on ownership of property, suffrage, and size of estate. These records were consulted by the historian of a half-century or more ago chiefly for descriptive material concerning institutions and social conditions; now they are sources of data compiled and analyzed for a variety of conclusions, in the spirit and manner of the Namier school.[19]

Since few local archives covering an extended period have been published *in toto,* the historian must use them in the local record offices unless, as in Maryland, they have been transferred to the state archives, or, as in Virginia, they have been photographed for security purposes and the convenience of centralized research. In copying programs the older records usually claim prior consideration, to the advantage of researchers in early American history. The lack of bona fide local archives in the United States (as distinguished from county and town clerks' record offices) has not been remedied to any appreciable extent; but the scholar can be grateful for the inventories of such records that were published by the Historical Records Survey under the Work Projects Administration of New Deal fame.[20]

Within the past few years two monumental projects have opened the way for a more direct approach to particular groups of material in the vast field of manuscript records. The approach by respository through their published guides, mentioned above, is now available on a nation-wide basis through Philip M. Hamer's *Guide to Archives and Manuscripts in the United States* (1961), the best startingpoint in the scholar's quest for his sources. The *National Union Catalog of Manuscript Collections* (1962-), projected as a long-time service of the Library of Congress, is co-ordinating data on such collections, supplied by the repositories, and presenting them in a format approximating that for printed books (the familiar LC catalog card). The nature of this project's operation precludes an alphabetic arrangement of entries or (fortunately) any attempt at subject classification. The comprehensive index to each volume is the key to its contents.[21]

Materials for American history in foreign repositories became the desiderata of a few historians in the second quarter of the nineteenth century, beginning with Jared Sparks. The guides to such materials, planned by J. Franklin Jameson and published by the Carnegie Institution of Washington during the early years of the twentieth century, are well known to students of American colonial history, especially through their use of the volumes compiled by Charles M. Andrews on Great Britain. The copying of British records under American auspices is a long, dismal story of limited aims and even more restricted financial resources, brightened by personal enthusiasm and intermittent efforts by individual states. The objectives were commendable, but the train of uncompleted undertakings and the lack of comprehensive planning among the states were regrettable. The Virginia Colonial Records Project, which secured both private and public support by association with the 350th anniversary celebration of the founding of Jamestown,[22] has come closer to completion than many of its predecessors. Selected records were microfilmed in England and mimeographed survey reports were issued by groups of records; but the reports, cued to the microfilm, still await an index to give the records maximum usefulness.

Students of early American history have also had frequent recourse to *Reports* of the British Historical Manuscripts Commission that pertain to sources on the colonies. Many of these were family papers preserved in manor houses and "not readily opened" to the scholar—to employ a euphemism that has often implied his frustration. In recent years, however, the financial burden of large British estates has worked to the scholar's advantage by bringing about the transfer of family archives to the county record office, where they are more likely to be accessible. Thus the trend toward centralization of manuscript collections in the British Museum has been modified, and preferably so. Fast travel "shortens" distance, microphotography is cheap, and there is much to be said for maintaining the association of records with the area of origin. The National Register of Manuscripts, established in the Public Record Office, serves as a clearinghouse of information, somewhat like the more highly organized National Union Catalog of the Library of Congress. Meanwhile, the results of a survey of these resources, B. R. Crick and Miriam Almon's *Guide to Manuscripts relating to America in Great Britain and Ireland* (1961), puts the scholar in debt to the compilers.

If one great corpus of manuscripts may be singled out for its impact on historical scholarship during the past decade, it is the Adams Family Papers. In the custody of the Adams Trust for fifty years and closely restricted in use, although important segments had been published from time to time since the mid-nineteenth century, the Trust conveyed these priceless archives to the Massachusetts Historical Society by deed of gift in 1954.[23] What followed, in accordance with plans already formulated, constituted a dual service to scholarship through microfilming on the one hand and historical editing on the other. The microfilming of the entire family archives down to 1889 and the offering of sets for sale represented an about-face from the conservative liberalism of the family who had felt an intuitive obligation to protect family privacy, allowing publication of those papers pertaining to public policy and national affairs[24] under the scrutiny of an Adams or a trustworthy Worthington C. Ford. An example of comprehensive microfilming had already been set by the State Historical Society of Wisconsin in making available the Draper Manuscripts. The National Archives had initiated a selective program of microcopying; later the Library of Congress became engaged in issuing its series of Presidential Papers by the same medium. More recently the Massachusetts Historical Society began a long-term project, with a grant from the National Historical Publications Commission, for microfilm "editions" of its most valuable collections, each supplied with a description of the collection and an index in pamphlet form.

This "editing" of texts on microfilm, which, some curators and historians maintain, obviates the need for letterpress editions of primary sources, is relevant to that more significant project involving the Adams Papers, *viz.* the multi-volume edition under the editorship-in-chief of Lyman H. Butterfield. The volumes already published provide irrefutable evidence in text and annotation of the contribution to scholarship made by editing of high quality. The *Adams Papers* are the peer of the *Papers of Thomas Jefferson*, edited by Julian P. Boyd, whose first volume (1950) ushered in the present era of comprehensive historical editing.[25] It is a phenomenon that has precipitated controversy among historians who enjoy its fruits but are men of little faith in the prolonged cultivation that will be required at the hands of future editors. This skepticism in turn has revived the old question of what should be the role of the historical editor, although no one could honestly deny that this art and craft have now reached superior levels of attainment.[26] It is worth noting that scholars in the early American period have been virtually the exclusive beneficiaries of all the *Papers* published thus far.

In diverse ways the historian's approach to his sources has been made smoother during the past twenty years by bibliographies and kindred reference works, whether concerned wholly or in part with early American history. Of a general nature, three compilations emulate the great work of Charles Evans on American imprints: Donald Wing's *Short-Title Catalogue . . . 1641-1700* (3 vols., 1945-51),[27] *A Bibliography of Canadian Imprints, 1751-1800* (1952), by

Marie Tremaine, and *The Voice of the Old Frontier* (1949) by R. W. G. Vail, who had completed Sabin's *Bibliotheca Americana* in 1936. Since a large percentage of the imprints recorded in Evans's *American Bibliography* (to 1800) are to be found in the American Antiquarian Society, here was an opportunity to make photographic copies for distribution. The Evans Microprint Project, under the direction of Clifford K. Shipton, has done more than bring all these texts within easy reach, for the preparatory work clarified and corrected numerous bibliographical details and exposed numerous "ghosts" that lurked among the Evans entries.[28] Another facet of bibliographical research of peculiar service to historians is illustrated by the five-volume *Catalogue of the Library of Thomas Jefferson* (1952-59) , meticulously compiled by Millicent Sowerby. It is a reconstruction on paper, according to Jefferson's own scheme of classification, of his great library of 1770-1815, sold to the Library of Congress and destroyed for the most part in the fire of 1851.

Early American newspapers have served the historian well because of the American Antiquarian Society's pre-eminence in this field. Clarence S. Brigham began making these resources known in detail through its *Proceedings* in 1913. The revised edition of this indispensable work was assembled and published in 1947 in two volumes as *History and Bibliography of American Newspapers, 1690-1820*, just as research in early American history was beginning to expand. Not long afterward appeared the *Virginia Gazette Index, 1736-1780*, covering all known issues of the Williamsburg newspapers and providing the only work of its kind for the colonial period.[29] The offer of a set of these papers on microfilm with the *Index*, or separately, lent further encouragement to photoduplication of early newspaper files which had begun to replace photostats before the war. By the end of the 1950's, the *South Carolina Gazette* files, 1732-1781, were available on microfilm through the Charleston Library Society. What had been accomplished by this technique, however, was entirely by individual initiative, whether educational or commercial, directed to a particular newspaper. Recently the American Antiquarian Society, prompted by its own distinguished collections, has launched a project in cooperation with Readex Microprint Corporation for microfilming all files of colonial papers not yet adequately done.[30]

In 1953 the Institute of Early American History and Culture began a series of conferences on Needs and Opportunities for Study which have dealt with a variety of subjects: science, law, architecture, the arts, education, ethno-history, and most recently technology. The purpose of each conference is to suggest opportunities in a neglected or relatively unexploited field, in part by surveying its development and evaluating its current status. What has the scientist or the architect or the lawyer contributed by way of reliable history and how can he and the historian work effectively to fill the gaps in historiography? The essay and bibliography in each volume provide a wide-ranging, yet concise, perspective with well-selected references that may serve as a point of entry into new research. It is encouraging to note that since Whitfield J. Bell's *Early American Science* (1955) and William N. Fenton's *American Indian and White Relations to 1830 ... [with] a Bibliography by L. H. Butterfield, Wilcomb E. Washburn, and William N. Fenton* (1957) were published, the increase in research has brought about the need for a revised edition of each.[31]

The conference on early American law did not bear fruit as a published volume in the series. This is regrettable because in the complex field of legal history many of the sources are fragmentary, including court records which the researcher might expect to find in the appropriate archives. Others are widely scattered in personal papers, unidentified and seldom preserved in "obvious" places. Under the sponsorship of the American Historical Association several well-edited volumes of colonial court records have appeared,[32] but financial costs have so restricted their length that they are little more than fine samples with limited value for research. The rise of the colonial lawyer and the growth of an American system of procedure, both subjects of far-reaching significance, must be investigated by diverse approaches. Even the substantial legal papers of John Adams, so skillfully edited by two young legal scholars for inclusion in *The Adams Papers*,[33] survived piecemeal and incomplete, many of them mere scraps. This three-volume work demonstrates forcefully the indispensable role of the historical-minded lawyer in making such records more generally useful to the historian, who likewise must appreciate them for what they embody beyond their original purpose.

The ramifications of early American history lead, via its sources and bibliographies, in many directions where fresh research beckons a younger generation of scholars—for example, in the advanced concepts of historical geography and re-interpretation of the Age of

Discovery and Exploration, now promoted by the Society for the History of Discoveries; by further evaluation and more critical use of local records, the most extensive category of untapped sources, whose peculiarities and omissions are audible to the scholar attuned to the frequencies of the era that created the records; by more intelligent appreciation of graphic materials as historical sources, correlated with the written record, fully identified, and carefully reproduced for publication; and always by well-tempered criticism of those reputable predecessors in the historical profession whose foresight is only our hindsight.

In the practice of his art the historian subscribes to no general laws. The essential elements in his method pertain first to the authenticity of the primary sources, next to the external and internal criticism he imposes on them, and finally to the historical context in which he uses them for information and interpretation. The historian's schematic translation of "facts" into "data" for scientific analysis and conclusions has benefitted from improved techniques in the social sciences, well illustrated by the application of "symbol analysis" and "content analysis" to historical sources.[34] Such procedures are conditioned equally by an application of sound principles and an awareness of the *limitations* of the sources. Scholars in the field of early American history have been hesitant about adopting such corollaries to historical method because of limitations caused by the attrition of time on survival of records, by lack of official data uniformly recorded through long periods, and by a society with a high percentage of illiteracy. Furthermore, the scholar cannot engage in oral interviews nor does he have recourse to recordings of contemporary voices. Nevertheless, because of the nature of his research he may find opportunities to employ punched cards and to accelerate his labors by computerized research.[35]

In his *Brief Retrospect of the Eighteenth Century* the Reverend Samuel Miller observed that "the historians of the present day lay their authorities before the reader, and their caution is excited, and their fidelity rendered more vigilant by the recollection that the same sources of information are open to others, and that contemporary rivals and many classes of readers, will sit in judgment on the truth of their narratives."[36] Although the present essay has been directed toward the sources for early American history and the media for publication, it is clear that the historical writing of the past generation has been motivated by a more acute spirit of criticism than Miller found a century and a half ago. "Contemporary rivals" have engaged in prolonged controversy over two fundamental issues: the nature of the American Revolution, broadly conceived; and Federalists versus Anti-Federalists in the framing of the United States Constitution and its application to the new national government. The power of ideas *vis-à-vis* economic and social forces has come full circle, producing the revisionist and precipitating the cry of "Revisions in Need of Revising."[37]

"The revisionist has, of course, a vital function to perform," as Wesley Frank Craven has wisely pointed out, "but the very character of the function encourages overstatement, which in turn can invite new revisionist efforts. What is most needed today perhaps is a little more tolerance by revisionists for other revisionists, past and present, and a little more awareness of the contribution each group has made. . . ."[38] In commending the high level of the historical monograph today, Daniel Boorstin offers the timely rebuke that "more recent scholarly works have too commonly tended to become efforts to arbitrate among other scholars' views."[39]

Among early American historians much of the historical criticism still stems from Charles A. Beard and Carl Becker, with occasional echoes of Frederick Jackson Turner. Fresh investigation of the records has been accompanied at times by questionable use of such tempting terms as democracy and classes, liberal and conservative; but no "thesis" worthy of that designation has appeared. Nor has a new "school" of colonial history taken form since Andrews' death in 1943. But a renaissance has emerged from the work of distinguished scholars and their promising protégés; and a few of the old masters still survive.

NOTES

1American Historical Association, *Annual Report for 1900* (1901), I, 47.

2In *The New History* (New York, 1912).

3Tremaine McDowell, *American Studies* (Minneapolis, 1948).

4*New England Quarterly*, XXIII (1950), 561.

5Each issue of *American Quarterly* carries this aim on the masthead (inside front-cover).

6Cf. J. H. Hexter, "The Historian and His Day," *Reappraisals in History* ([Evanston], 1962), 1-13.

7John Higham set forth this idea in "The Cult of the 'American Consensus': Homogenizing Our History," *Commentary*, XXVII (1959), 94-100, inflating a "new" viewpoint which had, presumably, swept the field. By 1962, however, "we can not conclude that an image of consensus has decisively replaced the old image of conflict. Perhaps a better keynote to contemporary historiography may be found in the frequent attempt to combine such antithetical principles as consensus and conflict without entirely negating either alternative." Higham, "The Construction of American History," in *The Reconstruction of American History*, John Higham, ed. (New York, 1962), 23. Perhaps it is not a "cult" but only a normal manifestation of differences of opinion among historians who do not begin by seeking "principles." The "cult" becomes sheer academic nonsense in its application to early American history by Dwight W. Hoover, in "Some Comments on Recent United States Historiography," *American Quarterly*, XVII (1965), 302-305.

8Dr. Swem had greatly improved the quality of the Second Series, 1920-43, over that of the first, 1892-1919, under the editorship of Lyon G. Tyler.

9*William and Mary Quarterly*, 3d Ser., I (1944), 91, 92. The first editor of the Third Series was Professor Richard L. Morton, College of William and Mary.

10Editors following Dr. Morton were Douglass Adair, Lawrence W. Towner, and William W. Abbot.

11For an evaluation of the magazine in its own pages see Keith B. Berwick, "A Peculiar Monument: the Third Series of the *William and Mary Quarterly*," in XXI (1964), 3-17.

12Under the editorship of James Morton Smith, 1955-66.

13A case in point is "Logmark Editions," a joint venture of the University of Wisconsin's Department of History and the State Historical Society of Wisconsin. My criticism of the purpose of these imprints and their physical quality as "books" appeared in the *News Letter* of the Institute of Early American History and Culture, No. 32 (April 1, 1963), 9-10. A reply, by Professor Irvin G. Wyllie of the Department of History, was published, *ibid.*, No. 34 (November 16, 1963), 9-11.

In the spring of 1966 the American Press Publications, Inc., aware of "the 'publish or perish' rule that prevails in many colleges and universities," sent out a form letter: "Dear Professor: Do you have a copy of your doctoral dissertation? We would like to consider it for regular book publication. . . . Our company has found that doctoral dissertations, in a majority of instances, are readily convertible into standard books which can answer the teacher's problem. . . ." Here is the publisher calling the piper's tune.

14Howard H. Peckham, *Guide to the Manuscript Collections in the William L. Clements Library* (Ann Arbor, 1942); second edition by William S. Ewing (Ann Arbor, 1953).

15The most recent edition is 1948. See also *National Archives Accessions* (1940-).

249

16The survey of Federal Archives in the States, under the Work Projects Administration, 1937-42, produced numerous mimeographed inventories, state by state. Many of these records are now preserved in the appropriate Federal Record Centers. Sargent B. Child and Dorothy P. Holmes, *Bibliography of Research Projects Reports: Check List of Historical Records Survey Publications*, W. P. A. Technical Series, Research and Records Bibliography No. 7 (Washington, Work Projects Administration, April, 1943), 1-14.

17In American Historical Association, *Annual Reports*, 1900-17.

18William Sumner Jenkins, *A Guide to the Microfilm Collection of Early State Records* ([Washington], 1950); and *Supplement* (1951).

19Contrast the use of such records by Philip Alexander Bruce at the turn of the century and by Constance McLaughlin Green, Staughton Lynd, Sumner Powell, and others in recent years.

20Cf. Child and Holmes, *Bibliography of Research Projects Reports: Check List of Historical Records Survey*, 61-69.

21See also Richard W. Hale, Jr., ed., *Guide to Photocopied Historical Materials in the United States and Canada* (Ithaca, 1961).

22Julian P. Boyd, "A New Guide to the Indispensable Sources of Virginia History," *William and Mary Quarterly*, 3rd ser., XV (1958), 3-13.

23L. H. Butterfield, "The Papers of the Adams Family: Some Account of Their History," in Massachusetts Historical Society, *Proceedings*, LXXI (1959), 341-353.

24Charles Francis Adams, ed., *The Works of John Adams* (1850-56), I, vi; VII, 3; C. F. Adams, ed., *Familiar Letters of John and Abigail Adams* [1875]; W. C. Ford, ed., *The Writings of J. Q. Adams* (1913-17); W. C. Ford, ed., *Letters of Henry Adams* (1930); etc.

25The other multi-volume *Papers* in progress, with the date of publication of the first volume, are: Calhoun (1959), Franklin (1959), Clay (1959), Hamilton (1961), and Madison (1962).

26Lester J. Cappon, "A Rationale for Historical Editing Past and Present," *William and Mary Quarterly*, 3d Series, XXIII (1965), 56-75.

27*Short-title Catalogue of Books Printed in England, Scotland, Ireland, Wales, and British America and of English Books Printed in Other Countries* . . . (Columbia University Press for the Index Society). A continuation of *Short-Title Catalogue, 1475-1640* (London, 1926).

28American Antiquarian Society, *Proceedings*, LXIV (1954), 261-263; LXVIII (1958), 186-189. Photography by Readex Microprint Corporation.

29Compiled by Lester J. Cappon and Stella F. Duff and published by the Institute of Early American History and Culture in 1950 (2 vols.).

30American Antiquarian Society, *Proceedings*, LXXV (1965), 4.

31The other volumes in the series are: Bernard Bailyn, *Education in the Forming of American Society* (1960); Walter M. Whitehill, Wendell D. Garrett, and Jane N. Garrett, *The Arts in Early American History* (1965); Brooke Hindle and Lucius F. Ellsworth, *Technology in Early America* (1966).

32Recent volumes: Susie M. Ames, ed., *Accomack-Northampton County Virginia, 1632-1640* (1954); Leon de Valinger, Jr., ed., *Kent County Delaware, 1680-1705* (1959).

33L. Kinvin Wroth and Hiller B. Zobel, eds., *Legal Papers of John Adams* (3 vols., Cambridge, 1965).

34Richard L. Merritt, "The Colonists Discover America: Attention Patterns in the Colonial Press, 1735-1775," *William and Mary Quarterly*, 3d Ser., XXI (1964), 270-287;

elaborated in his *Symbols of American Community, 1735-1775* (New Haven, [1966]); "The Emergence of American Nationalism: a Quantitative Approach," *American Quarterly,* XVII (1965), 319-335; *Comparing Nations; the Use of Quantitative Data in Cross-National Research,* with Stein Rokkan (New Haven, [1966]).

35"Computerized Research in the Humanities: a Survey," American Council of Learned Societies, *ACLS Newsletter,* XVI, No. 5 (May, 1965), 9-13. See Frederick Mosteller and David L. Wallace, *Inference and Disputed Authorship: The Federalist* (Reading, Mass., 1964), and review by Linda M. and Stephen S. Webb in *William and Mary Quarterly,* 3rd ser., XXIII (1966), 353-355.

36(New York, 1803), II, 132.

37Edmund S. Morgan, "The American Revolution: Revisions in Need of Revising," *William and Mary Quarterly,* 3rd ser., XIV (1957), 3-15.

38Craven, "The Revolutionary Era," in John Higham, ed., *The Reconstruction of American History,* 63.

39Boorstin, *The Americans: The National Experience* (New York, 1965), 433.

Historic Sites Archaeology in the Study of Early American History

BY WALTER MUIR WHITEHILL

Some among the army of historians investigating the American past recognize that written records are not the only keys to the understanding of human behavior. Those bold enough to venture along unexplored paths realize that the earliest settlers endowed posterity with artistic, architectural, and physical remains that offer exciting evidence of the way men lived and thought. No more eloquent spokesman for this viewpoint can be found than Walter Muir Whitehill. As director and librarian of the Boston Athenaeum, and as a member of the faculty of the Peabody Museum of Harvard University, he is familiar equally with the books and artifacts from which history is made. Dr. Whitehill began his loyal association with the Huntington Library in 1953 when he delivered the Founder's Day address. His contribution to this volume convincingly demonstrates that historians of early America must pay increasing attention to historic sites archaeology.

SCHOLARS TEACHING in universities and their colleagues who carry on research in museums, libraries, historical societies, and projects in editing and historic preservation sometimes seem to be travelling on separate roads that seldom converge. The university teacher is known through his production of students and—in these days of "publish or perish"—books, but the institutional scholar often devotes equivalent thought and research to problems whose solution remains anonymous or invisible. The correct dating and attribution of a document or an object may require long investigation with no more tangible result than a brief footnote or catalogue entry. The reasonable restoration of a small detail of a building often demands extended research, the details of which remain unpublished in a file-drawer. While the scholarly motives and processes of the two groups are identical, their results are frequently so dissimilar in form as seldom to meet on common ground.

When John E. Pomfret, President of the College of William and Mary, and Kenneth Chorley, President of Colonial Williamsburg, Incorporated, founded the Institute of Early American History and Culture in 1943, under the joint sponsorship of their two institutions, they created an imaginative organization that I have appraised elsewhere as "beyond question the most valuable asset to general American history contributed by the field of historic preservation."[1] In less than twenty-five years, with modest expenditure, the Institute has published dozens of distinguished books, raised the *William and Mary Quarterly* to high rank among American scholarly periodicals, and, through post-doctoral fellowships, nurtured the development of some able colonial historians. Through the annual spring meetings of its Council, and periodical conferences on needs and opportunities for study in various fields of early American history, the Institute has brought to Williamsburg, under singularly pleasant circumstances, scholars from many parts of the country. Thus it has been a remarkable meeting ground in which colonial historians of diverse interests have become better acquainted with each other, and have also had an opportunity to learn of the meticulous research that goes on behind the scenes not only of our most extensive project in historic preservation but of the near-by activities of the National Park Service at Jamestown and Yorktown. Since the beginning of my first association with the Institute in 1949, when Jack Pomfret was still the presiding genius of the College of William and Mary, I have been in Williamsburg at least once each year.

The gardens, the buildings, and their furnishings are attractive in any season, even when the travelling public rolls in like breakers on the shore, but the greatest fascination of the place lies in the research offices, drafting rooms, laboratories, storerooms, brickyards, and other areas where the real work is done. There one realizes the extent of historical and archaeological research that has been carried on in the forty years since the late John D. Rockefeller, Jr., began to give substance to the Reverend William A. R. Goodwin's dream of a restored Williamsburg. For many years the research reports upon which architects, craftsmen, and gardeners based their re-creations remained in files, largely unknown outside of the staff. Happily that is now changing. A Williamsburg Architectural Series was inaugurated in 1958 with the publication of Marcus Whiffen's *The Public Buildings of Williamsburg, Colonial Capital of Virginia, An Architectural History*, which was followed two years later by the same author's *The Eighteenth-Century Houses of Williamsburg, A Study of Architecture and Building in the Colonial Capital of Virginia.* Then in 1965 seven volumes of Williamsburg Research Studies were printed for distribution through the University Press of Virginia.[2] These made available in inexpensive form reports from the files of the Research Department, originally prepared for some internal use. Some are chiefly compilations of documentary sources relating to a subject; others are more interpretive. All, however, contain material that is both welcome and useful. And in 1963 Alfred A. Knopf published for the general reader *Here Lies Virginia, An Archaeologist's View of Colonial Life and History* by Ivor Noël Hume, since 1957 Chief Archaeologist at Colonial Williamsburg.

Mr. Noël Hume's book brings home forcibly to American historians the truth of Professor Grahame Clark's observation that "archaeologocial methods can profitably be applied to any phase or aspect of history insufficiently documented by written records, however recent in time; indeed, archaeology can not only be used to fill gaps in the documents, but also to corroborate them."[3] In a paper presented at an Institute conference in the Needs and Opportunities for Study series in 1964, when I remarked that: "The more thoroughly one brings to bear all possible techniques of history, geography, and archaeology upon the study of the early American arts, the more rewarding will the results be," Mr. Noël Hume made the following corroborative comment:

It is my belief, and I think we prove it here in Colonial Williamsburg every day, that archaeology provides documentary evidence which is just as valuable to the historian as are the letters, diaries, bills of lading and so forth which are normally his sources. I do not suggest that the archaeologist is frequently likely to correct the historian—nor would he wish to do so. Documents are inevitably more precise and more easily read than is the evidence of the spade. Nevertheless, archaeology can frequently fill in gaps left amid the documents, and more often it will round out the historical evidence to give them a substance they might not otherwise achieve.[4]

One has only to visit Mr. Noël Hume's laboratory and consider the implications of what he has recently dug out of a Williamsburg well to understand the variety of documents that archaeology can furnish the colonial historian. But even if one does not have that stimulating experience, a careful reading of *Here Lies Virginia* or of his Smithsonian Institution report "Excavations at Rosewell, Gloucester County, Virginia, 1957-1959"[5] will make the point abundantly clear.

Most historians still think of archaeology in terms of the distant past—of prehistory in the Dordogne, of Troy or Egypt—rather than in terms of American sideyards. Historic sites archaeology in the United States is an affair of recent decades, with relatively few skilled practitioners. Like most specialties, it has developed in response to a need, and this particular need is one that became really pressing only forty years ago when work began at Williamsburg. The two chief public buildings of the town—the Capitol and the Governor's Palace—had burned so long ago that no one knew what they looked like. To find out, it was necessary not only to search widely for documents but to explore the sites of the buildings themselves. And at the beginning there was no one trained in the discipline of historic archaeology of the American colonial period. As Mr. Noël Hume puts it,[6]

The techniques of archaeology, which all stem from an understanding of the principle of stratigraphy, are applicable to any site. It makes no difference whether we are excavating the remains of a Roman villa or a nineteenth century brewhouse, we are faced with the same practical problems of digging, recording, and preserving and we solve them in much the same ways. But there the similarity ends. The man who can identify and date a Roman amphora within fifty years would be somewhat out of his depth when called upon to pronounce on a yeast sieve made in Baltimore in 1854. Failure to identify the yeast sieve as such, might very well result in the loss of vital evidence. The same problem immediately presented itself in Williamsburg. The architects, who were primarily interested in uncovering old foundations and fragments of buildings, suddenly found themselves confronted with quantities of broken wine bottles, ceramics, tobacco pipes, buttons, shoe buckles, gun parts, kitchen hardware, and so forth, none of it having anything to do with the lives of their colonial owners. Although immediate efforts were made to find people who knew something about these excavated artifacts, the sad truth dawned all too quickly; they just were not to be found. There were collectors and museum curators who specialized in the study of the fine and decorative arts of the eighteenth century. But a broken chamber pot hardly came under these categories, nor, indeed, did the majority of the objects that were being recovered.

Thus Colonial Williamsburg was forced to develop its own experts in the excavation and interpretation of colonial sites "through the dangerous school of trial and error."[7] And so over the next third of a century the burgeoning of projects in historic preservation, with their very specific demands for information needed for the restoration or reconstruction of buildings, led to an increasing development of historic sites archaeology.

Similarly the expansion of the activities of the National Park Service, created within the Department of the Interior in 1916, particularly after the passage of the Historic Sites Act of 1935, led to a flowering of historic sites archaeology. In 1947, for example, the National Park Service began excavation on Roanoke Island, North Carolina, in the hope of locating and identifying the site of Sir Walter Raleigh's "Lost Colony." There were no contemporary maps, drawings, or written descriptions of this first English colony, but only a rise in the ground traditionally reputed to be the site of the "Citie of Ralegh in Virginia." An exploratory trench soon produced evidence of an old earthwork, but it had to be determined whether this was indeed the remains of an Elizabethan or a Civil War fortification. Eventually the approximate size and shape of the whole earthwork was determined, and it became apparent that this was a typically mediaeval fortification, almost identical in plan with one built by the colonists on the island of Puerto Rico, while en route to Roanoke, of which a contemporary sketch fortunately survived. It thus became clear that this was indeed the remains of the 1585 fort, and in due time a reconstruction of it was achieved as a feature of the Fort Raleigh National Historic Site. But when the excavation began in 1947 the National Park Service had no necessary conviction that reconstruction would be either possible or desirable: the original purpose was simply the location and identification of the site and the hope that archaeology might, as indeed it did, supplement the scant documentary evidence concerning Raleigh's colony.[8]

On Jamestown Island, Virginia, a group of National Park Service archaeologists began in 1934 to explore the site of the first permanent English settlement. This work, ably directed by J. C. Harrington, with the assistance of the Civilian Conservation Program, continued until the beginning of World War II. In 1954, with the approach of the 350th anniversary celebrations, excavation was resumed under the direction of John L. Cotter, who by 1956 had systematically explored some thirteen acres of the Jamestown townsite.[9] Through the conscientious intelligence of the National Park Service, the anniversary celebrations were not allowed to encroach on the original site. No reconstructions were attempted there, but the old foundations were, after study, reburied and their outlines marked on the surface by low brick walls. The exhibition buildings of the 1957 Jamestown Festival, together with a reconstruction of a seventeenth-century fort and mooring for the replicas of the 1607 ships, were kept off Jamestown Island in order to preserve the integrity of the archaeological site. In many parts of the United States, throughout the 26 million acres of land in the custody of the National Park Service, archaeology has been usefully employed in the study and interpretation of historic sites, not only of the colonial period but of more modern times.

While the development of historic sites archaeology in the United States owes much to the pragmatic necessities of projects in historic preservation and of the National Park Service, prehistorians and anthropologists have made remarkable contributions that are not always sufficiently known or appreciated by American historians. The most remarkable account of these is *Franciscan Awatovi, The Excavation and Conjectural Reconstruction of a 17th-Century Spanish Mission Establishment at a Hopi Indian Town in Northeastern Arizona* by Ross Gordon Montgomery, Watson Smith, and John Otis Brew, which appeared in 1949 as volume XXXVI of the *Papers of the Peabody Museum of Archaeology and Ethnology, Harvard University*. The Peabody Museum, founded a century ago through a gift from George Peabody of London, was the first definitely anthropological museum in the United States. Although a professorship in American Archaeology and Ethnology, now held by John Otis Brew, the present director of the museum, was endowed by George Peabody, the institution has never limited itself to the American continents. While its archaeologists have excavated extensively in Ohio, the Mississippi Valley, the Southwest, Mexico, Guatemala, and Peru, members of its staff make themselves equally at home among the pygmies of the Kalahari desert in southwest Africa and in the jungles of the Solomon Islands and New Guinea.

They dig at Les Eyzies in the Dordogne, measure skulls in the Caucasus, and collect masks in Liberia. In addition, when their shovels encounter a historic site of the colonial period in the United States, they excavate it with like care and sympathy and publish reports highly useful to students of American history.

For the five years from 1935 through 1939 the Peabody Museum Awatovi Expedition, under the directorship of Dr. Brew, conducted field research in the drainage of the Jeddito River, which lies partly in the Hopi and partly in the Navajo Indian reservations in northeastern Arizona. During this time twenty-one sites were excavated, ranging from the second half of the first millenium A.D. to the beginning of the eighteenth century. Among them was the site of the Franciscan mission of San Bernardo de Aguatabi, which was known from meager historic references to have been still inhabited at the close of the seventeenth century. *Franciscan Awatovi* is the lucid, beautifully written and illustrated history of this mission, which was one of the most remote extensions of Spanish colonization and evangelization.

In the introduction Dr. Brew tells of the surprises the site produced.

Even then we underestimated its extent and importance. The low remnants of standing walls, as we eventually discovered, marked only the residence of the friars, their offices and schoolrooms, and the rear wall of the main church. No signs existed above ground of the foundations of two large churches our excavations were to reveal. Familiarity with colonial protestant religious structures in the farming districts of the Mountain States led us to envisage a small church of thirty feet or so in length and a primitive outpost residence of a few rooms. We failed completely to realize two important factors in the problem we were about to tackle; the extent to which the Franciscan friars "kept their form," even in this farthest outpost of Spain, and the fact that from the very beginning the friars were building for the future and so erected an extensive establishment far beyond any possible needs of the one or two fathers who were originally quartered in it.[10]

When the church turned out to be more than one hundred feet in length, the prehistorians sought the help of Ross Montgomery, a California church architect steeped in the architectural and historical aspects of early Spanish missionary efforts, who had restored the Santa Barbara mission after the 1925 earthquake. Montgomery joined forces happily with the Harvard group. The result was a four-part report in which Dr. Brew dealt with the history of Awatovi and the excavation, Mr. Montgomery provided an analytical restoration, and Mr. Watson Smith reported on the mural decorations. Thus a remote Franciscan outpost, for which precious few written references survive, has risen like the phoenix from rubble.

Dr. Brew's observations on this collaboration deserve quotation in full as a classic statement of the relation between history and archaeology.

One of the primary aims of archaeology is to reconstruct conjecturally not only the buildings and industries and arts of a bygone time but also the way of life of the builders of those buildings and the practicers of those arts. Why did they build as they did? Why did they draw certain designs and not others? What did they think as they stood on the doorstep and surveyed their environs, as they sat talking with their neighbors, as they read in the privacy of their own rooms and made plans for the activities of the morrow? It is in such speculations that archaeology and anthropology meet and it is by answering these questions that archaeologists justify their labors.

Montgomery has provided us, in his section of the report, with an anthropological interpretation. It is the most ambitious attempt of this kind that I know. His intimate knowledge of modern Franciscans and members of other divisions of the Roman Catholic Church and his extensive historical researches have enabled him to present a conjectural reconstruction of the life of 17th-century Spanish Awatovi, as well as of its buildings. In his inspired descriptions the bones take on flesh and we follow the workings of minds as well as the flash of the axe and the track of the trowel.

The reader must always, however, remember that the presentation is *conjectural*. And this is as it should be. The archaeologist who strives for "complete objectivity" is pursuing a phantom. In his introduction Montgomery points out that another architect would have built somewhat differently upon the foundations with which we have provided him. Similarly no other anthropologist or historian would see life at Awatovi just as Montgomery has seen it. There would be variation in details and variation in emphasis. We shape our reconstruction on our own experience and on our knowledge of the work of contemporaries and predecessors. The usefulness of our results depends on the extent of that experience and knowledge and upon the skill with which we apply it.

When it is skilfully applied, however, we see a new technique which modern research is providing. It is composed of the blending of the disciplines of anthropology, archaeology, and history in studies of those fascinating periods, found all over the world and in most cultures, which have been labelled as "historic" because of the existence of written documents but which are very imperfectly known because those documents are so limited. A partial development of this technique has long been part of the kit of the classical scholar of the Mediterranean but it is now being extended to include Early Christian Ireland, Mediaeval Europe, the Middle and Far East, and Colonial periods in the countries of the New World. The bracketing of prehistory with anthropology in American universities is preparing archaeologists for their part in this development. The programs of excavation and restoration of colonial sites by the National Park Service in many parts of the United States and the work of private institutions, as at Williamsburg, Virginia, are now providing historians with new and different material to use. The Book of Kells and a few contradictory king-lists give little insight on the way of life during the Late Iron Age in Ireland. Similarly, although 17th-century Awatovi is an "historic site," we have found *no document* which we know to have originated there and the few references to it in contemporary record, as will be seen, are very meager indeed. Archaeology can go a long way toward filling these great gaps in our knowledge of early historic periods. But this added ability, achieved by the expansion and improvement of our excavating technique, is also an added responsibility, to which both the archaeologist and the historian must rise. Fortunately for us, Montgomery has.[11]

I have the impression that too few American historians are aware of the extent to which archaeology and anthropology can contribute to their re-creation of the past. If this be true, the archaeologists are not to blame. Although Dr. Brew's remarks which I have just quoted were printed in a somewhat forbidding-looking anthropological series which began publication in 1888, the distinguished National Park Service archaeologist, J. C. Harrington, brought a similar message to the American Association for State and Local History a good fourteen years ago. His paper, *Archaeology and Local History,* read at an annual meeting, was published by the Association in February 1953 as volume II, number 6 of its *Bulletins.* Moreover in 1965 the Association published still another essay of Mr. Harrington's *Archaeology and the Historical Society.*[12] One of the problems is set forth in chapter III of the latter work, under the heading "It is not easy to dig up an archaeologist."

There he remarks: "Unlike engineers and architects, it is harder to find an available archaeologist than a Chaucerian scholar. The classified section of the telephone directory is of no help!"

The rub is, of course, that historic sites archaeology is, as we have seen, relatively new. The few qualified practitioners are mostly fully occupied. As Mr. Harrington observes: "A member of a university faculty can sometimes be employed for a short-term project, and a major program may extend over a long enough period and be sufficiently challenging to entice a man away from his current position."[13] But too often the undertakings are too long to be fitted into a summer, and too brief, or too short of funds, to induce a scholar to leave a permanent post. Sometimes such matters can be usefully arranged, as in 1957 when, through Dr. Brew's interest, Mr. Oriol Pi-Sunyer, while a graduate student at Harvard, came to Monticello to excavate the Mulberry Row industrial area for the Thomas Jefferson Memorial Foundation.[14]

The Peabody Museum and the Department of Anthropology, Harvard University, continue to show a helpful interest in historic sites archaeology. The Ph.D. thesis of William S. Godfrey, Jr., accepted in 1951, was entitled "Digging a Tower and Laying a Ghost, The Archaeology and Controversial History of the Newport Tower." This study, based on excavations in the summers of 1948 and 1949, blew away a lot of pseudo-Viking nonsense and established the fact that the puzzling tower had been built in colonial times.[15] Dr. Stephen Williams, Associate Professor of Anthropology and Curator of North American Archaeology, in a seminar on archaeological method and theory frequently leads his students into the historic period.[16] One of them, Norman Porthun Barka, in 1965 submitted an extensive Ph.D. thesis on "Historic Sites Archaeology at Portland Point, New Brunswick, Canada, 1631–c. 1850 A.D." At this New Brunswick site Dr. Barka unearthed the remains of Fort La Tour, a French fur trading post of 1631-45 and of the Simonds, Hazen, and White trading post, established by Massachusetts men in 1762, which probably lasted into the late eighteenth century.

In a preliminary chapter, Dr. Barka summarizes the extent of historic sites archaeology. He lists 109 excavated historic sites of European origin in North America—military establishments, trading posts, settlements, missions, and industrial sites—as well as 60 excavated Indian sites at which trade goods were found. It is encouraging to have him say that of the 109 European sites he lists, the reports of 23 were published in the period 1930-49, while 45 appeared in the 1950's, and 41 in the first four and a half years of the 1960's. This statistic happily suggests that the pace is accelerating and that in the predictable future we may have more qualified men able to meet the standards of the Brew-Montgomery *Franciscan Awatovi* than in the past. This is a good goal to aim at.

[1]Walter Muir Whitehill, *Independent Historical Societies* (Boston, 1962), 476.

[2]This first group makes available Jane Carson's *Colonial Virginians at Play; James Innes and His Brothers of the F.H.C.; Travelers in Tidewater Virginia, 1700-1800: A Bibliography; We Were There: Descriptions of Williamsburg, 1699-1859;* Hugh F. Rankin's *Criminal Trial Proceedings in the General Court of Colonial Virginia;* James H. Soltow's *The Economic Role of Williamsburg;* and *The Negro in Eighteenth-Century Williamsburg* by Thad W. Tate, Jr.

[3]Grahame Clark, *Archaeology and Society. Reconstructing the Prehistoric Past* (London, 1957), 20.

[4]Walter Muir Whitehill, Wendell D. and Jane N. Garrett, *The Arts in Early American History, Needs and Opportunities for Study* (Chapel Hill, 1965), 22-23.

[5]United States National Museum, *Bulletin* 225, Paper 18, 153-229.

[6]*Here Lies Virginia,* 95.

[7]*Ibid.,* 96.

[8]J. C. Harrington, *Archaeology and Local History* (Harrisburg, 1953), 158-160; Ivor Noël Hume, *Here Lies Virginia,* Chapter II.

[9]John L. Cotter, *Archaeological Excavations at Jamestown, Virginia* (Washington, 1958. *National Park Service Research Series,* Number 4); *Here Lies Virginia,* Chapter III.

[10]*Franciscan Awatovi,* p. xix.

[11]*Ibid.,* xx-xxi.

[12](Nashville, 1965).

[13]J. C. Harrington, *Archaeology and the Historical Society,* 35.

[14]*Thomas Jefferson Memorial Foundation, Report of the Curator* (Charlottesville, 1957), 9-11.

[15]For published reports, see William S. Godfrey, Jr., "The Newport Puzzle." *Archaeology,* II (1949), 146-149; "Newport Tower II." *Archaeology,* III (1950), 82-86; "Vikings in America; Theories and Evidence." *American Anthropologist,* LVII (1955), 35-43.

[16]Professors Williams and Brew very kindly lent me a large number of reprints and bibliographies on historic sites archaeology from their own reference libraries, which I read with interest but could not summarize here without unduly extending the length of this article. I am indebted also to Miss Margaret Currier, Librarian of the Peabody Museum, for letting me see the theses of Dr. Godfrey and Dr. Barka.